First
Wilderness

My Quest in the Territory of Alaska

BY SAM KEITH

Author of *One Man's Wilderness*

REVISED EDITION
with Color Images

ALASKA
NORTHWEST
BOOKS®

First Printing of Revised Edition 2018

This edition:
ISBN 9781513261652 (paperback)
ISBN 9781513261829 (hardbound)
ISBN 9781513261836 (e-book)

The Library of Congress has cataloged the earlier edition as follows:

Keith, Sam.
First wilderness : my quest in the territory of Alaska / by Sam Keith.
pages cm
    ISBN 978-1-941821-09-1 (paperback)
    ISBN 978-1-941821-19-0 (e-book)
    ISBN 978-1-941821-34-3 (hardbound)
1. Keith, Sam. 2. Keith, Sam—Travel—Alaska. 3. Wilderness areas—Alaska.
    4. Outdoor life—Alaska. 5. Frontier and pioneer life—Alaska.
    6. Pioneers—Alaska—Biography. 7. Adventure and adventurers—Alaska—
    Biography. 8. Proenneke, Richard—Friends and associates. 9. Kodiak Island
    (Alaska)—Description and travel. 10. Kenai Peninsula (Alaska)—Description and
    travel. I. Title.
F909.K28A3 2014
979.8—dc23
                        2014017710

Edited by Tricia Brown
Maps by Ani Rucki

Alaska Northwest Books®
An imprint of

GRAPHIC ARTS
BOOKS®
GraphicArtsBooks.com

Proudly distributed by Ingram Publisher Services.

Printed in the United States of America.

GRAPHIC ARTS BOOKS
Publishing Director: Jennifer Newens
Marketing Manager: Angela Zbornik
Editor: Olivia Ngai
Design & Production: Rachel Lopez Metzger

To my sister, Anna, and my wife, Jane.
I think of you and I think of home.

The Land of Beyond

Have ever you heard of the Land of Beyond,
That dreams at the gates of the day?
Alluring it lies at the skirts of the skies,
And ever so far away;
Alluring it calls; O ye the yoke galls,
And yet of the trail overfond,
With saddle and pack, by paddle and track,
Let's go to the Land of Beyond!

Have ever you stood where the silences brood,
And vast the horizons begin,
At the dawn of the day to behold far away
The goal you would strive for a win?
Yet ah! In the night when you gain to the height,
With the vast pool of heaven star-spawned,
Afar and agleam, like a valley of dream,
Still mocks you a Land of Beyond.

—From *Rhymes of a Rolling Stone* by Robert W. Service

Contents

An Unmet Friend

BY NICK JANS

I never met Sam Keith, but wish I had. His Alaska sojourn ended in 1955, the year I was born, and he arguably had more in common with my father (a fellow child of the Great Depression and a Marine combat veteran of World War II) than I. Yet Sam and I traveled parallel trails, decades apart. We were both young English majors fresh out of back-East colleges, yearning for something more, a wider horizon on which to stretch our dreams. That hope, and our shared, abiding love of the natural world, led us across the continent and northward thousands of miles to Alaska. Neither of us had a fallback plan; half-broke and boxed in, we just went, led by the eternal optimism and inexhaustible energy of youth. And The Great Land proved everything we hoped for, and more. Its sprawling, careless beauty became woven into our being, inseparably twined with the stories of our lives.

Alaska being the almost unimaginably vast state that it is, Sam and I ended up many hundreds of miles apart. But as I read *First Wilderness*, I can imagine myself alongside Sam on Kodiak Island, pulling long, hard hours working in the company of rough men; catching his first salmon; tagging along with his soon-to-be lifelong friend, Dick Proenneke, on a bear hunt; camping at the mouth of a remote stream as a neophyte fish warden; navigating a stretch of wild Kenai Peninsula rapids in an outboard skiff. The words ring true and vivid. Keith's writing bursts with exuberance. At its best, it exhibits a crafted, visual style verging on brilliance:

> *During the next few days, Bruce showed me a flock of sandhill cranes settling in a moose meadow. Some of them almost somersaulted as they landed. . . . They had an ethereal presence as they rose, wheeling above us like vapors clouding, spreading, thinning, and coming together again. They made a whooping, purring racket that descended upon us.*

More often, the writing tends toward sturdy, workmanlike cadences, suited perfectly to the story at hand. Always, the prose is engaging and fast-paced, almost breathless; we sense the raw excitement of young Sam scribbling late at night in his journal or penning letters home, searching for the words to describe a land so wide and deep, and to capture the essence of the people he meets along the way.

Though the narrative revolves around a series of on-the-move adventures set against the backdrop of Alaska's territorial days, the more profound journey is inward. Above all, *First Wilderness* is, as the subtitle states, the story of a quest: a young man searching for a direction and purpose in life. Alaska, no matter how alluring, ultimately proves waypoint rather than destination for Sam Keith. We can feel the pull his beloved father, Merle, and sister, Anna, exert, drawing him back to that other world. Throughout the tale, too, the beauty of Alaska competes with Keith's yearning for feminine companionship. Equally as beguiling as snowcapped peaks are a head-turning beauty on a Seattle bus and a redhead on the Coast Guard base where Keith serves as a civilian construction worker. These connecting threads lend thematic undercurrents that pulse through the book.

Given the distinctly autobiographical perspective, what Sam Keith chose to omit from *First Wilderness* offers telling insight.

There's not a word about Sam's experiences as a bomber crewman just a few years earlier; no mention of his being shot down over the trackless ocean and surviving. He seemed to have consciously resisted mining the dichotomy between the destructive power of war and the restorative properties of nature, à la Hemingway, though it offered an obvious and natural theme to explore. Why indeed would a born storyteller avoid so much as a reference to what must have been the most harrowing and dramatic experiences of his life? According to his daughter, Laurel, "I think he simply saw the war as something he had endured and survived. It was in his past and he always wanted to focus on the future." And truly, that forward-focused optimism brims throughout *First Wilderness*. Alaska provided a new beginning for Sam Keith, in every sense of the word. He went on from there to find the purpose he yearned for, as an educator, through someone he met in Alaska; and later on, he met Jane, the love of his life, at a home movie showing of his adventures.

Through understated foreshadowing, Keith sustains narrative tension, preparing us for his eventual farewell to Alaska. Close attention to the text hints he clearly sensed his trail diverging from that of Dick Proenneke, whose classic story of solitary wilderness living and self-sufficiency Sam would later carve in *One Man's Wilderness*. He seemed to realize that his own destiny lay in the company of others, rather than alone. Throughout the rest of his life, though, Proenneke's experiences served as a reminder of the trail not followed. Sam and Dick's long-distance friendship, constantly renewed through hundreds of letters, would keep Alaska welded to his soul. Dick Proenneke was truly both avatar and doppelganger for Sam; no surprise that the two friends passed from this world just weeks apart.

Sam Keith lives on, through his family and those whose lives he touched; and no less so in his enduring contribution to Alaska literature. *First Wilderness*, this posthumous offering, cements that legacy.

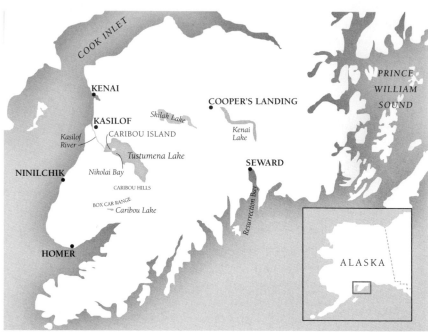

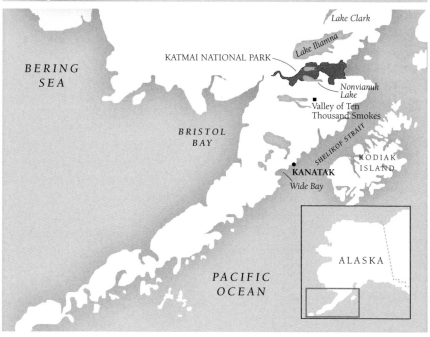

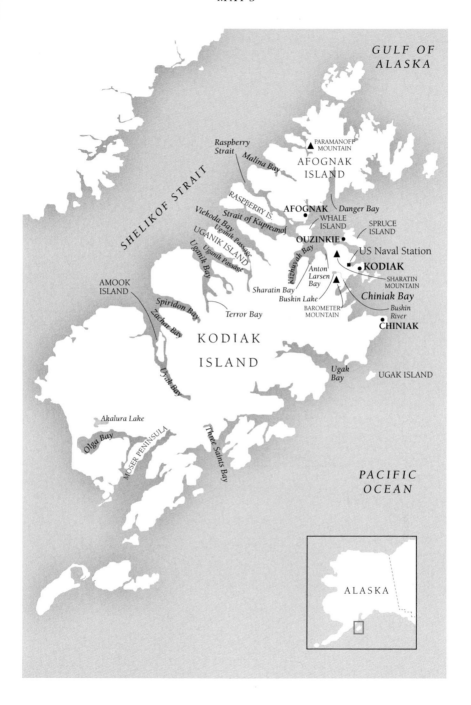

GULF OF
ALASKA

Raspberry
Strait

PARAMANOFF
MOUNTAIN

Malina Bay

AFOGNAK
ISLAND

RASPBERRY IS.

Strait of Kupreanof

AFOGNAK

Danger Bay

WHALE
ISLAND

SHELIKOF STRAIT

Viekoda Bay

Uganik Passage

UGANIK ISLAND

Uganik Passage

Uganik Bay

OUZINKIE

SPRUCE
ISLAND

US Naval Station

KODIAK

Kizhuyak Bay

Anton
Larsen
Bay

SHARATIN
MOUNTAIN

AMOOK
ISLAND

Spiridon Bay

Sharatin Bay

Buskin Lake

Chiniak Bay

Zachar Bay

Terror Bay

BAROMETER
MOUNTAIN

Buskin
River

KODIAK

ISLAND

CHINIAK

Ugak
Bay

UGAK ISLAND

Uyak Bay

Akalura Lake

Olga Bay

MOSER PENINSULA

Three Saints Bay

PACIFIC
OCEAN

ALASKA

13

Sam with a landlocked salmon, Aroostook County, Maine, 1942.

Buried Treasure

BY BRIAN LIES

This is a book that almost didn't happen.

Sam Keith, the author of the award-winning book *One Man's Wilderness*, passed away in 2003. Four years later, his widow, Jane, moved from their retirement home in Anderson, South Carolina, back to Massachusetts, where Sam and Jane had lived for many years. Jane's new apartment didn't have much storage space, so during the move, a dozen archive boxes of Sam's—filled with letters, journals, unpublished manuscripts, photographs, and slides—went instead to a garage . . . our garage.

You see, I'm married to his beloved daughter, Laurel.

Laurel and her father were kindred spirits. For years after his death, the boxes sat untouched on steel shelves at the back of our garage. Opening them was just too painful.

The boxes collected dust until the winter of 2013, when thoughts about their contents started to nag me—I knew there were stories in there that Sam had written, but never published. A junior-high-school English teacher for twenty-six years, he routinely came home after school, napped in his favorite chair, then wrote. He kept a journal almost every day of his life.

Sam had written *One Man's Wilderness* in 1972, recounting the story of his longtime friend, Dick Proenneke, who'd chosen to build a log cabin in remote Alaska and live a subsistence lifestyle. Using interviews, notes, and Dick's journals, Sam had written a best-seller. Now, forty years after the book's initial release, and long after it was reissued in paperback, sales were still strong.

Standing in our garage, I looked at the shelved boxes and wondered, *What if there's another publishable manuscript in there?*

Pushing past our snow thrower and Christmas decorations, I began to pull the boxes from the shelves. Inside one, I found a smaller cardboard box. On its lid were the words *Raw Quest* written in Sam's distinctive handwriting. I lifted the lid to find a thick stack of onionskin paper, a typed manuscript. A quick look told me that this was Sam's autobiographical account of his first trip to Alaska, during which he met and shared many adventures with Dick Proenneke, as well as other remarkable men whom he befriended. *Wow*, I thought. *This could be it.*

I started reading the pages, hoping that there was a real story there, rather than just journal entries. Soon I realized I was no longer reading because the author was my father-in-law, whom I'd respected and loved. I was reading because this man's adventures in the Territory of Alaska were at turns harrowing, funny, and fascinating—a letter home from a different time, and from the one remaining wilderness in North America. I couldn't wait to tell Laurel what I'd found.

When she read it, she discovered a facet of her father that she'd never known. Laurel agreed—this story needed to see daylight.

Sam's life before the events in this book was already marked by adventures. He was born in Plainsfield, New Hampshire, in 1921 and raised by loving parents with his younger sister, Anna, whom he adored. Sam's father, Merle Vincent Keith, was a talented wildlife artist who never found the success he yearned for, and who worked a variety of manual jobs to try to support his family. The family moved frequently, from New Hampshire to Massachusetts and then to Bayside, on Long Island, New York, where Merle felt his proximity to the New York publishing world would offer more opportunities for success.

But the Great Depression hit them hard, and the publishing work never materialized. The family's financial difficulties left lasting marks on Sam—personal scars from being forced to accept government aid as a boy, and feelings of obligation to family—which stayed with him throughout his life. To the end of his days, he was extremely humble, downplaying his own skills and talents, and poking fun at his own mistakes.

Merle Keith taught Sam and Anna about hunting, nature, and outdoor skills. Nature was a release from the hardships of life, a place both real and imagined in which a person could survive and even flourish, given the right skills and mind-set. Nature was a sacred thing, to be honored and conserved. It would play an important role in his writing. He hoped one day to write a story that his father would illustrate, and the two would find success together.

On graduation from high school in 1940, Sam joined the Civilian Conservation Corps, and spent a year building fire suppression roads in Elgin, Oregon. Then he returned to Long Island to work as a landscaper before enlisting in the Marines in May 1942. He would serve as a radio gunner in the "Billy Mitchell" Marine bombing squadron the Flying Nightmares, and survive being shot down over the Pacific Ocean. Later, he was awarded several decorations for his military service.

After the war, Sam attended Cornell University on the G.I. Bill, earning a degree in English Literature in 1950. He filled countless journals with his observations about nature, people, and life—the stuff that might later become stories.

But after graduation, a sense of duty drew him back to help out at home. His mother had passed away while he was in college, and his father remarried. The household now included Merle, his new wife, Molly, and mother-in-law, Mrs. Millet. Instead of striking out and pursuing his dream, Sam took a job in a machine shop. He began to chafe. He wanted more. He needed an adventure, a purifying experience in which he could find out what he was really made of. The territory of Alaska had always called to him, and at last, he made up his mind to go.

The following adventure stories from Alaska begin in 1952,

and in them you'll meet that man in search of adventure and acceptance. You'll read about how he met Dick Proenneke and how their lifelong friendship began. And you'll meet a number of colorful characters who inhabited the place that would, in 1959, become the forty-ninth state.

Sam wrote this manuscript in his after-school hours of 1974. Neither his wife nor his daughter was aware that he'd written another book. In preparing it for publication, Laurel and I, working with our insightful editor, Tricia Brown, have changed as little as possible. Occasionally, we found that his letters or journal entries about a particular event were fresher or more vivid than the manuscript version and would be more interesting to a modern audience. So we've tucked them in. We've included excerpts of his letters home, shedding additional light on his thoughts or actions. And we've also pared away some small bits—overly long descriptions or observations—that got in the way of telling the story.

The following is Dad's distinctive voice, already familiar to the many thousands who have read *One Man's Wilderness*.

So—please meet Sam Keith, at last telling his own story, in *First Wilderness*.

Longings

A t a party in Massachusetts one winter evening in the early 1970s, several of us men drifted away from our wives and gathered in front of a snapping blaze in the fireplace. We sipped our drinks and stared into flames that turned our conversation from current events to our primitive longings. We strayed easily from talk of the trans-Alaska pipeline. . . .

"I was all set to go, in '48," one said. "Right down to the military jeep and two spares. But we never got the show on the road. My roommate up and decided he wanted to go on for a master's, and I met Nancy."

Another man leaned in. "I was another casualty. I had it all figured out. I was going to be a wilderness trapper way back of beyond somewhere. The Porcupine. The Pelly. The Athabasca. I dreamed about marten and lynx and wolverines and sourdough biscuits. Read all the books. Still have 'em somewhere. I settled for my father's meat business. In it ever since."

"You won't believe this. Right after I got out of the service, all I could think about was Ketchikan. Commercial fishing—that was the life for me. I had a name all picked out for that forty-footer I was going to own: *The Northern Lady.* Somehow, it just don't sound the same plastered on a canoe."

I had heard the same sad tunes before. On and on stretched the tombstones with their eroded epitaphs of what was going to be, yet never came to pass.

We all have our Alaska, in one form or another. It's a place we never got to see, a goal we never reached, a dream that stayed that way.

I was one of the lucky ones. I mined some of those dreams we talked about as boys, before responsibility descended with its straitjacket. I saw things I dreamed of seeing. I did things that I dreamed of doing. I prospected *my* Alaska, and discovered new placers in myself. That big, awesome land brought out the pieces, like flashes of gold in black sand.

CHAPTER 1

Out of the Nest

M y father, Merle V. Keith, tilted his head to appraise the sketch he was making of a drake wood duck, sighed softly, and peered up at me over the top of his glasses.

"You really going?"

"My mind's made up," I said. "There'll never be a better chance than right now. No excuses, and the longer I wait the more I'll have a chance to make them. I'm single and have five hundred bucks stashed away. I'm busting to head out. Find something to write about."

"You sound like a teenager, not a thirty-year-old."

"Maybe it's delayed action. Marine Corps, then college, and that damn machine shop. I'm wound up like a spring. Anna's all set now, and you're off on another tack. I'm all turned around. I'm not sure what I want to do, and even if I did . . . I don't feel ready to do it. Alaska's been talking to me day and night. And that's partly your fault. You planted *that* seed a long time ago."

Dad smiled. His bald dome gleamed beneath the fluorescent lamp, and his gray fringe of hair made me think of a victor's wreath. He stared right through the sketch he was drawing.

"There are strange things done in the midnight sun by the men who moil for gold," he recited. "The arctic trails have their secret tales that would make your blood run cold."

"You introduced me to them all," I said. "Not just Robert Service. Jack London and Rex Beach and James Oliver Curwood and Stewart Edward White."

Dad bent forward on his stool and made the drake on the paper come alive with a highlight in its eye.

"I'm not sorry about that," he said. "You can take away a lot of things, but you can't take away a man's dreams." He looked up at me with those gentle blue eyes. "I can understand the way you feel. You're like a bird dog casting the cover for a scent. One thing you want to remember, though . . . you don't always find the birds in the cover that's the prettiest or the farthest away." Dad dabbed his brush at the palette to pick up more paint.

"I read a poem that I've never forgotten. I've looked for it for years, but I'm ashamed to say I don't even know the name of it. It starts off like this: 'There is a legend that often has been told; Of the boy who searched for windows of gold; The beautiful windows he saw far away; When he looked in the valley at sunrise each day.'"

Dad had been looking at the ceiling as he recited, but now he turned back to me.

"He had to see those golden windows. One day he climbed up there to see them, but they weren't gold at all. They were just plain windows. When he looked back across the valley to his own house, though, the windows there had turned to gold."

Dad paused for effect. "But that's enough philosophy. Go to it. I might see that big country, after all. I hope you find what you're looking for."

He knew my dream was to make a living with my stories, to be a professional writer. Despite my best efforts, that just hadn't happened yet. Dad's eyes dropped for a moment as he made deft strokes to bring out the drake's crest. "To find it, you've got to have some idea what it looks like."

I was going to miss my visits with my father in his studio, there in West Bridgewater, Massachusetts. It was a delightful

Merle Keith at work in his studio.

mess with its paintings, sketches, photographs, carvings, plaster casts, animal skulls, specimens in formaldehyde, driftwood branches, paper wasp nests, birds' nests, cocoons, swamp grass, reeds, milkweed pods, garlands of bittersweet, bird skins, tubes of paint, and palettes blotched like autumn leaves.

The place smelled of linseed oil and the fresh pine shavings that littered the floor. Sayings were tacked on the wall. *A quitter can't win* was a saying that rallied his persistence whenever it flagged. Another was the Golden Rule. Yet another read, *Don't wait for your ship to come in. Row out to meet it.*

Here was Dad's escape from the world. His illustrations of my unsold stories were not only reminders of my failures, but endorsements of his striving spirit.

I WONDERED IF EVERY YOUNG MAN was as mixed up as I was.

I had taken advantage of the G.I. Bill and attended Cornell University in the fall of 1946. Torn between majoring in English and Wildlife Conservation, I had chosen the former and filled in with the latter wherever I could. It had only been three years since my mother's death. Her passing marked the end of *home* as I knew it. Dad had remarried quickly, and my sister, Anna, and her family had moved into the old house.

After graduation from Cornell in 1950, I had boarded with Anna and pounded out articles and short stories that earned a steady income—of rejection slips. A small inheritance from my grandmother and income from odd jobs had furnished the necessities while I sat behind the typewriter and watched the mailbox. My account petered out about the same time Anna obtained a divorce. With three kids and a big house, she needed help.

I had taken a job in a machine shop. It paid more than some of the other jobs available, and a neighbor who worked in the plant provided the transportation.

"A college graduate and you're working here?" That was a question I could neither answer to my satisfaction nor to the one who asked it. It was a matter of expediency. I was dazed, confused, and even bitter. I was a young Indian brave waiting for a vision. I wrote often in my journal, a habit I would keep up for life and one that helped me sort through colliding thoughts.

Author's journal, June 15, 1950
I can't allow myself to fall into a rut,
now that I am fresh out of college. I must be
on my guard, for pitfalls are numerous.
I hear the call of northern places and
soon I must heed their pleadings.

THE GREAT DEPRESSION HAD LEFT UGLY psychological scars on my family. How often I thought of Dad being forced to make a living as a laborer, something he despised, because he had a family to support. He was first an artist, but he had only been able to play at his calling. That wasn't going to happen to me. But what *was* going to happen?

How I envied the boys in high school and later those in college who knew exactly where they were going. Everything they did was tailored to a pattern. Everything I did was trial and error.

I also had a hang-up about women. I looked upon a woman as doing me a favor to tolerate my attention, and never from the viewpoint that she might be flattered by it. I stuttered. I stammered. I didn't consider myself much of a bargain.

Neighbors and acquaintances did their best to make a match for me. I was not only cheating myself, they said, I was cheating some nice girl out of the good life. From my warped perspective, marriage was a trap. I regarded it as an ending rather than a beginning, a stifling of the adventurous spirit, a sentence I wasn't ready to accept.

Dad had made a very necessary adjustment after my mother's death. He was starting anew. He didn't have many years left, and he wasn't going to live them in the past. His new wife, Molly, was good for him, but from my selfish standpoint, she had stolen him from me and remodeled him.

Dad and I had been so close. The canoe was lonesome without him in it. The grouse cover lost its appeal without him along to share it. It became difficult to talk with him. There was always a timetable he had to follow, a call he had to make, a concert he had to attend, a planned interruption. I no longer felt part of his life, but rather an interference. Dad needed Molly more than he needed me.

Even with Anna, the belonging I once felt in the old homestead just wasn't there anymore. I was intruding in her private life. She washed my clothes and fed me like a lumberjack, but something was missing. Reminders were everywhere of what used to be and wasn't anymore. They were Nature's subtle ways of pushing me out of the nest, pressuring me to do my own building, but I just wasn't ready to pour the foundation.

With my job at the machine shop, I could contribute to the household and put aside some savings, but I loathed the place. What had happened to Dad was happening to me. I looked at the painted windows that kept out the sun. Rooted at my thread-grinding machine, I became a robot with programmed moves. Motherly women in the department delighted in making me a guinea pig for their recipes, and I ballooned from a trim 180 to a paunchy 215. I became restless, irritable, and silently critical of my fellow workers. Many had been in the shop all their lives. No end was in sight other than retirement or death. I saw a life sentence in a world of whirring belts, turning gears, and monotonous repetitions. Not for me.

When Anna remarried, I glimpsed the daylight I had been seeking. Jim Anderson was a good, hardworking man who loved Anna and the kids just about as much as I did. I knew I could trust him to take care of the family. With the yoke of responsibility off my shoulders, Dad's dreams of the land of the Midnight Sun came back to me. I began to hear the voices that came on the wind and stirred the leaves and furled the surface of the pond on the way to Siberia. Alaska was in the sound of the geese. It was in the first glow of morning, and in the flames of a sunset. It was all I could think about.

I made my plans. Slowly I readied the essentials of my gear. If I needed other things, I could pick them up along the way or send for them when I got settled. I scrubbed the South Pacific out of my seabag. That old veteran was going to be moving out again. I splurged on a pair of custom-made, ten-inch moccasin boots from L.L. Bean, along with some heavy shirts and a pair of Ballard cloth pants. I decided to head for Seattle, Washington. That would be my jumping-off place to the North.

And then it was time to actually say my good-byes. I drove to Dad's studio the night before I left, my mouth dry.

"I wish I was twenty years younger and a whole lot richer," Dad said, looking beyond the walls of the studio. "There's a thrill in heading off somewhere, but there's a bigger one in coming back. There's a difference between motion and action, too. I hope you discover that someday." He squeezed my hand, grasped my shoulder, and drew me into him.

"I want to hear all about it. When you see that first big bear. When you see the northern lights. When you tie into that first rainbow." His eyes twinkled. "And don't forget to look what's at the end of him."

I hurried out of the house and into the darkness. I didn't want him to see my tears. That big guy had always been a shelter I could run to in a storm, and now he just didn't seem to be there anymore.

I HAD DECIDED TO TAKE A bus instead of a plane. That way I would have more time to think about what I would do when I stepped off in Seattle. Anna drove me into Boston to the Greyhound Terminal. Her four kids were in the backseat. In my pocket was an envelope that the neighbor had dropped off with instructions to not open it until I was on the bus. The handwriting on the front was Dad's.

Anna stopped in front of a huge travel poster. It depicted a dizzy sweep of mountain peaks spidered with snow. "I don't blame you," she said. "They're so beautiful and scary at the same time."

I didn't like the shivery tenseness building up inside me. A knot writhed in my stomach, untying and pulling tight again. Even though it was still an hour before my departure, I felt it was best to get the good-byes over with. I kissed Deena and Betsy first, then baby Joyce. Skip, the little man at eight years old, screwed up his face and pushed it up close with his eyes closed.

"Men shake hands," I said. His hand was warm in mine. He laughed nervously, then turned away.

"Time to go, Anna," I said. "If you need anything. . . ."

She pressed her hair against my cheek, her arms tight around my back. "Jeepers," she whispered. I kissed her. Her blue eyes glistened. *Gee*, I thought, *she looks so much like Mom.* She turned abruptly and walked away, the kids scurrying in her wake like baby quail. Deena turned to shout, "The mukluks, Uncle Sam. Don't forget!" I tried to swallow the lump growing in my throat.

To kill time after checking my seabag, I decided to get a haircut. The barber left his newspaper almost reluctantly, motioned me to the chair, and tucked the apron hem into my collar in a tired way.

"Just a trim," I said. "Not too much off the top."

"Coming or going?" he yawned, flicking a comb through my hair.

"Heading out," I said. "I'm off to Alaska." The way it sounded sent a thrill through me.

"Married?"

"Uh-uh. Not ready for that yet."

With sluggish motions he moved the electric clippers up the side of my head. "No hurry," he breathed, half to himself. "Get yourself a bundle. Don't go into it with nothing. You'll be in debt for the rest of your life."

There it was again. This man was serving his sentence, too.

I walked out smelling of hair tonic and sat down on a bench to examine my string of tickets. Wisconsin . . . Minnesota . . . North Dakota . . . Montana . . . Washington. They'd be new places for me. I'd seen Idaho and Oregon in my Civilian Conservation Corps experience, building a truck trail and dwelling at the Fire Guard station in LaGrande, Oregon. I had my wallet in one breast pocket and my Traveler's Cheques in the other. Both flaps were buttoned down. When the loudspeaker announced loading time, I moved out, my small bag in one hand, my two fishing rod cases lashed together in the other.

The same feeling came over me that I had had so many times as a boy. I used to drag my sled up the hill that loomed white and awesome against the night. Once on its summit, I would wait until all the others were sliding away fast. Alone up there I felt kingly as I surveyed the down-swooping path of frost, my breath condensing in clouds and evaporating against the stars. I waited until all forward motion of the sledders had stopped. Then I rushed at the slope, slammed belly down on the sled, picking up speed, plummeting over the crust. . . .

"Their ride is over," I muttered to nobody in the bustling bus terminal. "Mine's just beginning."

Author's journal, July 9, 1952
The big day at last. The knot of nausea
in my stomach, writhing there as if untying.
Almost wanting to throw up and yet I knew the
feeling. I'd had it many times before. When you
leave something, when you leave persons you
love, you feel that way. You feel sick inside and
wonder why the hell you have to leave.

CHAPTER 2

The Jumping-Off Place

The Greyhound growled out of the terminal, past the parked taxicabs and into the traffic stream of Boston. It was raining. I fingered Dad's envelope out of my pocket, hesitated for a moment, then ripped it open with my thumb. His words were to the point:

> *I once told Anna you were lazy and irresponsible. You were wasting your education. I was wrong. You're a restless dreamer. You can be so much more than you are. You're holding out for what you want to do and you won't settle for what you have to do. Keep following your star and please accept my apology.*

I pursed my lips. "You were right the first time," I muttered. "No need to apologize." The seat beside me was empty. I hoped it would stay that way. I didn't feel like talking. I had a lot of thinking to do.

I lay back in the darkness, listening to the singing of the tires in the rain. Trucks droned like huge hornets zipping past the window. I never realized before how much freight moved over the roads while most people slept. Those drivers hurtled their rigs through the dark with hours on their minds and a clock to beat. I dozed fitfully, waking now and then to the sounds of snoring or a baby crying, then drifting off into a limbo again. I was startled when the lights flicked on, and from far off the driver's voice announced a rest stop. For a moment, I had no idea where I was.

In New York City, a frail, slight man with heavy-rimmed glasses sat down next to me. Before we left the city, conversation started to flow. At thirty-three, he was an eye surgeon. Here he was, just three years older than I, and professionally established. I was still groping.

"I make my living here in the city," he said. "A very good living . . . and I hate it. The people are callous. If you fell down on the sidewalk, they'd walk over you before they stopped to help you get up."

He told me how he had no time to himself at all, how patients came with their problems and left them with him to solve, how meetings of medical societies stole the precious moments of privacy that emergency operations failed to claim.

"So," he said, "I'm going to my sister's place for ten days and didn't tell a soul where I was going."

"I envy you," I told him. "You've arrived. You're right on course." I confided that I still didn't know what I wanted to do in life, but I was headed to Alaska to find out.

The doctor laughed. "Envy me? Why I'd give a whole lot to be going with you. When I started high school, everything was all planned. Mapped out. I'm sure life is much more exciting your way. The quest is much more stimulating than the goal."

So we sat and talked, each envious of the other, each good for the other, and yet I felt that his was the better way to go. He was doing something worthwhile, contributing unselfishly of his time to society, and I was still a boy who wanted to play.

I didn't like to see him leave when he got off the bus.

"It's been a most pleasant experience," the doctor said. He handed me a card and we shook hands. "If you're ever in New York again, please look me up."

"It would be fun to compare notes someday," I said. I watched him hurry off, blurring into the crowd and the anonymity he sought.

SCENES FLASHED PAST THE WINDOWS OF the bus as we hurtled west. In Ohio, I was amazed at forests of television antennae. Chicago was in the throes of the Republican convention with "I Like Ike" placards, searchlights, and a barrage balloon [blimp] in the sky. Wisconsin towns impressed me with their washed streets and neat shops. Minnesota's bodies of water, large and small, danced with sunlight.

North Dakota? A huge, undulating golf course and clumps of trees. Flat Montana rose up into the Rockies. The road was a precipitous rock wall on one side and a guard rail—dizzying nothingness beyond it—on the other. I could only smell the evergreens of Idaho as we roared through it in the night. Southern Washington seemed desolate with sage and rock. It felt like we were in the southwest. Then enchantment came outside of Ellensburg— the snowy Cascades jutting their proud peaks above the dark foothills. Black-striped, orange-barked pines towered amid the firs, and I felt I was moving through a canyon bordered with great living columns. Fog patches curled and ascended the slopes. The clear waters of the Yakima River raced along beside me.

Finally, upswooping, cloud-crowned Mount Rainier . . . and Seattle.

I shaved in the large restroom of the terminal. Soldiers were stripped down, dipping into suitcases, sprucing up and appraising their reflections. A thick-armed giant shaved next to me and splashed water like a grizzly emerging from a creek. I felt dwarfed beside him and wondered where he came from and what he did. I decided he had to be related to a Douglas fir.

Five days on the bus had exacted a toll. I didn't realize how tired I was until I broke out on the streets of Seattle. I'd claim my seabag as soon as I got settled somewhere. *Which way to go?* I flipped a coin. Heads one way; tails, the other. Tails directed me to the Georgian Hotel. Not fancy, but in my price range, and it was clean. I soaked luxuriously in a hot bath, crawled between fresh sheets, and drifted into a deep sleep. When I woke, I couldn't believe it! I had slept almost twelve hours.

I lay there staring at the ceiling. Thoughts bombarded me. Was I running away from life, or running toward it? Wouldn't problems from back East follow me like birds in the wake of a ship? When was I going to realize I couldn't be a boy forever? Well, I'd come this far. I'd play the hand out. With a frowning concentration, I dressed and went out to see the town.

Signs were all over the place:

ALASKA, LAND OF OPPORTUNITY.

FLY TO ALASKA! $79 TO ANCHORAGE WITH
55 POUNDS OF LUGGAGE, 30¢ FOR EXTRA WEIGHT.

STEAMSHIP CRUISE TO ANCHORAGE,
$115 WITHOUT TAX.

SEE THE LAST FRONTIER!

The promoters were going on all cylinders. Such a lavish display made the whole business feel like a sucker's game to me. Round-trip tickets weren't mentioned at all. I wasn't going off half-cocked. It was now Monday, July 14. I'd look around. If I didn't line up an Alaska job here by Friday, I'd light out for Anchorage or Fairbanks without one, and take my chances.

I bought an Alaskan newspaper. I could see there was much unemployment up there in the land of opportunity. Her cities were crowded. There were many references to men stranding themselves without funds. Several pleas in the advertising section alarmed me. "Young man desperately needs work." "Young man will do anything."

I checked the *Seattle Times* carefully to see if anyone was driving up the Alaska-Canada Highway (also known as the Alcan) and wanted a passenger. That was like trying to fill an inside straight, but I'd continue to keep my eyes open just the same.

I wandered the streets to get oriented. Soldiers and sailors prowled the sidewalks singly and in bands, looking into windows, and moving in and out of the shops. Nobody seemed to notice them. They didn't give the impression of being proud of their uniforms. I remembered how proud I'd been of mine, but times were different then. The country was together.

I strolled along the waterfront. Sockeye salmon, gutted and slab-sided, lay on beds of crushed ice. SEND A SALMON EAST, a sign read. AS LOW AS $10.50. Anna would be pleased with one of them, I decided, so I sent her one. I wasn't surprised that it cost me $12.50. The low price advertised must have been reserved for the east bank of the Mississippi, the farthest west you could be and still call it "East" here. Piles of crabs rested on folded legs. Men in short rubber boots hosed the wooden and cement floors, sloshing debris off the edges. The smell of fish and seaweed hung in the air. Masses of brown-leaved kelp waved in the Puget Sound swells, like fronds of coconut palms. Packing cases, cans, and papers bobbed in the water around the pilings.

If you don't know what to do with something, I thought, *just throw it off the pier. The ocean will take care of it.*

I walked into the spacious People's Savings Bank to cash a Traveler's Cheque. I was still wearing my moccasin boots. Even though they felt like gloves, I needed something more appropriate for town wear. A squat character pounced on me from the ambush of his doorway.

"What size you wear? Come in. Come in. You come to the right place. I sell cheaper than any other place in town. Where you from? What kind of work you do, sir?" I let him rattle on until I was able to indicate what I wanted. Then I sat down. He unlaced a boot and slipped a loafer on my foot. I didn't even say I'd take the shoes. I thought he was looking up another style. Instead, he was wrapping up the loafers.

"You don't wear big, heavy shoes. People think you're from the country. Wear these. Look like a civilian. Eleven ninety-five," he concluded.

Think you're from the country. In the next few hours, his words rang in my brain. I decided to do some investigating. I took the shoes around to various shoe stores and tried to find out whether or not I had been taken. Of course, the proprietors dismissed my queries by saying that they could not put down a competitor, but in doing so they gave me the slight hints I was looking for. I watched their faces when I told them what I had paid. Finally, an old Swede, bless his heart, told me that they were cheap shoes, that he sold them for $8.00. I could have kissed him.

I stomped back to the first store like a Nazi Storm Trooper. "Here's the boy with the big shoes back and he wants his money!" I said. I slammed the shoes on the counter. "Those shoes are worth about $8.00. When you size up a sucker next time, look a little farther than the shoes he wears." He argued. If he was bigger, I think I'd have swung at him. I got my money back and I returned to the old Swede's shop and bought a good pair. I felt I had won my fight. If I couldn't trust people, I could now be on my guard and weigh every dealing with cold suspicion.

> *Author's journal, July 15, 1952*
> *I wasted the day wandering through the streets. A brooding concentration. Did I try to run away from life? Am I ashamed of what I have done with college up until now? Whether I get a job or not, I must go to Alaska. I must go for pride will not let me return yet to the east. And yet I can't help but think that this "land of opportunity" rage out here is a sucker's game.*

I had no idea what I was going to do, but it was time to find a job, any job.

During the next few days I visited the offices of several contractors with jobs in Alaska. They were interested in tradesmen, not laborers. Laborers they could hire on the scene. College didn't count unless you were an engineer or an accountant. College just put you in a different league. I wondered how many educated derelicts there were wandering on Skid Row. I stumbled on a notice posted by the Navy. Laborers were being hired for Adak and Kodiak.

IF INTERESTED, REPORT TO THE
ALASKA RECRUITING OFFICE AT PIER 91.

I was walking, and by Pier 63 I decided that Pier 91 would be easier reached by trolleybus. I didn't know what the fare was. I fumbled for change, revealing my insecurity in my surroundings. As I sat down, I didn't notice the girl sitting next to the open seat. A few minutes later I was surveying her shapely legs, the perfect swelling of her calves, the thin ankles dropping into black, high-heeled pumps. Her eyes were a sparkling blue, her lips moist and the red of strawberries. I kept stealing glances at her.

"Pier 91 and Carleton Park," the bus driver announced.

The girl got up to leave. I followed her out. I guess I still looked bewildered by my surroundings, because the girl smiled.

"Pier 91 is over there," she said.

"Thank you," I said. She smiled again. Her teeth were like the first snow and her eyes flashed. I walked away, thinking how pretty she was.

A sailor at the gate issued me a pass, and I proceeded to the Alaska Recruiting Office. After filling out an application, I was told to report the next day for a physical. If I passed that, then the deal was to sign a one-year contract. Free air transportation would be provided to Adak or Kodiak, and if I completed my year, the trip back to Seattle would be gratis also. I would have the option of signing over again, too. *Not too bad*, I thought. *This could be my Alaska meal ticket.*

Back on the street, I hailed the trolleybus. I climbed aboard, and for a moment I thought I'd never gotten off. There, across the aisle, were those legs again. The girl I'd sat next to before! She smiled at me. It was almost an invitation to introduce myself and sit beside her, but I stayed where I was and lamely thanked her again for her help. My damned shyness and Yankee reserve . . . I'd never get rid of it. Afraid to make a move and be refused. That would hurt too much.

The bus driver turned when he stopped again. "You two chasing each other around? Too hot for that. Go find a shady spot."

Even with this assist, I remained tongue-tied, but managed a shy smile in her direction.

Finally, she got off. Her arm brushed mine. I watched her walk across the sidewalk to a store window, then turn and smile. I grinned back as the bus moved off. The driver shot me a sour glance. I got off at the next stop and walked hurriedly back toward the girl. I was going to throw all caution to the winds. It was just too damn lonesome in this town.

Then I noticed a passing bus. My hopes evaporated. There she was again, smiling and waving. I waved back, trying to communicate to her to get off, but she didn't pick up the vibrations.

"Damn it," I said out loud.

~

I WENT TO THE LIBRARY FOR some guidance, and decided to look up some information on Adak and Kodiak. I immediately ruled out Adak. Not a tree on the island. But, Kodiak . . . that held promise. I wondered what the fishing was like.

On my way back to the hotel, I passed a Girlie Show, all lit up and glittery with revealing posters beneath the marquee. Girls in flesh-colored G-strings and hammocks of fishnet supporting their heavy breasts seemed to squirm right out of the pictures. Their mouths were drawn into "Os" and their eyes were big and round. I hesitated for a moment, then walked on.

Back at the hotel room, I took a bath. As I toweled myself off, the roll of blubber around my middle was emphasized in the full mirror on the door. How did that accumulate so fast? It wasn't that long ago when my stomach was drumhead tight and the muscles showed.

You're going to seed, I thought as I jutted my chin and shaved critically.

Don't blame Seattle, I answered. *It's not as unfriendly as you think. There's things to do, but you're holding on to your wallet.* I rinsed off the blade.

But my wallet's my security blanket until I get to Alaska, I thought, splashing my face with a spicy lotion. *All right, then*, I told my reflection, *so stop bitching about Seattle.*

The next morning, I returned to Pier 91. The smell of the sick bay was familiar to me from my Marine days. So were the needles the corpsman jabbed me with. I saw on the screen of my mind the long line snaking into the tent, the marines emerging from the other end of it, holding their arms, grimacing, and shouting for the benefit of us waiting to be punctured. "Look out for the hook!" "It's a square needle!" "Jesus, that butcher struck bone." An occasional trickle of blood down an upper arm made believers out of us. Some boys even fainted in the tent before the needle touched them.

I felt the swollen pressure of the rubber tubing around my bicep as the doctor squeezed the ball and watched the gauge.

"How's it look?" I asked.

"See that you don't get too heavy," he said. That did it. Removal of the lard would have top priority.

After filling out forms in duplicate and triplicate, after swearing not to overthrow the government and swearing solemnly that I never had been or was presently affiliated with a Communist or Fascist Party, after indicating my preference for Kodiak, I was told to report again in two days. Okay, then, two days to be a tourist—to see Seattle with new eyes.

I spent the rest of the day in a waterfront aquarium and finally in a theater, where I saw *The Wild North*, a movie about a desperate man in some of Canada's roughest mountains.

Cars sizzled along the street in a steady rain, their lights glistening on the pavement. People hugged close to the buildings as they hurried along the walks. The rain felt good hitting me in the face. Just for a change of pace, I stopped in a bar to have a few drinks. I sat at the bar with a young, homesick soldier. He was drinking beer because there nothing else to do. The place was full of people with nothing else to do. Women were waiting to be picked up. I didn't want that kind of trouble.

"Don't stay in here too long," I said to the soldier. "They'll keep looking better and better."

Usually I walked upstairs to my room instead of bothering the clerk to take me up in the elevator. Tonight, I was later than usual.

I noticed the handle to the closed door leading upstairs was missing. Was this a precaution against unwanted guests? The only way up was the elevator.

When I opened my room door, I found a note had been slid under it. *Lonesome?* it read. *You don't have to be, you know.* There was a number to call. Now, who had put it here? I hesitated, then slowly tore up the note and tossed the pieces into the wastebasket.

I brushed the curtain back and looked down on the street. There were lots of lonesome people in this world.

I hoped Kodiak was the paradise I heard it was. I intended to work hard, play hard, and save my money. When I saw my family again, I'd be richer, both in money and experience.

July 16, 1952
Dear Dad, Molly, & Mrs. Millet:
    This is only going to be a short letter. I took off without my Marine Corps discharge. Everytime I go away, although I check and recheck my gear, I always manage to overlook something. Because I will probably need it when I get to where I am going, would you please send my discharge to me by the fastest way possible? I think you will find it in one of the trunks at your place. . . . Mail it to:
    GEORGIAN HOTEL
    ROOM 307
    SEATTLE, WASHINGTON.

    I went over to the Naval District Headquarters and inquired about Civil Service jobs in Alaska, and much to my satisfaction, found a few laboring jobs open. . . . The woman at the desk told me I had the job as long as my physical did not in any way reject me. I have to sign a one-year contract and as far as I know, I will be in Kodiak, Alaska. The pay is just *under $2.00 per hour.*

Please hurry along my discharge. Hoping all is well.

Love to all,

Sam

I HAD BEEN EATING IN THE Sportsman's Cafe. The food was excellent, and I enjoyed sitting at the counter and watching the chef do his job. I have always been fascinated by people doing things well. Harry Mae, the chef, had many orders going at the same time. His movements were flowing, and he wasted none of them. He was tall with sunken cheeks, deep-set eyes, and features like Abraham Lincoln.

This particular evening was slow when he placed the steak platter in front of me. It must have been obvious to him how I savored the brown-crusted, red pieces of beef.

"How's the steak, bud?" he asked, leaning on the counter.

"Best ever. You can cook my grub anytime."

He dumped more salad on my platter. Then he got a piece of pie and a cup of coffee and came around to sit beside me. We sounded each other out. I was enjoying his company and hoping that customers would stay away for a bit.

"You have to go down deep for king salmon," he said. "Bounce three and a half ounces of lead off the bottom and ripple a sewed herring along about a foot above it. Picture three hundred to four hundred boats trolling the bay. You sock into a big king and then he starts his run. All them lines out there. You bring him to the boat, and you're a fisherman." He pointed to a picture of himself with a sixty-four pounder he had caught. Then a chance remark revealed that he had been to Kodiak.

"How's the fishing up there?"

He grinned. "Tie a rope on a broom handle," he said. "That's all the gear you need. Wait till you see that water. So clear you can drink it." He got up as a group sauntered into his restaurant.

I smelled the sweet scent of the woman before I saw her. Her hair was a tumble of black brown curls, snapping with glints of copper, and bouncing on her shoulders. She sat a few stools away from me, tipped her head back like a sunbather, and her hair shimmered. Her knitted suit hugged the swell of her breasts and communicated the mold and movement of every muscle. She moved a leg to cross over the other. I glimpsed her calf muscle roll and bulge against the nylon. The idealist part of my nature still controlled the animal. I didn't hear her voice. She was just a beautifully alive creature that entranced me, that made me linger over my coffee like an old man watching the glory of a sunset. She never looked my way at all. If she had, I would have turned crimson.

⌁

STATEMENT OF LIVING AND WORKING CONDITIONS
U.S. Naval Station, Kodiak, Alaska
26 November 1951

GOVERNMENT: The U.S. Naval Station, Kodiak, Alaska, is under regular Navy jurisdiction. All civilian employees are subject to Seventeenth Naval District and regulation, including naval discipline, during their presence on the station, whether during or outside regular working hours.

GENERAL: The station is part permanent and part temporary. It might be termed to be in "Pioneer State" without paved streets, walks, etc. Prospective employees should not expect metropolitan conditions.

CLOTHING: Civilian employees should provide themselves prior to departure from the United States with heavy clothing for winter, rain clothing, and overshoes for both winter and summer. Work clothing, rain clothes, and overshoes and boots are obtainable in the town of Kodiak. Prices for all of these articles are higher than in the States.

⌁

BEFORE I LEFT FOR KODIAK, I needed some gear, so I bought a suit of neoprene rain gear, a Filson cruiser jacket, and several sets of Duofold long-john underwear. I was beginning to feel like an

Alaskan before I even got there.

My departure date was approaching fast. At the Alaska Recruiting Office I filled out a few more forms and was told to bring all the gear I wanted shipped.

My seabag had all it could hold. I lugged it down to Pier 91, went to Transportation to establish my priority for the Sunday flight, and got my orders from a Navy clerk who had the charisma of a stereotypical undertaker.

At 11:35 A.M. on Sunday, July 27, I would meet the Navy bus and proceed to McChord Field in Tacoma. My last chore at the pier was to transport my bulging seabag across a high footbridge to Household Effects. Sweat poured in trails all over my face when I arrived and deposited the fat, canvas sausage. The neatly dressed woman who checked my gear was careful that I didn't get too close to her and gave me the definite impression that the sooner I left with my perspiration, the better.

Harry Mae served me a thick, orange fillet of king salmon with cream sauce for my last supper.

"The kid's going to Kodiak," he announced to several others along the counter. That started something.

"You'll be walking across the backs of salmon," one said.

" . . . want to fish near the crick mouths when the tide's turning."

"When you see a bear stand thirteen feet high, then you seen something!"

"It's rugged with them winds up there, but you won't find a better place to save money . . . if you don't gamble. Lots of that— and drinking, too—man, oh, man!"

Harry poked around under his counter. "Try these," he said. "Tied 'em myself." He handed me several artificial flies, some attached to Colorado spinners. "Take these plastic bags, too. Just as good as a creel. And," he added, "drop me a line."

At 1:30 P.M. I arrived at McChord Field. The flight was not scheduled to leave until 4:20 P.M. Things hadn't changed much since my service days.

The DC-4 transport plane had bucket seats, heavy canvas stretched over metal crossbars. A blanket was spread out in the aisle, and a Black Jack game was in progress around it. Some sailors, slouched and sullen, were showing the effects of their leaves; others hinted of anxiety. Several civilians were reading magazines. A Navy Chief sat with his head hanging, dropping lower and lower until it rose abruptly, only to loll on his chest and start a new cycle.

The motors roared. I fastened my seat belt. The plane began its taxi into position.

So long, Seattle, I thought. *We didn't really get acquainted.*

Two time zones away to the north, Kodiak waited in the Territory of Alaska.

Territory. That had a good sound.

> *Author's journal,* circa 1952
>
> *I am anxious to get started and get settled once more. Kodiak lies ahead, a land that I have never seen. Just a point on a map, a place where a giant bear lives. And now I will enter a new field of vision, and I must like what I see there, for I have bound myself for twelve months. I must work hard, I must be faithful to my notebook, and if I do these things I might someday show some doubters that I had the stuff after all.*

CHAPTER 3

The Transplanting

M y face pressed against the window. The Alaskan coast was coming into view. Conical spikes reared out of vapor that ringed their chocolate-colored bases like feathers. Cloud layers sliced mountains across their middles to give the illusion of floating triangular peaks. Beyond them loomed the alpine monarchs, giant, thrusting spearheads chiseled from alabaster, dwarfing their spruce-skirted subjects. Clouds piling against the jagged land upheaval reminded me of heavy surf caught with a high-speed camera just after its explosion against the rocks. On we drifted over a white desert that hid the sea.

One of the passengers pointed to a hole in the fleece.

"Anchorage," he said. I didn't see a city. All I glimpsed was a mountain veiled in the freshest green, then some planes on a landing field, just before the clouds erased the earth again. Kodiak wouldn't be far now. The plane began to buck and stagger, now plummeting, now surging in a fizzy, floating upwards. I pulled my seat belt tighter.

When we finally slanted in for the Kodiak approach, I looked at my watch. It had been ten hours since we left McChord.

Subtract two for the time difference. We hit with a shuddering jolt and bounced. The engines thundered. Concerned, frightened looks, almost panic, and then everyone jabbered with relief as the wheels touched down again, this time on the runway.

Nobody seemed to know what to do with a group of men arriving after midnight. In bewildered knots, we tied and untied over the hangar floor until a Navy bus arrived, blinking its headlights. The sleepy-eyed driver didn't seem to know or care where he was taking us. At the first stop, there weren't enough bunks available for everyone. Success at the second stop.

As I collapsed into my bunk, my head throbbed. In the bunk next to me sprawled a sailor as pale as a corpse. I asked him if I could get him anything, but he just smiled weakly and shook his head. His ashen face was the last thing I remembered.

I awakened in the morning to the far-off whooping and guttural calls of ravens. I looked out to steep green hills that ascended into the mist. There were gullies down their sides and scars of raw earth. Spruce and alder choked the ravines. A fine rain was falling.

Kodiak, Alaska
July 29, 1952
Dear Dad, Molly, & Mrs. Millet:
Ten long hours in an Army transport plane.
Bucket seats. We followed up along the coast of
British Columbia. Below could be seen the patches
of snow in the mountains, lakes half sealed with ice,
bare places on slopes and snaky paths that betrayed
lumber operations, smoke pluming up from a fire in
the forest, a line of jagged snow-shrouded ramparts
seeming to march beside us. . . .
I'm not going to include all of the details of my
final arrival here. It was as I expected. Nobody
seemed to be expecting us. Typical naval procedure.

*My ears ached from the drop into a normal pressure,
my head ached and I was dead tired. . . .*

*I am hardly settled here. My job is that of a
typical laborer with pick and "muck-stick" (Alaskan
lingo for a [he-he] shovel). This afternoon I could
see my breath in the air.*

*I hear a lot of fellows got stranded for jobs on
the Alaska mainland. I'd have been foolish to have
joined them.*

*This is a very incoherent letter, but I just wanted
to get word to you.*

Love to all,

Sam

*P.S. The pilot undershot the runway coming in and
had to gun his engines at the last minute. We hit
like a ton of bricks, and barely missing going in the
"drink." (Oh, well, he was an army pilot.)*

AFTER A BREAKFAST REMINDFUL OF MY service days, a paunchy fellow with a jutting jaw checked our papers. He chewed on a toothpick and enjoyed our confusion. He pointed to the ghostly shape of a mountain.

"That's Barometer," he said. "Our weatherman. If you can see Barometer, it's going to rain. If you can't see it. . . it's raining." He glanced slyly over the group to see if his comment made us any more miserable than we were, then dispatched us to the various checking-in stations that were scattered across the base.

There weren't enough rooms to go around in the civilian barracks. I had to share one with a southerner who probably resented my presence as much as I felt uncomfortable in his. A calendar hung crookedly on the wall. The days of July were crossed out up to the twenty-fifth, which had a red circle around it, inset with the word *Hooray.* My instructions were to unpack, get into some working clothes, eat lunch, and report to the superintendent's office, wherever that was, by one o'clock. It was now almost noon.

I made it.

Then I waited for perhaps an hour in an atmosphere as cheerless as the rain that hit like sand grains against the windows. Apparently, a laborer was one of those low forms of animal life not deserving of a welcoming word or a handshake. I was moved gruffly along from the superintendent to the foreman and finally to a seamy-faced straw boss with a Wyatt Earp mustache. He didn't introduce himself or ask me my name, so I stubbornly kept my mouth shut. He deposited me into a ditch with a shovel. His grunts and hand signals communicated that a leaky water pipe had to be exposed.

I scrabbled up shovelfuls of shale and mud until I had the pipe uncovered, but not for long. The water welled up around it. My feet got soaked. The steady cold rain seeped through the shoulders of my denim jacket. I had foolishly decided against the rain gear. A pump was started, the intake hose lowered to me, and the pipe appeared once more. The boot-ed plumbers then took over after I dug a sump hole for the end of the hose.

After that, I was whisked away in a truck to a large building. Compressors breathed and bellowed like shuddering metal monsters as they supplied air through the black hoses to the jackhammers that rumbled from within the clouds billowing from the entrance. Men were breaking up the cement floor. They were just shapes in a gray haze. While some trembled over the hammers, others shoveled up chunks into wheelbarrows. I was handed a pair of giant nippers, and as the lumps fell away from the probing of the bit, I cut the embedded steel mat of reinforcement rods. Again I felt involved with a nameless society. Discontent hung in the air like the cement dust. Between the stuttering bursts of the hammers, I caught their comments:

"I'm finishing the week and that's all she wrote for *me*."

"To hell with the contract. They can shove it. I'll pay my own way back."

" . . I've had a bellyful. . ."

Sam in his room at the naval base on Kodiak Island.

"Who they kiddin'? *This* ain't Alaska. They sent us to Siberia!"

One fellow loading a wheelbarrow showed me his hands, raw and blistered. His face was flushed. His hair and eyebrows were powdered with dust.

"All right for farm boys," he muttered. "They're used to it. Hell—I'm a musician." He played a sax in the evenings in some joint in town. Something had to break for him soon besides his back. He couldn't stand much more of this, he said. "Not even a respirator," he grumbled. I just kept cutting and listening. This wasn't as bad as the ditch. At least I was out of the rain.

About ten minutes to five, we loaded into the back of a truck and bounced on the plank seats as the vehicle careened over the gravel road. Men hurled epithets at the driver.

"I get stuck on this rock much longer," one bearded character said, "I'm grabbin' me one of them jacks and jumpin' off a pier."

We stopped in front of a low building with a sign on it: LABOR POOL. The musician nudged me.

"Spelled wrong," he said. "It should read: FOREIGN LEGION." We piled over the tailboard, out of the truck.

A gang clustered in a sloppy line around the time clock. They were eyeing its face, waiting for the minute hand to lurch to freedom. Young and old, white, black, brown, and Indian. They were like convicts doing time. My eyes roved over their faces. All had their reasons for being here. I wondered what they were.

Were they putting on an act for the new man? Well . . . they weren't going to discourage me. I had a job and I intended to keep it. Hard work was what I needed. I'd done it before. Now I was going to jolt myself back into shape again.

CHAPTER 4

Taking Hold

T he days wore on.
I progressed from sore hands to blisters, from blisters
that rose in hard bubbles across my palms, to blisters that broke
and burned like fire and peeled away, to stinging slits that healed
into calluses. Jackhammer, "muck-stick," pickax, and sledge were
my insensitive taskmasters.

Unloading cement sacks from piled-high flatbeds, staggering
with heavy vats of mess hall slop, muscling up heaped rubbish
barrels to be emptied into a truck—all contributed to my
shrinking waistline and the return of the old firmness to my
arms and shoulders. I found myself reflecting on those Parris
Island boot-camp days when we drilled in the sand, when I kept
myself going by glaring at the Drill Instructor who drove us to
exhaustion, when I blew at the sweat running down over my face
and kept repeating under my breath, "I can take anything you
can, you son-of-a-bitch."

What boosted my morale more than anything else here was
getting a room to myself. The physical punishment of the job
was as nothing compared to the aggravation I felt returning to a

roommate whose habits were the complete opposite of mine. He either had a cigarette bobbing on his lips or a bulge of tobacco in his cheek. Draining sinuses caused him to snort and sniffle almost continuously. Long after midnight, he kept a light burning, and the large can beneath his bunk was not only the target, often missed, for his cigarette butts, lungers, and jets of tobacco juice, but also a convenience for his urine. One evening he came in glassy-eyed from town and vomited all over his blanket.

He draped things anywhere that would hold them and piled his laundry into a neglected heap in the corner. Continually, he bragged of his sexual conquests. All conversation soon deteriorated into either lewd, detailed descriptions of his successes, or the agony, complete with facial grimaces, of some potent venereal disease he had contracted south of the border. When it seemed that I could stand his presence no longer, he happily announced the evening before my first day off that he was all through. To hell with this prison camp. He needed a woman, and was going back to civilization. With a suitcase jammed with dirty clothes, he left with my blessings the next morning.

I lost no time moving his bunk into the barracks storage area. Other men had private rooms, and I was going to have mine. The fishing could wait. Right now the room had top priority. I declared a field day, and transported everything into the hallway. I opened the window wide, swept out the place, scrubbed down the walls, and then with a clean swab and hot, pine-scented soapy water, I sloshed suds all over the floor. After going through several rinse waters, I felt I had purged the place.

When I stood back from the open door after mopping the floor dry, I knew the contentment of a thorough housewife. The window glistened. The floor gleamed. The air smelled fresh and clean and free again. I tried to picture how it would look with the red print curtains I'd seen in the Montgomery Ward's catalog. Surely they would provide a finishing touch.

Heavy rain discouraged my fishing plans for the afternoon, but I was jubilant just the same. I had redeemed something that seemed hopelessly lost. Privacy was beyond all price. I lay on my bunk, hands folded behind my head, and listened to the onslaught of the rain. I dreamed of streams and mountains, but most of all I just stretched out in an atmosphere filled with the sounds and scents of my own.

Friday evening
Oct. 10, 1952
Dear Dad, Molly, & Mrs. Millet:
Your last letter was handed to me on the job. I started to read it, and the rain drops made the ink run, and I had to put it in my hunting coat. About an hour later when the asphalt trucks stopped coming, I got a chance to read it. . .

I get time and a half for all over 40 hours, but do not get double time for Sunday. The government takes out such a big slice that it is foolish to work too many hours. I made $140 last week. The withholding tax amounted to $25. Since I have been up here, I have saved $365 besides paying the $85 I owed Wards and another $30 I spent for logger boots and other accessories. If I watch my step I should have at least $2,000 by next August.

I bought some red print curtains for my room. They really made it look as "homey" as a farm kitchen. After I do my washing and hang up the clothes to dry, how fresh and clean smelling is the air in my little home! And, Molly, I change my underwear every day as I do my socks. I have a big wash every week, but find it easier to get clothes clean if they are not too dirty to begin with.

These letters are not very interesting, I'm sure. But neither is asphalt paving, and that is what my life has been lately—shoveling that steaming stuff and watching the black path stretch in the wake of the tireless machine. . . .

We were paving the other day. Off in the distance the scary, purple clouds began to swell and hide the mountain ranges. You could see the valley begin to haze in the distance and you knew that rain was on the march. The roller operator, who is built surprisingly like a roller with his great, round body, squinted at the sky.

"Pull on your slickers, boys," he said. "In just about two

minutes, it's going to rain like a cow pissin' on a flat rock."
It did, too. . . .
So long, love to all,
Sam

I HAD EXPECTED THE "NEW MAN" treatment. I was assigned the Sunday garbage runs and the heavy work that others craftily dodged. I was being tested. I was the unknown gunslinger drifting into town, and the top guns had to find out how fast I was, constantly watching and listening for some weakness or flaw.

Although my fingers sometimes cramped on a jackhammer handle, my stomach rolled from the stench of maggot-writhing slop, my back stabbed as if the pick I was swinging was driving its point into me instead of the shale, I hid my feelings behind a smile. They played their little games, and I played mine.

I was determined to live up to my idea of what an Alaskan was. He faced things head on and didn't whimper. He did the job that had to be done. If he couldn't, then he didn't belong. He wasn't worthy of the name.

The civilian workforce came from all over. Some merely passed through like storm fronts, raised hell, and moved on. Others stayed in spite of their griping. They had set goals for themselves. A fellow called "Rogue River" was going to buy a logging truck and be his own man in the big timber country. "California" planned to save a bundle and set himself up in a landscaping and nursery business. "Arkansas" dreamed for a bottomland farm, free and clear of any bank. "Illinois" was going to drive home down the Alcan in a brand-new station wagon with Alaska plates.

"Big Time" had other notions. "Ten thousand be about right," he said, a wistful smile spreading over his dark face. "First get me a Cadillac, long and low like them cigar-smokin' fat cats drive. Here I go to Chicago or Detroit, and watch me spend a thousand a week. Different women every day. Hoo-wheeee! When it's all gone . . . I'm gone, and all them women would say, 'I wonder where that rascal's at?'"

What struck me was that nobody planned to stay in Alaska.

They were here for a stake. The gold rush was still on.

There were others in the barracks, too many of them, whose dreams went only as far as the weekends. They were the lost ones. They would stay as long as they could hold their jobs. On Fridays, the cabs waited for them. The cabbies brought them, smiling and prosperous, into town, then hours later delivered them as defeated hulks that slobbered up the barracks stairs. They sprawled in the corridors. When aroused from their stupors, they hurled curses, struggled to their feet like huge, sluggish turtles righting themselves, and weaved grim-faced and groping along the walls, only to fall against their doors. On Sundays, they pleaded for drinks and fell prey to the loan shark demands of "Oasis," a man who accepted IOUs, payable the next check, for tapping his plentiful supply. Miraculously, they reported for work on Monday to build up the payday thirst and start the cycle all over again.

Oasis fascinated me. He was a Syrian man who always wore a suit coat and a soft gray Stetson. He kept his shirt buttoned up to the collar. His eyes were brown and sad with dark circles under them. A wart on his forehead was almost as prominent as the diamond that flashed on his finger. He smelled of incense and spoke with an accent out of the Middle East. When he talked in his soft way, I could picture him dealing cards on a Yukon steamer, or spilling dust from a moose-hide poke onto a scale.

In some barracks rooms, wild-eyed, sweating men talked to dice, shook them in their fists, and rattled them off the walls to decide the fate of their paychecks. There were the card games, draw poker and seven-card stud and Black Jack, that attracted players like night creatures to a beacon. They were consumed by a fever. They not only risked what they had, but even what they hadn't earned yet.

Winning big drove them on. Winning was the smiling siren, always retreating from them. A winner one moment was beckoned to become a loser the next. The next pot was more important than the present gain. I wondered who finally pocketed most of the cash. Were professional gamblers shearing the sheep? I wasn't about to find out. I didn't have the kind of courage to throw away hours in minutes.

There was frontier-like recklessness in the air, a "don't give a damn" attitude that surfaced in checkered woolen shirts, swagger, and bravado. Perhaps it could be traced to the special flavor emanating from the word *Territory*, as opposed to *State*. Men talked of going "Outside" or to the "South Forty-Eight."

It was not only in the language. It was in the Northern Cross in the night sky, on the Big Dipper shoulder patches of the town police, and in the daylight which stretched far into the evening. I was caught up in it. As proud as I once felt of the Marines' globe and anchor I'd worn, I now felt a similar pride in working to become an Alaskan.

━

I LEARNED I COULDN'T BE TOO trusting. I'd read too much about the trapper's code and the unwritten laws of the North. You didn't have to lock doors—that was only done in cities. Stealing was out of the question.

My first wash jarred me back to reality.

After scrubbing my clothes in the community sink (which I later discovered was also used as a urine can rinse, a mop bucket, a fish cleaner, and a king-sized ash tray), I hung my laundry on the lines in the drying room. When I returned to check it, I noticed that a set of lightweight long johns, a large thirsty towel, and two pairs of socks were missing. That wouldn't happen again. Back in my room, I strung up a clothesline of my own. I bought a washtub, too. Evidently, cleanliness was a virtue some of the inhabitants enjoyed at the expense of someone else's efforts. "It's easy to be dirty," my mother used to say, "but it's work to keep clean."

I didn't lend any money, either. When I first arrived, I had some Traveler's Cheques left. I played as broke to whoever approached me for a loan. If men wanted to blow their paychecks, then let them suffer for it. I didn't intend to bail them out, nor did I expect them to come to my rescue either. I was going to steer my own ship. I certainly didn't intend to go under because of the indiscretions of men I hardly knew.

The food in the cafeteria was plain, and there was plenty of it. I had the choice of sitting at a long counter off to one side of the serving line and ordering pretty much what I wanted, but the price reflected that luxury. I was working hard. Fancy food didn't appeal that much to me. Quantity was more essential than quality. Anything hot was good. I listened to the old, familiar complaints that came loud and often: "All them cooks know about seasoning is salt and pepper, and they leave that up to you." "That'd gag a maggot!" "That goddamn grease is pluggin' up my drain."

⌒

FOR ALL OF THE FISH TALES I'd heard in Harry Mae's café, I limited myself to the role of a spectator. The bay resounded with the splashing of salmon. Sailors lined the ramps and piers casting hardware into the clear salt water that swirled and flashed with fish. I enjoyed the action, the frustration of tangled lines, the hopeless backlashes, and the sight of many salmon in the air at one time. As tempted as I was, I left my gear in the room. I wasn't going to let the salt corrode the innards of my reels. Besides, it really wasn't my kind of fishing. Crowds weren't for me.

Fishing was a private affair, or something you shared with a companion who loved it as much as you did. A few of the streams we had crossed during the garbage run to the dump were more to my liking. They were worth more than a few hours after supper. A man could lose himself walking their banks toward the mountains where they began.

To make up for working Sunday, I had a day off in the middle of the week. That suited me just fine. At last, it was time to get out of here and wet a line on the Buskin River. I bought a frying pan at the commissary to go with the tea pail, tin plate, and enamel cup I had brought with me. I also picked up a few supplies that included a small piece of bacon, some bread, a package of tea, salt, flour, and cornmeal. The game pockets of my canvas coat bulged when I left the barracks with an unstrung fly rod swinging on the end of my arm.

Although it had rained during the night, passing vehicles swirled up a faint dust. The green slopes that rose to one side of me blushed with the blooms of fireweed. Now and then I followed the flight of a magpie that blurred black and white and iridescent out of the alders to float over a tall growth that displayed giant white umbrels like Queen Anne's lace. I passed beneath tall cottonwoods that lathered the road edges with a froth of catkins. Through the quivering leaves, I saw the high peaks, and I could hear the salmon splashing before I came to the bridge.

I looked down into the clear water sweeping beneath me. The pool was restless with shapes and shadows and flashes that hurried over the rounded, flat stones of the bottom. Salmon arced in playful rolls. Everywhere the plunging and thrashing of them, the flirting of their tails, and the ringing slaps of their mingling sides. I was alone with them, thrilled.

I slid down the banking of loose shale. I strung the fly rod and tied on one of the Colorado spinners that Seattle chef Harry Mae had given me. My hands were shaking. The lure dropped with a tinkling into midstream, and I watched the tiny blade twirl into the throng. I felt it nudge one fish, then another. Suddenly the line hissed tight and sliced into the current. My reel screeched. Out he came, scattering the water white. I kept a steady pressure on him, following him along the bank as if he were a spirited dog on a long, fragile leash.

My heart raced as I worked him into the shallows and up on the stones. He gasped with a metallic glitter of gill covers. His upper jaw overhung his lower, and his back rose into a narrow-bladed hump. Viewed from above, his snout tapered like a shark's. He was not quite as bright as the fish in the bay. Olive green, flecked with black, irregular ovals, shaded the upper half of his body, while through his midsection gleamed a silver and lavender streak to his spotted tail. The inside of the lower jaw and tongue were black. I had caught my first humpback, pink, or black-mouthed salmon. He would weigh perhaps five pounds, much more fish than I needed. I watched him revive in the shallows, then feebly wag back to where he had come from.

I caught several more. Their frenzied splashes mingled with my whoops of delight. The females were beautifully streamlined, smaller-headed, and reminded me of large rainbow trout. My wrist ached from the fish I had landed as well as those I had lost. Not all had struck the lure. Some had been accidentally snagged in the fin or the tail. I had been introduced to salmon. Now I wanted to meet the Dolly Vardens.

As I followed the curving of the creek bank, I noticed definite changes in the salmon. The farther I moved upstream, the more aged they became. They were losing their glitter. The males were developing hooked beaks and grotesque humps. Dorsal fins masting out of the current were margined with a white fungus.

I came to a small, abandoned bridge. My attention was drawn to what I thought was a phoebe or some other kind of flycatcher, flittering about and disappearing into the shadows of the girders. Suddenly this foolish bird dropped into the current, swam like a field mouse, and popped into full view once more atop a moss-covered rock. He bobbed as if doing calisthenics. His upright stub of a tail gave him the appearance of a large, gray wren. Fascinated, I watched him submerge and forage along the bottom. He surfaced powder dry, his bill full of wriggling things, and flew up beneath the bridge to silence the shrilling of the nestlings there.

"Son of a gun," I muttered. "That's got to be a water ouzel."

Along the hillsides grew large-butted alders, their trunks sheathed in moss for several feet before giving way to a bleached, scaly growth sprinkled with reddish caps. These thickets were dappled in gloom. The hoarse yelps of ravens, the complaining gulls sliding their shadows over the black sand before me, and the thrashes of spawning salmon provided fitting background music for a dramatic entrance. I looked about apprehensively. It wasn't hard to imagine a shaggy Kodiak shouldering out of the tangle and towering on his hind legs to look me over.

I stopped at a glassy run where many salmon hovered and flirted above their gravel territories. Holding positions below them were the barely visible, sleek, gray shapes . . . the Dolly Varden waiting for the eggs to flow.

I cast the small spinner and fly across the current, letting it swing downstream, twitching my rod tip to make the lure twinkle. A gluttonous flash . . . *WHOP* . . . that abrupt downward swipe of the tip and the telegraphing into my wrist of squirming life. The trout writhed on the surface like a bright grub doubling itself to get out of the light. He tumbled and thrashed until he ran out of water. I studied his fifteen-inch length and wished I had a camera. Although he resembled a brook trout, he was more slender, and his tail was slightly forked.

I had read that the name "Dolly Varden" came from either a pattern of cloth or a Charles Dickens character who wore brightly colored petticoats, but the present silvery sheen of the fish from a sojourn in the sea had all but erased his red spots and mottled shades of green.

"So you're the salmon-egg pirate that used to have a bounty on your tail," I mused. I released him and grinned at my reflection. "Really something . . . letting a fish go because he's too big for the pan."

I tied on a small, orange wet fly. This proved to be more selective, and I began taking trout in the nine- and ten-inch class. I could have filled a bushel basket. I kept three, dressed them out, and wiped them clean and dry with moss.

A pond-like offshoot of the stream glimmered an invitation to camp. There were trails mashed through the grass and slides down the banking and heaps of dung that gleamed with fish scales. Otter sign reminded me of my trapping days in the marshes back home, but I had never seen such a profusion of it. I startled a sheldrake family. A brood of ten surfboarded wildly in the hen's wake. Aspen limbs gnawed clean of bark betrayed the shadowed tunnel of a bank beaver just beneath the surface.

A made-to-order spring issued a frosty trickle out of some stones. Here I half-filled my tea pail. Then I snapped some dead limbs from the spruce that grew out of the fireweed and lupines, and soon I had a fire crackling. The mosquitoes gathered and whined, so I slopped more repellent on my face, neck, and hands, and dribbled some of it all over my red felt timber cruiser's hat. I cut a green stick for a crane, jabbed one end of it into the banking, and propped it with stones.

I hung my tea pail over the flames from the notch on its other end. When the water boiled, I swung the pail away from the fire, dropped in several pinches of tea, and let it steep. Next I cut my bacon piece into slices that soon made music in the pan set on the coals. In my plastic bag of flour and cornmeal mix, I shook the trout until they were coated. Then I laid the bacon slices on a shelf of moss to drain and crisp.

The trout dropped with sizzling sounds into the fat. When they were browned, I transferred them to the tin plate, draped the bacon over them, and fried up two slices of bread. I sat by my fire, cross-legged, munching pink-meated trout, bacon, and fried bread, sipping tea, and waving at mosquitoes.

I watched crowds of fingerlings pouncing on larvae that wriggled on the surface film. They moved in close, like curious children, peering up at me with big eyes. I broke up my extra bread slice and tossed in some pieces. The minnows scattered in panic, then regrouped to tear at the bits, punching them about until they disappeared. Salmon cruised in, some of them wagging into the beaver's entrance and drifting out again. I watched an eagle perched on a cottonwood snag working on his feathers.

"Boy!" I muttered through a mouthful. "Perfect . . . just perfect."

I wiped at some mosquitoes around my neck. "Almost, anyway."

I cut a few green alder branches and tossed them on the coals to make a smudge. The acrid smoke smarted my eyes and drifted wherever I sat.

I scoured my gear in the black sand and rinsed it. As I doused my fire, a wind came up, blowing cool from the mountains, and did a better job on the mosquitoes than the repellent or the smoke.

I wandered upstream to where salmon were dead and dying. Gulls and ravens picked at the carcasses. I saw one eyeless salmon, his hump rotting away, still moving upstream. It must be true that gulls straddled them and picked out their eyes. . . .

I felt I had walked through a generation. I had seen surging youth, savage courtship, the splashing, darting abandon of getting the job done, and finally death. It sobered me. Salmon returned to fresh water to die, but there was a purpose in their pilgrimage. They left precious seeds in their passing. There had to be a purpose in everything. *What was mine?*

⌐

IT WAS LATE AFTERNOON WHEN I arrived back at the barracks.

"Where's the fish?" greeted an old man sitting on the outside stairs and squinting at me.

"Still in the creek," I grinned.

He wrung his hands slowly, looking down at them. There was a trembling about his chin. Strangely, he made me think of the eyeless salmon. "Wish I liked to fish and could get around more," he said. "Then I could enjoy this country. It's the spare time that kills me. Them damn days off. Wish I worked every day."

Days off, I thought. *I wish I had more of them.* Where did the roads lead from the naval base? What was behind the wall of mountains? I wasn't going to just sit and look at the scenery. I wasn't going to see it from the roads either. The smell of the wood smoke in my canvas coat hinted of things to come. Kodiak was spread before me like a great banquet table.

Author's journal, July 30, 1952
Guys who don't like the outdoors have no business up in this country. To them, there is nothing to do. To me there is more to do than I seem to have time for.

CHAPTER 5

Local Color

Curiosity rather than need prompted me to take the base bus into town. At the main gate, I casually appraised the marine sentry. He looked lean and unwrinkled in his cut-down shirt, and he had the haughty bearing of one impressed with his role. A braided cord looped from his shoulder and ended in the butt of his sidearm.

He still feels it, I mused. *It didn't last too long for me. I lost it somewhere when I began to feel too owned.*

The bus droned along the road, swirling up a thin dust that dissipated into the spruce boughs heavy with cones. In red letters a sign blared SLIDE AREA. Soon we swept along a shelf in the side of a mountain, and the tires spun stones over the guardrail. I looked up. I could imagine boulders toppling from the outcroppings, growing larger until the slope was in motion like a wave. I looked almost straight down at the sea. It flurried white against the brown cliffs. Gulls milled above the kelp patches.

We descended into the clutter and sprawl of buildings that was Kodiak. What caught my eye was the church with its bulbous towers, like spikes growing out of bright onions. The Russians had left their mark. Every other establishment on either side of the muddy main street seemed to be a barroom or a liquor store. Twenty-five cents for a bottle of Coke. Three-fifty for a haircut and shave. That was double the price of back home. There was the smell of fish and salt air, the crying of seabirds, and at the far end I could see the masts of the fishing boats spearing from the harbor.

I wandered out on a pier, stopping now and then to look down at the pilings, at the large sea anemones sprouting big-stalked out of their sides like mushrooms on trees, at mustard-colored growths on a bottom speckled white with shells. Here a starfish ... a moonfish; there a flashing of minnows as they chased the teeming organisms I couldn't see. My eyes swept over the boats, big and small. *Where had they been? Had it been a good season? What about commercial fishing next summer?* I had a long time to think about it.

I strolled along, peering into shop windows, going inside to browse. One of the heavy woolen shirts in Donnelly and Acheson's would be something Dad would appreciate. In Kraft's, I priced a pair of ornate mukluks. Much more than I intended to pay, but I ordered them anyway to be picked up later on. Deena would be in her glory wearing those to school. I saw other things that would complete my Christmas package.

An Alaska Native man rocked unsteadily before me as if trying to decide on the most comfortable place to fall. His black hair stood up like the bristles on a paintbrush. I tried to imagine him in a skin boat, whirling his two-bladed paddle, his eyes glittering in the glare of the sea, but when I saw him suddenly pitch into a sodden heap, my picture vanished.

I felt ashamed of what my race had introduced. He had been better off in his cleaner world. I didn't linger long in the atmosphere of commercialism.

⌐

THE FIRST HOT ROLL IN KODIAK got underway, and I was part of the paving crew. We worked seventy- and eighty-hour weeks to beat the frost. The paychecks were fat, but the days off were lean. I had to content myself with what I heard and saw on the job.

Wrapped in the stink of hot asphalt and the vapor from its 300-degree heat, I stole glances at the long-tailed ducks. Out in the shimmer of the bay they were feeding, swimming proudly, and sailing in tight circles. The tails of the drakes were sharply pointed. The black-and-white-splashed bodies dove, making rings on the water that scrambled into each other, and then the surface was lonesome without a ripple. Soon it began to dimple again as heads popped up like frogs. The air resounded with their high-pitched Canada goose calls.

While I sipped coffee during a break, I watched an eagle spread against the sky, rocking on the air with stiffened wings, his primaries separated into great dark fingers. He rose lazily, drifted past a cloud, and I saw his shadow slide over the high slope. I was cruising the sky lane with him.

My eyes followed him until he was a speck above a far peak. What was he seeing that I wasn't? As I squinted after him, I felt my heart beating against my shirt. No one else seemed to have noticed him at all.

Each morning was a repetition of the last. I rolled tiredly out of the blankets, washed up, and trudged to breakfast. One of the waitresses was a woman who always started the long day off right. She stood to one side of the grill, her arms folded across her big breasts, her round, happy face flushed from the heat, barking our orders to the cook.

"Short stack!"

"Fry two!"

"Two in the water four minutes!"

"Fry four on two!" She always had time in between for her bright-eyed comments: "Cheer up, Sam, the first hundred years are the hardest." "Come on, Andy, get with it. You look like you're walking around to save funeral expenses."

Whenever I could, I sat with "The Historian" in the cafeteria. He always wore a perfectly knotted tie. His clean scalp showed through his white hair, and the expression in his bulging, pale eyes gave him the quiet dignity of a basking turtle. With the air of a schoolmaster, he was always ready to dispense his vast knowledge of Alaska and its history.

"The Katmai eruption was back in 1912," he said, fingering the folds of flesh beneath his chin. "Katmai is just a hundred miles north of here on the Alaska Peninsula. She literally blew her top. They say the first explosion could be heard all over Alaska. It caused a blackout for more than two days and must have seemed like the end of the world. They say the rain stung like acid. You'll have to see Katmai National Monument and the Valley of the Ten Thousand Smokes. That peninsula still boils and rumbles. I've felt earth tremors here. It's no secret. This country could go berserk."

This was country I had to see for myself, not just through the eyes of The Historian.

Over the weeks, I slowly made acquaintances other than on the job. Many of the boys had been to other parts of Alaska and had played roles that fired my imagination, like "Skunk Bear."

Skunk Bear had trapped along the peninsula and on the mainland. I loved to listen to his tales. He had a reddish beard and dark brows. Even though his face cracked and his body shook when he laughed, his eyes held the glitter of a cornered animal's. He had a violent temper when drunk, and men gave him lots of room.

"I had me a sixty-mile trapline on the mainland with a cabin or lean-to every ten. I used to bring rice, lots of sugar, and Karo syrup to mix with berries. I could live fine on fish and rice every day," Skunk Bear said, advancing his hard-earned knowledge of trapping.

"You have to be able to read sign. Two fellers trapped an area one winter and caught one mink. They didn't know mink travel under the ice in winter. What they thought were mink tracks were really marten tracks. They set in the water and you don't catch marten in the water.Now, you don't get many wolverine. They're travelers. They don't make their own kills. They have to cover lots of country to make a livin' off the leavings. His problem's appetite. That's more powerful than his brains." When he had run out of trapping advice, Skunk Bear waxed on about the glories of the Far North.

"I been up and down this lonesome land. Seen sunrises and sunsets most as pretty as four ladies in a hand of draw poker."

Skunk Bear gave me a big bear tooth. I drilled a hole in it, passed a piece of rawhide through it, and wore it as a watch fob.

My stomach was flat and hard again. My hands were ridged with calluses. My fingers felt thick and strong. I wore my red hat, grayed with dust, and the brim turned up in front.

When I pulled out my bear-tooth watch fob, I felt that if I wasn't fast becoming an Alaskan, I was at least playing the part of one.

September 7, 1952

Dear Dad, Molly, & Mrs. Millet:

I'm anxious to weigh myself to see if I've lost any weight. I'm afraid I haven't. At least what I carry now is solid. My arms are rock hard from the heavy work I've been doing and my stomach feels as though it is reinforced by something other than a belt. I eat like a horse. Now that we have a new cook, I'll probably eat even more. The grub was pretty poor for a while, but this new fellow seems to have awakened quite a few dormant appetites.

So long, love to all,

Sam

CHAPTER 6

Winter Smorgasbord

The paving went on so long that autumn escaped me. I had missed out on the coho run and had to be content with the tales I heard of those leaping silver fish. I began to wonder whether or not I had my priorities properly established. My bank account was growing. *Was that why I was really here?*

The morning came when Barometer wore a gleaming white crown. I watched the rich blue behind it change to a rosy glow as the sun came up.

The snowline dropped relentlessly down the slopes until the mountains were wrapped in their robes of winter. There was a sharp, refreshing bite to the air as darkness came on earlier.

"Long Gone" was one of the men who was ready to move on with the coming of winter. A chilly-eye cynic, he was tall and blade thin. His face tapered like a wedge. He often misquoted lines from the classics, and he smoked cigarettes out of a silver and ivory holder. He'd been all over Alaska but never in one place for very long. I came upon him folding a canvas tarp in the toolshed.

"Thinking about camping out?" I grinned.

"I'm making a sailboat," he snapped, "so's I can sail out of this hole. It's Southeastern for me. I fell down so hard on the ice yesterday, I didn't give a damn whether I got up again."

He was fun to work with and made the hours fly.

When we pulled into the dump with the garbage truck, the gulls were waiting in gray and white ranks. They were much larger than the gulls back home. We had just finished a long garbage run, and the gulls sensed we carried a choice cargo. They wheeled in a cloud around us as the bed of the truck lifted and disgorged its slop.

Long Gone picked up what was left of a slice of prime rib. The bone was easily eight inches long and an inch and a half wide.

"Watch this," he said, tossing it toward a gull that lurched forward with its bill open. It snatched up the bone, gulped like a sword swallower, and amazingly the whole thing slid out of sight.

Long Gone shook his head. "I don't believe it," he muttered. "Look at 'em.Look at 'em go at it. See that wide-open beak? That's the same as a closed fist being shook. There's the fat cats getting all the gravy. Look at them others just standing around waiting for what's left. Looks familiar, don't it? There's the whole story laid out right there. Greed . . . stealing from each other . . . stepping all over each other . . . the poor devils that get left out. Hell, man, that's the Outside you're looking at. See that sorry-looking son of a bitch over there? That's me."

I saw something else. As I listened to the whacking of their bills and their shrilling cries, I was taken by the deterioration of a species. They were adjusting to handouts. They didn't have to get out and scratch anymore. All they had to do is wait. Long Gone saw society in general; I saw an aspect of it in particular.

"You boys complain about working in the weather," Long Gone said, fitting a cigarette into his holder. "This is nothing compared to Adak. Oh, that wind! Damn williwaw knock you down. You got to walk around with rocks in your pockets. They planted a tree out there once, only one on the island and they called it Adak National Forest. If I stayed in that dismal place much longer, they'd have sent home a coffin . . . and I'd be in it."

One day, we were digging in a ditch when a Great Dane that belonged to one of the officers came up to inspect our work. His big paws touched off a small landslide of shale back into the hole.

"What the hell you think *you're* doing?" roared Long Gone. "Now I got to shovel all this up there again. Ain't you got any respect for a working man at all? Suppose you were down here and I was up there doing what you just did. How would you like it?" The dog cocked his head, moved his ears attentively, and stepped back, flicking his tongue as if ashamed of himself.

When Long Gone finally left, I hated to see him go. I hoped he made it to Southeastern. He'd blown his check in town the night before he left and had to sell some of his things to get plane fare. I picked up the Michigan-type trail snowshoes that he'd won in a poker game.

The Historian had something to say about those who were leaving, too.

"Men come up here," he observed, "and they think they're going to save a lot of money. For a month or so they stick close to their rooms, put money in the bank every week, and they feel good that things are turning out the way they planned. Then the day comes when it gets to them. The roof caves in. They find themselves in 'The Snake Pit' or one of the joints in town.

"All of a sudden they've found something that's too good to be without. Life is too short. That's when the trip downhill begins. They borrow money. They take days off. Their next week's pay is gone before they get it. Look at Everson. His contract was up last August. He didn't have a dime to go Outside, so he figured he'd hang on. Now he hasn't got as much as he had in August."

In spite of The Historian's sage advice, I went on a shopping spree and did some damage to my wallet. I was able to send home a Christmas package that included the mukluks for Deena, a heavy woolen shirt for Dad, and some pieces of Alaskan jade set into ivory for Anna. For my Christmas present, I asked her to ship me the Ansley Fox twelve-gauge shotgun as soon as possible. Now that the snow was here, I had ptarmigan hunting on my mind. Skunk Bear had told me enough about these grouse of the high country to make me anxious to get acquainted.

I learned how to dress for the job in all kinds of weather. I loved the warm hug of the "long handles." If I could keep my hands and feet comfortable, and keep moving, I didn't worry about the elements. I washed my woolens often in lukewarm water and squeezed the suds all through them. Clean wool was warmer wool. I wore deerskin chopper mittens over woolen liners, and I wore loose arctic boot covers over my work shoes.

Often the williwaws rattled the windows in their frames and showered grit against the panes. I felt an eeriness in the stillness between the blasts.

Even when rafts of ice floated in the bay and the wind blasted pellets of snow into my parka hood, I ran the jackhammer with a frenzied energy until my blood flooded heat all through my body. With numbed face I laughed at the gales. I didn't know the frost of fifty below yet, but I felt I was an Alaskan just the same. The winds belied the thermometer. Coming in out of the weather to a warm room, I welcomed the burning feel in my face.

A great change came over the mountains. They were severe in their white wraps that were creased with blue shadows. I loved to look at them when a few stars still had their lights on.

> *January 3, 1953*
> *Dear Dad, Molly, & Mrs. Millet:*
>   *I finally bought my camera. It is an Argus C-3.*
> *It cost $69.50, so it ought to be fairly good. I'll*
> *take some black and white pictures first before I go*
> *fooling around with color slides. It is 35mm and a*
> *shutter speed up to 1/300th of a second. I should be*
> *able to get some swell pictures. . . .*
>   *My laundry bag is bulging at the seams. I'd better*
> *get busy.*
>   *Love to all,*
>   *Sam*

I OFTEN ENTERTAINED MYSELF WITH MY new 7x35 Rangemaster

binoculars and my *Field Guide to Western Birds*. In the open water, there were large gatherings of ducks. During low tide, when dark green weed rolled in the shallows, the mallards laid their throats on the surface, and the ripples played from the sifting action of their bills. Pintails, mostly females, fed on the same fare while a few of the drakes, clustered out of the wind, displayed their gray-etched feathers and stretched their slim necks and white shirt fronts.

Rafts of bluebills bobbed farther on. Here and there a pair of goldeneyes slanting up and slanting down on the swells, a boisterous knot of long-tailed ducks, and blocky bodied eiders headed into the wind; now and then a surfacing merganser in close, his crest like a boy who combed his hair too quickly and didn't get the spikelets down in back. Once what appeared to be a swimming toucan turned into a loon attempting to swallow an oversized fish.

Sometimes I got the hurry-up call to ride atop a sanding truck on a frosty night when the mountains loomed like an encampment of enormous ghosts in the moonlight. We'd start at the end of the runway. The bed of the truck would lift slightly, and off we'd go, the blades of the hopper spinning out the sand that poured into the chute. I kept driving my shovel into the black grit and pulling it to where it fell away. It was much the same motion as paddling a canoe very fast. My arms got so tired, there seemed no strength in them, but I kept flailing, and the sand whirled out and freckled the ice in our wake until the bed was empty. My lungs heaved in drafts of the night air. It was pure physical exhilaration.

Back at the sand-loading area one evening was where I first met Vard Smith of the Roads and Runways crew. His drawl and ready smile invited conversation. He lived on the base with his wife, Myrtle, and two children. He talked the language of the shotgun and the field, and before the night's work was done, he gave me an invitation. I said yes. We were going ptarmigan hunting.

～

THE JEEP WHINED ALONG THE CREEK road, taking the turns tightly and growling up the grades. Vard crouched over the wheel, now and then squinting at the peaks that glared in the sun as white as plaster.

"They'll be down today," he said. "Snow's covered their feed up there. We ought to find 'em in them willers along the bottoms."

He swung the jeep off on a widened shoulder, cut the motor, and swept his arm over the brush-sprinkled valley. "They're out there," he said. "Let's go find 'em."

We unstrapped the snowshoes from the roof.

"Quiet as a graveyard," I said, lacing a snowshoe sandal tight against the toe of my boot moccasin. "Not a stir."

"It'll wake up," drawled Vard.

It was a wonderfully clear day, and there was no wind to water the eyes. I hauled in deep breaths of the frosty air as if there wasn't enough of it, exhaling sharply to watch the vapor clouds. The mountains ringed us, appearing much closer than they were, hatchet-edged against the blue. A raven, hunched on a cottonwood snag, ruffled its feathers and broke the silence with a guttural complaint. The snow twinkled. Ice-sheathed twigs of alder and willow flashed and glittered. It was a world of crystal that beckoned.

Vard and I slogged about fifty yards apart through patches of reddish willow tips that speared from the snow. I dropped a seven and a half shot into the right barrel and a number six shot into the left. The brass ends of the shells glistened from the chambers. I snucked the barrels shut against the breech with the solid sound that well-machined parts make meshing and locking into each other. The Ansley Fox had arrived just a few days earlier; now it was an old friend from home cradled across my arm. I could hear the whispering of webs, the slithering of the snowshoe tails, and far off the whooping of ravens in a discussion of our arrival.

About ten minutes out, I noticed the first sign: myriad trails lacing the willow edges. Droppings curved atop the snow like smooth-hided caterpillars. Here a curled white feather and there a twig snipped off in the feeding. Not very fresh. Probably yesterday. There were wide paths through the brush left by the hobbling, big-footed rabbits. I saw the dainty prints of a weasel leading into a blue-shadowed hole.

Then I noticed the tracks of a larger hunter: the graceful, winding line that betrayed a fox's trail. How desolate it all seems, I thought. Like a white desert. But the signs are plain enough. Life is hidden here.

I spotted two tunnels about a yard apart. In one of them I glimpsed a movement of something quickly withdrawn. As I eased toward the place, a snow-powdered red fox erupted almost in my face. His tail flopped from side to side as he scampered off, heavy-bellied. He stopped and turned his puffy face to look me over.

"Vard," I yelped. "Looks like this guy already has his limit." The sound of my voice launched the fox into frantic scrabblings and abrupt stops until he disappeared over an outcropping blown bare by the winds. I looked down into his U-shaped sleeping quarters. I could have easily shuffled past, unaware of his presence beneath the winter blanket.

Croaking sounds came to me. I wondered why I hadn't heard them before. Perhaps the fox had been too much the center of attention.

"Vard?"

"What's up?"

"Sounds like frogs up ahead. Hear them?"

"That's what we come for. That's ptarmigan talk." He was poised like a bird dog on a point. Then he motioned ahead. We advanced slowly.

The snow seemed to be moving. White shapes materialized in the willow whips less than a hundred yards away. Some were extending their necks and rocking on their tails. Others were jabbing at twigs, scissoring off the tips. Now they were herding on ahead, croaking softly to each other. Those in the lead trotted long-necked and squat-tailed across a clearing. The others huddled after them in wriggling motions through the willow whips.

"Pick out a bird," coached Vard. "Looks like a big cloud of white leghorns when they flush, but there's lots of space around 'em. Watch."

Sam with his bounty after a winter ptarmigan hunt.

Four birds exploded closer than I expected, and then on ahead everything moved as the willows flickered and blurred with bodies hurtling out of them like a squall of giant snowflakes. "Crrr . . . uck . . . uck . . . urrrrrrr."

I shoved off the safety and pulled up on the closest one. At the jolt of the shot, the feathers jumped out of his back. He folded floppily and bounced on the snow. I swung on another one planing low to my left, and as the shot exploded, I knew I was behind him. I watched him scale away to the ridge. About five hundred yards ahead, the main bunch flurried into a settling down again. They were talking over the experience.

I shuffled to where my bird sprawled in the red-spattered snow. He resembled a plump white pigeon. I picked him up so that his back rested across my hand and his head hung limply. His neck feathers fluffed. His breast swelled round and solid. I fanned his small black tail and frowned, inspecting the feet. They looked like a rabbit's, as if furred instead of feathered.

Vard lifted his webs toward me. He held up two birds. So engrossed in my own action, I hadn't even heard him shoot.

"They'll come a little harder now," he said.

Squinting ahead, I picked up the birds again. They were a whiteness moving over whiteness, their teardrop shapes snaking and huddling through the wolf willows. Then they were stretching their necks, balancing on tiptoes, and suddenly in a flowing surge they arrowed over the drifts, their feet twinkling trails in their flight. Into the tall alders they scuttled.

Vard's shot crashed and echoed. My head swiveled to see a lone bird somersault in the air and hurl into the snow like a wadded white rag.

"Good shot," I yelled.

We barely got into the alders when the birds began catapulting up through the branches, whirring and croaking. The heavy thuds of our shots mingled with the startled sounds of their departures. I wasted my first shot by shooting too quickly, more in self-defense than with deliberation. Then I glimpsed a white blur thrusting through the branches like a big snowball thrown against the blue of the sky. I swung with him. As the shot rocked me, it had the right feel to it. Twigs rained down. I saw the bird hitch beyond the maze and fall away, a great, white, helpless butterfly. I marked him down and threaded my way toward the place.

Several falls and many oaths later, I found my ptarmigan slumped at the base of an alder as if asleep. I examined him ritually, then worked him into the game pocket with the other. After checking my barrels for plugged snow, I moved toward Vard's shout. The lumps nudged me through the canvas.

"They're no set-ups in this stuff," I panted. "More like the grouse back home."

Vard had picked up another bird. "These boys that bring in a sackful," he drawled. "They ain't wing shootin'. They're sluicin' 'em right on the snow."

A rabbit squirted out from the top of Vard's snowshoe.

I could see its bugged black eye as it raced away. It dodged nimbly and glided along the brush edge. Vard fired. The rabbit spun kicking on its side, then lay there, jackknifing.

Vard snatched him up by the hind legs and rapped him solidly behind the black-tipped ears. The rabbit jerked, then stretched long and still from the end of Vard's arm.

"Rabbit's good eatin', too, you know," he said. He slit the rabbit down along the paunch, then slung the entrails with a snap into the snow. Into his coat he slipped the furry bundle. A big hind foot stuck out of the game pocket.

By noon we had ten birds between us and the rabbit. That was enough. We stopped in a spruce thicket to have lunch. First we made a snapping fire from the dead limbs we broke off the trunks, and soon the little pail filled with snow was hanging over the blaze. I kept adding more snow as it melted down. Then I threw in a few handfuls of coffee. When the contents boiled over in a brown foam, I swung the pail off the fire, and tossed in a snowball to settle the grounds. We toasted our sandwiches, sipped strong coffee, and later on washed down a generous slice of Myrtle Smith's homemade cake.

"Great country," Vard observed, his cheek bulging with dessert. "All you need is the get up and go to appreciate it."

While we lazed around our fire, a band of redpolls busied themselves in the alders, flicking their wings and shivering their tails as they foraged. The pale rose on the breasts of the males gleamed against the snow. A chickadee inspected the snowshoes that stood on their tails in a drift. Spruce cone flakes were sifting down through the needles. I could hear the crossbills before I saw them. They dangled their reddish bodies from the cones and jabbed with their bills. A golden crowned kinglet came within a few feet of my face.

That night at Vard's place, I enjoyed the hunt all over again. We skinned the ptarmigan and split them down the middle. First Myrtle parboiled them with onion slices and salt and pepper. Then she dried them off, dipped them into a pancake batter, and fried them in butter in a covered skillet. She used the onion water to make a white sauce that was ladled over rice and the crisp, golden ptarmigan pieces. Every mouthful was a delight in an atmosphere of home.

"We'll have to do this again," Vard said as I left.

And we did. Many times.

I OFTEN WENT OUT ALONE INTO the white stillness beyond the roads. I stood in awe in the high passes, absorbed in the silence until a raven's hoarse note or an eagle's cry startled me as if a gunshot had suddenly crashed in my ears.

The peaks called to me in stirrings of strange communication from within. They were patient grandfathers beaming down on the babe that played in their snowy beards.

I had to go high to find the rock ptarmigan. He was smaller than the willow, with a black eye stripe. I found him alone or in small groups where the wind had blasted the crags bare. Often times, up high, I packed my snowshoes and walked the crust until it was time to take the express route down.

I held the snowshoes and shotgun across my lap and tobogganed down the slope on the seat of my pants. I zipped over the shining crust incredibly fast, and there were times when I wondered if I would hurtle to my destruction. Somehow I always managed to dig my heels into braking plumes of snow.

I sent skins of both species of ptarmigan home to Dad.

One day a light package arrived. Nestled in shredded paper, I found a gray whorl of driftwood and perched upon it an exquisitely carved pair of ptarmigan. They were just what my tabletop needed. They expressed the high places and love.

Author's journal, March 14, 1953

I have decided to get a movie camera and a telephoto lens and typewriter. That means taking about $300 out of the bank, but I must do it. You've got to invest if you want a return, and I want more of a return than just interest on my deposits.

I spent most of the day writing.

I should be able to get the scenes I want with a five-power telephoto lens and a Kodak

movie camera with good lens to begin with. I
think I can see how a fellow becomes a miser.
I'm going to draw out the money Friday, and
see how it feels to spend some money again.

SEVERAL ROOMS AWAY FROM ME LIVED Old Mac. He had seen me many times coming back with the snowshoes. Those sightings started conversation that led to a happy relationship.

Mac drove a fuel truck. Every time he heard a base vehicle siren of an evening, he'd grimace and grumble that he knew where his first stop would be in the morning. In his early fifties, he wasn't really old at all. He just looked that way.

There were deep seams in his face that ran like cracks from the corners of his small, steely eyes. His skin was a parchment yellow. The veins made blue lumps on the backs of his hands, and there was a trembling in his fingers. A few strands of hair were plastered over the swollen dome of his skull.

For two years now he'd been away from the bottle, and he could thank Dick Proenneke for that.

When Mac introduced me to his friend Dick, I liked him at once. I didn't know it at the time, but Dick was to influence my life greatly. He was several years older than I and in splendid physical condition. "Just an Ioway farmboy," he said. He had a quiet assurance that communicated to me he could do anything. Although he was a diesel mechanic, there was an emanation from him of the packboard, the canoe, and the mountains. He met the high standards I had ascribed to the true Alaskan.

Dick had rescued Mac from a career of weekend binges, had gotten him interested in bear hunting, and had supplemented this interest with a membership in the base rifle club. They had gone on several bear hunts together, but Mac had never been in the right place at the right time to "bust that fatal cap." As a result he became a target of ridicule for some of his former drinking associates. "Old Bearless," they called him.

He tilted his head and studied me with his bright eyes. "Where are you from?" he seemed to say.

Several of Merle Keith's wood carvings, mailed to Sam in Alaska.
(Tricia Brown photo)

One evening Dick projected a reel of his eight-millimeter movies. There was Mac walking a bear trail. There was Mac glassing the slopes, the wolverine fur trim of his parka blowing in the wind.

"There's McCullough, skunked again," drawled Dick. "The green grass comes and goes, and there's McCullough still grumblin'." He added, "There's McCullough swearin' at a bruin goin' over the mountain."

Mac blatted good-naturedly. "I'm an even-tempered old bastard," he said. "Miserable all the time."

Mac had a lot on the ball. We often wondered what had blown him off course.

"I'd take a belt," he said, "then have to drink the rest because I was afraid it would spoil." He never confided completely in us, but a remark now and then hinted of frustrations after being grounded as a pilot of Tri-Motor Fords because of poor depth perception. There had been a woman, too. She had an ethereal presence in his reminiscences and seemed to color his assessment of all females in general.

Mac was obsessed with the Kodiak bear. Dreams of the shaggy giant had made it possible for him to adjust from a pitiful drunk to a determined Jason in quest of a golden hide. Tacked on the back of his door was a poster-sized illustration of a bear towering out of some brush. Beneath it was printed: RUSH ORDER. A large map of Kodiak, Afognak, and Shuyak Islands was mounted on the wall. Red lines, like capillaries, traced his previous wanderings into the various deep-cut bays with Dick. Prominent red stars indicated bear sightings. Always something had happened to prevent the kill.

"That's McCullough's jinx chart," Dick said.

In spite of the trembling in his hands, Mac became an excellent target shot. His total involvement in the small-bore base matches and his fastidiousness about his weapons were second only to his consuming desire to shoot a Kodiak "as big as a circus elephant."

We often sat in his room of a winter evening amid the smells of his tobacco and Hoppe's nitro solvent and listened to him extol the virtues of his .300 Magnum Winchester Super-grade Model 70, his Leica camera, and his bear-finder Bausch & Lomb binoculars.

One night I smelled smoke. I opened Mac's door and went out into the hall. From beneath the door of the next room I saw the smoke curling. I rapped loudly. No answer. The door was unlocked, and I went in to see one of the perennial lushes sprawled on a smoky bed. I rolled him on to the floor, grabbed up the scorched bedding and mattress, and dragged it off down the corridor and out the door to let it smolder in the snow. We got another mattress from the storeroom, aired out the room, and rolled the protesting hulk back on to his bunk again.

Mac pursed his lips and shook his head. "Smoking in bed. That scares the living hell out of me," he muttered. "That bird's going to do me in yet. He's bad news. He was cleaning a .257 Roberts one night and the damn thing went off. I almost lit on the ceiling. The slug chewed my closet apart and blew a hole clean through my parka."

"Is that how that dog-bed coat got aired out?" grinned Dick.

"Glad I wasn't in it," Mac grunted. "He ought to fall off the wagon and let it run over him."

Dick looked at me and winked.

May 18, 1953
Dear Dad, Molly, & Mrs. Millet:
   I'm tired tonight, but I'm going to write this letter.
I think I have a lot to say. I got in this morning at
11:30 after nine days on the 38-foot fishing boat,
"Elizabeth," with water-wise Johnny Malutin at the
wheel. It was one of the most absorbing trips I have
ever experienced.
   Marion G. McCullough, "Mac," makes laugh so
much I get the hiccoughs and my eyes begin to water.
Mac squints out across the distance and says, "I
always wanted to shoot one of them bastards. You'll
see a one-shot bear kill." Mac's been hunting Kodiaks
for about three years now and bad luck has always
plagued him.
   Mac and Dick Proenneke are a pair. They are
close friends and they're bantering with each other
at every opportunity. At this point I should tell you
about Dick Proenneke, a tireless fellow who loves the
outdoors, a fellow who has shot his bear and says, "I
kinda like to see the old boys. I won't shoot another
one unless I have to." Dick makes me think of an
Indian scout. When I look at him, I can see him in
buckskins and a long rifle across his arm. . . . .
   I'll try to tell you more in my next letter. Right
now I've got to quit.
   Love to all,
   Sam

SCATTERED IN AMONGST THE SNOWSHOE HUNTS and the long

treks into the mountains were the nights of square dancing at the Civilian Club.

Big John Yourkowski had dared me to participate. Big John was a heavy equipment operator with enormous hands and a red face. He was as rugged as a tree stump, yet gentle as big men often are. He was the best bulldozer man on the base and also operated the different type shovels and loaders. Big John could cast a dragline bucket like a fishing lure. He viewed the country in terms of its hazards to his equipment and how he could change its contours.

I didn't know a thing about square dancing, but it looked like so much fun that the fiddle music finally thawed out my feet. I went out on to the floor to make a damn fool of myself.

The dancers were patient, and before long I was whirling the full-skirted wives to the lively music and the caller's chanting magic.

"Allemande left with the old right hand!"

"And now you're home and swing that pretty little girl."

"Everybody swing . . . "

I looked forward to pulling on my Frisco jeans and plaid shirt and waiting for the squeal of the fiddles. There were always husbands who didn't care to dance and wives who did.

One dazzlingly beautiful redhead almost made my heart stop. She was single and a delight to swing, but her ever-present convoy of adoring sailors presented a competition too forbidding and too frustrating to endure. So I retreated. I rationalized it was better that way. *Why get involved?*

The wives were less of a threat to my freedom than the redhead, but she was a lovely vision that often came into my mind. I had the feeling I was back in the pioneer days as the fiddles wailed and colorful skirts whirled past the beaming face of Big John, who stomped his feet and beat his huge hands together.

One evening a knock sounded on my door.

"Come in," I said, looking up from my magazine. It was Mac.

"Like to speak to you about something confidential," he said, his eyes probing at me from his wizened face. He settled with a sigh into the company chair. "We plan on chartering a fishing boat about the tenth of May and going out for a spring hunt around the other side of the island. Uganik, Terror Bay, Zachar, and Amook Island. We wondered if you'd like to come along."

"Would I?! I sure as hell would."

"Nothing definite yet. Keep it under your hat for the time being."

"Gee, Mac, I sure appreciate you asking me."

"Dick suggested it. We figured you had the right temperament for a trip like this. You don't drink and you're highly interested in nature. You don't have to hunt. Just be along to help me peel off the hide and drag it off down the mountain." He let out a short blast of laughter.

"Could be the year," I said. "Your luck's bound to change."

He lit a cigarette and examined it reflectively.

"Fire on one end," he muttered, "and fool on the other." He took a deep drag and blew out the thin smoke. "Hell's fire, a man can't give up all his vices. Who wants to be perfect? Anyways, I've already alerted my boss that I want ten days come spring. 'Put that in the book right now,' I told him. 'That the only reason you signed another contract,' he says, 'because you didn't get a bear last fall? Is a bear all that keeps you in this country?' 'I wouldn't be surprised,' I told him. 'I'm not burning all this ammunition for nothing.'" Another laugh escaped him as he rose to leave. "You better start working on your boss, too," he grinned.

I listened to his footsteps moving off down the hall. Spring couldn't get here fast enough.

Author's journal, April 28, 1953

Mac and Dick have beautiful rifles. Mac has three mounted with scopes. I learned that trying to hold a fourteen-pound rifle with a ten-power scope on a fifty-foot target is quite a trick. That bull just floated, and I couldn't steady it. I'd be afraid to see what I'd shoot offhand. Dick molded plastic wood on the butt of his pistol to fit his hand.

CHAPTER 7

Days of the Bear

The flats were crowded with geese, and the wide-awake air resounded with their choruses. Canadas, specklebellies, and brant. Their bills grabbled greedily in the ooze. They tipped forward and chased one another like feathered lances. They pointed their beaks at the zenith and snaked their necks in sun-gazing rituals. They left wide tracks all over the soft mud as they wandered and visited, talking to each other in nasal overtones, as if discussing the land that was stirring from the winter sleep.

Through tatters of snow, the mountain peaks showed their nakedness. Bird songs fluted from the slopes, and rosettes of wild celery leaves appeared beneath last year's dried, broken stalks.

Several times I had packed my seabag, checking and rechecking the gear, so when I tossed it in back of Dick's red pickup along with cartons of foodstuffs, I felt I had left behind no essentials. Mac and Big John added their duffels to the heap. Off Dick and I went into town. Stowing the gear aboard the *Elizabeth* the night before would assure an early start in the morning.

"There she is," pointed Dick. "That old girl will be home for a spell."

The dull red-and-white, thirty-eight-foot salmon seiner rode at anchor in the shimmer of her reflections. Her skipper was a Native man named Johnny Malutin, who greeted us at the dock. He was crease-faced, stocky, and broad-shouldered. He spoke softly out of tight lips. I liked his bright red shirt open at the throat to show his black woolen fisherman's underwear. When I saw his loose boots, I thought of what Dick had told me. "They wear 'em loose," he said, "so's they can kick 'em off if they go over the side."

"You fish with me this season, Dick?" Johnny asked.

"Got to pass up this one, Johnny. Maybe next year though. Any luck this last trip?"

"See nine. Hunter miss big sow with last year's cub at sixty yards. Scope must be haywire. Only three days in bear country. We see nine. That pretty good."

We lugged the gear and the food cartons down the steep wooden stairs to the dock and loaded it in the red dory. Johnny stood up in the dory facing the bow and pushed at the oars with a shrugging of his shoulders until we reached the *Elizabeth*. There we transferred our cargo, placing all the canned goods in a metal trunk on deck next to the water barrel, and tossing the duffels onto the bunks. It would be cramped quarters in the cabin. Dick and I would set up a tent aft on the ample deck.

Johnny rowed us back in, then returned to his boat alone. When we left, there was a light in the cabin of the *Elizabeth*.

"Johnny's doin' some house cleanin'," Dick said.

"That's sure a fancy king-sized yacht out there beyond him," I observed.

"Charlie Madsen's boat," said Dick. "The *Kodiak Bear*. He caters to them Outside dudes. They want luxury and he gives it to 'em for a hundred-plus a day each. Johnny charges us thirty-five a day, and split four ways that ain't hard to take for seein' the same country. If you want luxury though . . . don't ship out on the *Elizabeth*."

Author's journal, May 8, 1953
Now a possible great adventure lies ahead.

> *My eyes must always be open, my ears open,*
> *and my memory sharper than it has ever been*
> *before. Here is my chance to really collect some*
> *material. I hope I can look back in later years*
> *and say of this trip of tomorrow, "There was*
> *the beginning." Now we shall see what the next*
> *week brings.*

AT 5:15 THE NEXT MORNING WE left Kodiak harbor under a low-hanging shroud of cloud and a spitting rain. All the way in from the base, Big John kept chuckling over what had been at the door of Mac's room. It was an enormous piece of driftwood, knobbed on one end and shaped like a club. A man wouldn't want to lug it more than a few steps. A picture of a bear dragging a man by the arm was pinned to its grayed face along with a note that read:

> *Here's you a bear-hunting stick.*
> *Don't swing until he gets close.*

Once into the channel, the *Elizabeth* surged on smoothly, churning a proud wake as the red dory chased along in tow.

Big, white gulls wheeled above the boom, calling in questions, soaring and rocking on the wind. Johnny peered out of his round pilot hole. His thick, square hand kept turning and nudging at the wheel, and the lines that hitched to the tiller wires creaked as they wound and unwound on the shaft.

"Piling up around the point," Johnny grunted. "Kind of lumpy. Maybe we get tossed around out there. We see what she look like when we get around Spruce Cape. Still lumpy we duck in Anton Larsen's Bay. Easier to get breakfast."

A flock of eiders, wingtip to wingtip, skimmed the waves in a long, ragged line, the drakes blaring black and white in contrast to the brown of the hens.

"There's your sea parrots," Dick yelped, gesturing toward the birds that scrambled before the prow. Their wings slapped the water as they rowed in panic. At first they looked bald-headed, and then I realized it was their bright thick bills that made them

Johnny Malutin, captain of the Elizabeth, *and Joe Byrd.*

appear that way. They lifted, spraddle-legged, their round bodies glancing off the waves like stones skipping before they labored into the air. Smaller birds with white wing patches tumbled out of sight, surfaced, and dragged their red feet into flight. "Sea pigeons," Dick said.

Several trembling formations of geese passed over us. I watched them until they were limp threads in the distance. I stood in the stern, feet wide apart, my hair blowing all over my face, taking it all in deliciously, feeling the shudder of the engine running through the planks and listening to the hiss of the foam that sang in our wake.

The big swells met us off the Cape. They came into us like moving green hills. The *Elizabeth* pitched upwards, and for a moment nothing seemed beneath us. The bow rolled, then plunged downward. Dishes clattered in the galley racks. Water smashed against the windshield and ran down over the glass. I felt the deck rise against my soles, and then the sinking in my stomach as the bow dropped dizzily away. Suddenly I was in a valley of foam. The spruce-lined shore went out of sight as a heaving, green, translucent mountain erased it, its crest shuddering, frothing

Dick getting in some rowing practice.

white, tottering against the sky, and I felt myself lifting again on the frightening power of the sea.

We left the wild water and threaded through the narrow place that was the entrance to Anton Larsen Bay. Dense spruce, heavy with cone clusters, grew out of the pinkish rock bluffs. Hanging from snags that reared starkly against the greenery were wads of dark growth. Moss hummocked the forest floor. Against a dim mountain, an eagle soared, giving me the impression that all he looked down upon was his.

In this quiet bay of the Flower Pot Islands, we had our bacon and eggs.

Mac wanted to go ashore and check out his rifle just in case the scope had been bumped out of line during the loading of the gear. As I rowed the dory, I thought of pirates going into a strange beach. Dick paced off two hundred yards, anchored a carton down, and tacked a target he had fashioned aboard on the side of it. It was a crude circle of black grease about eight inches in diameter on a section of newspaper.

Mac made himself comfortable on his belly. "Boys," he said, glancing up at us, "you'll now see what the world's finest bear rifle can do." He slid a cartridge into the chamber, squinted into his four-power scope, hauled in a breath, and let it sift slowly out. WHAM . . . the carton winced.

Mac's head hung. "Boys," he muttered, "I'm bloodied." He looked up. Blood branched over his nose and dribbled on to his cheeks. "Damn scope."

"Blood in his eyes," chuckled Big John, as Dick trotted over to retrieve the carton. "That's a good sign."

"In the black," Dick shouted.

"Close enough," grinned Mac, pressing a handkerchief between his eyes. "No doubt about it, boys. This trip you're going to see a one-shot bear kill executed with neatness and dispatch."

Dick tossed the carton back into the dory, and we shoved off. "I guess you'll live, McCullough," Dick said. "Target shootin' is one thing, but. . . . "

"Never you mind, Proenneke. Just you show me the bear."

We headed for Whales' Pass, moving past steep-sided islands where sea parrots dropped from their tunnels in the cliffs and sliced away in long swoops over the swells.

Ahead shimmered a lone island with a screen of gulls.

I wasn't surprised to hear Dick announce, "There's Clipper Ship Rock." It resembled an old square rigger bearing down upon us under full sail. As we drew closer, I noticed the gulls were smaller with black wingtips. The impressive structure was a kittiwake rookery. Birds nested all over its rocky shelves, and its sides were bleached white with their droppings.

"Them eggs are interestin'," Dick said. "More narrow on one end than the other. They roll in a tight circle. Reckon that's nature's way of keepin' 'em from fallin' into the sea?"

Johnny shrugged. "Eggs good to eat, too."

"How do you tell the good ones?" I asked.

Johnny grinned. "Native people go to island. Throw all eggs they find in water. Go back next day. All eggs they find fresh."

"No flies on—hey, what's that?" I yelped, stabbing with my arm to point at what I'd just seen. Out it came again, rolling its long, glistening length out of the sea, arcing smoothly, like a great fat tire turning and sinking out of sight.

"Blackfish," grunted Johnny. "Small whale. Twenty feet long, maybe. See lots of them."

We surged on through the seething rips and whirls of Whales' Pass, on through the Straits of Kupreanof, and then through Uganik Passage to where we anchored late in the afternoon beneath a mountain that brooded over Viekoda Bay.

In the evening a flat-faced, flare-nosed Aleut man, wearing a watch cap and a parka over striped coveralls, came to visit by skiff. He lived on the beach. His Labrador retriever, who had followed in his wake, kept swimming around the *Elizabeth*. Finally he sensed he wasn't welcome aboard and headed back in. The Native did his best to convince Mac that at least five bear were up on the mountain that shadowed us.

"They are up high now," he said. "They feed on berries covered by the snow since last fall. You can go up there with hardtack crackers yourself and live off the berries. I never see bear come down on the beach till June." He wanted our company and something to drink.

"No booze on this boat," said Johnny. "One season long before war, me and other feller partners. We trap peninsula. I lend him trapping outfit. He trap one bay. I trap other bay. He try get in skiff from boat when drunk. Fall in. Go down just like stone. I can't get him." He shook his head. "They find him later. He have my sets for link and wolverine. I never find them. Seventy traps I lose. No booze on my boat no more after that time."

Dick and I pitched the tent atop a tarp near the stern, unrolled our sleeping bags, and turned in. The last things I remembered were the creaking of the towrope against its cleat, the lapping sounds of water, and a pale star peeking through the flap.

~

Second Day

WHEN I WOKE THE NEXT MORNING, Dick's sleeping bag was empty. In the half-light I looked at my watch. It was 3:30 in the morning. Then I heard the knock of an oar. I lifted the flap.

"Sam," Dick whispered, beckoning me into the dory, "I got

Big John and Dick Proenneke.

somethin' to show you."

I dressed quickly and joined him. He rowed to an island in the mist. We beached, clambered up the rocks, and stalked across the brush to its far side. Dick pointed. There below us on a mahogany-colored reef, draped like slugs, some dry and some shining like wet rubber, were hair seals. They made noises like men with severe cases of indigestion and scratched at themselves with their flippers. Dick decided to get closer for a shot with his still camera. A few terns intercepted him and began to screech and flare. He took a few pictures, then suddenly jumped up, waving his arms. The reef exploded into seal-like fragments, and their heads bobbed and reared in the lather of their commotion. They reminded me of boys surprised at a skinny-dipping swimming hole. There they were popping up to see who was going to run off with their clothes.

Returning for breakfast with Mac, we moved out into the Shelikof. Across the blue water, rising like tiers of snowy pyramids that floated on the sea, were the peaks of the Aleutian Range. A volcano sent up a lazy plume of activity.

I could almost hear The Historian beside me. "When Baranof sailed these waters, the Aleuts practically lived in their bidarkas. They paddled their little skin boats all up and down the peninsula with their feet curled under them."

Dick sang out, "Sea lions ahead."

Mac and I focused on the island and saw the pale brown forms hauled up on the rocks and draped amongst the kelp.

"Why don't you give up huntin' bear, McCullough?" Dick said. "Why don't you settle for a bull sea lion? Cut his flippers off and you'd have a big brown hide."

Mac was fumbling at his camera when he tripped on the dory towrope and stomped heavily against the deck.

"Don't fall in," grinned Dick. "We can't stop to turn around."

"I'm going to squeeze off another masterpiece," Mac said.

"Hey, Dick," called Big John, "didn't you tell me the guy Mac bought the Leica off of never took any good pictures either?"

The island jumped and flickered and slid into motion like ripples of huge, disturbed cockroaches. The sea lions rocked over the kelp and poured into the sea. They surfaced in groups, thrusting their tapered heads. Only the giant bulls held their ground, posing haughtily on their flippers, nodding their heads, and bellowing their hoarse challenges. The stink of them whipped on the wind and tainted the salt-charged smell of the ocean. We left the swimmers forming an island of their own in our wake.

Cleaving the reflections of Spiridon Bay, we cruised into a bight, where a waterfall spilled from a saddle in the brown and white mountains. The sound of our engine muttered back to us off the slopes.

"Drop the hook," called Johnny.

The anchor splashed. Its chain rattled out. The line stopped, then quivered tight as Dick threw several half-hitches over the cleat.

"Good, this place," Johnny observed, looking up at the high places. "See plenty bear here."

We spent a good part of the day glassing the slopes along the snow streaks. Dick had his spotting scope set up on its tripod just in case a find needed the higher magnification of its twenty-, forty-, or sixty-power eyepieces.

In the early afternoon Johnny said, very quietly, "Bear on the beach." At first I thought he was fooling, then he pointed to the head of the bay. My eyes strained greedily into the binoculars. I let out a soft gasp as my first bear drew up sharply in the lenses. I saw the hump on his back. I saw him splashing, then moving ponderously to nose at the kelp patches on the black sand.

Dick checked him in the scope. "Good hide," he said. "We'll go after him."

Big John buckled on his .357 Magnum and drew the dory alongside. Dick slung his Springfield "ought six." I stepped in with my camera. Taking up the rear was Mac, who tripped on the cleat and almost threw the world's finest bear rifle overboard.

"Don't get panicky, McCullough," Dick grinned, as he wrapped some rags around the oarlocks.

"Bear hear good," muttered Johnny. "Can't make too much noise."

Dick headed into the wind that blew from the bear to us, and finally beached in a cove well above him. Single file, we followed Dick through the alders that curved out of the brown grass, moving slowly and not talking. Then a deep creek halted all forward progress. We hadn't noticed it from the boat.

There was no possible way to cross without swimming. Dick decided to go back and bring up the dory.

"Hurry up, Proenneke," muttered Mac over and over again. "Hurry up . . . for God's sakes, hurry up. . . . " He had a cigarette half out of its package.

"Better not, Mac," I said. "The wind could shift."

Finally Dick drifted into view. He brought the sad news that the bear had left the beach in a hurry.

Mac didn't want to believe it. "We'll have a look anyway," he growled impatiently.

We studied the bear's tracks in the mud and sand.

"Average," mused Dick. "No circus elephant. He's just another star on your chart, McCullough."

We examined a log the bear had torn to pieces. The smell of his fresh dung was in the air, strong and nose-wrinkling. A worn trail wound up through the grass. It was deep-rutted with depressions where the pads of bear had trod for generations. I walked in the path of the giants and had to stretch my legs uncomfortably to match the stepping places.

Mac dragged deeply on a cigarette, flung it down half-smoked, and mashed it with his moccasin. "Come on! Let's go after him."

"Shoot," Dick said, "that old boy's over the mountain by now. You don't catch up to a bear when he's on the move."

"I hope the bastard breaks his neck," stormed Mac. He kicked at the log fragments and almost upended himself. "Or ate a poison grub."

"Now what kind of a way is that for a bear hunter to talk?" Dick scolded. He shot me a look.

When we got back to the *Elizabeth* late in the afternoon, Johnny had good news. He had seen two bears up in the snow.

"We see 'em in the mornin'," Dick said, "we'll go up after 'em."

*

Third Day

JOHNNY SPOTTED THEM BELOW THE ASCENDING mist. Even in the lenses, they looked tiny up there in the snow. They made me think of leeches moving back and forth across the whiteness.

"Big bear," Johnny breathed. "Mating, I think. Don't go far. Same place as yesterday."

We readied for the climb. Big John would stay behind this time. He rowed us into the beach and returned to the *Elizabeth*. From the cabin roof, he would signal the position of the bear from us using a white towel.

We plodded up the wet, black sand and filed up over a knoll and down past some cottonwoods that rose mossy-barked beside a pond. A pair of sheldrakes flurried from its edge, wingtips slapping the water until they lifted into the air, and arrowed long and slim past the branches. An eagle lumbered off its huge nest of sticks in a high crotch, uttering a shrill whistle as it glided in a circle around us.

And then we began to climb, gradually at first, through the brushy birches, and then more steeply up the long brown grasses and into the tangled, forbidding thickets of alder.

The alder trunks crisscrossed and curved before us in surrealistic patterns. Some of them were stripped of bark as much

After the bear came ...

as six feet off the ground, and I knew how deep the snow had lain when the white rabbits had been hungry. Their pellets were sprinkled all over the moss.

Hard canes of salmonberry raked our hands. The dead stalks of wild celery rattled and crackled as we pushed through them. Here and there were the fresh green spikes of skunk cabbage, hellebore, and the rosettes of other wakening vegetation.

Dick went on tirelessly in the lead. I herded Mac on ahead of me. The steep climb was sapping his stamina, but he gamely staggered on. First he shed his parka. I rolled it up and lashed it atop my packsack. Next he passed me his camera and his binoculars. And then he just looked back at me, and without a word I knew he wanted me to sling his rifle. "I ever climb again," he panted, "it'll be in long handles and tennis shoes."

Patches of snow were beginning to appear. In some of them were old bear tracks. They stood out in high relief.

The snow had thawed around them and left the prints in a crooked trail of dirty lumps.

Mac sprawled on his belly beside a tiny stream that tinkled through the overhangs of grass. He put his face into it and sucked in several mouthfuls. "Best brand there is," he gasped, dragging a sleeve across his flushed face. He sat there, chest heaving.

Dick had just checked Big John's signal from the *Elizabeth* that floated like a bright leaf far below us. I saw him swing his binoculars up the slope, and then he was making scooping motions with his hands for us to get up where he was.

"I got plenty of wind," moaned Mac. "I just can't blow it out fast enough. Now what in hell ails Proenneke?"

"Let's find out."

And up we climbed.

"You don't need glasses to see them babies," Dick whispered, pointing. "Listen . . . you can hear 'em."

About seven hundred yards up and to our left, the two great bears wrestled and cuffed and bit each other, now rolling apart in the snow, now closing back together again with muffled snarls that carried down to us. One was knocked into a sliding backwards down a bank. In the middle of his descent, he reversed himself. He shambled back into the fray with a hind dragging gait, and his hide appeared too big for his body. The savage sounds rolled and echoed.

"If that's love, I'm glad I got left out," gasped Mac. "God Almighty . . . that's a record bear. If I could see a trunk, I'd know it was an elephant. Biggest animal I ever saw in my life."

"Let's get a closer seat," said Dick, moving on.

The snow patches soon merged into all snow. We sank to our knees as we struggled through it, slinging our legs and throwing our shoulders. One minute we could walk on the crust; the next we were plunging through it.

A dull throbbing sound carried to us from below. Another boat was moving into the bay. Dick had just topped the ridge that hid the bear from us. He was down on his belly now, urging us to get up to him. I gave Mac back his rifle. He suddenly staggered on drunkenly, falling, and getting up to go lunging on. Suddenly, a popping and then a whirring shattered the stillness. It was an outboard motor on a skiff, and it droned like a giant bee. I looked up to see a bear scrambling straight up to the highest ridge. He covered in minutes what would have taken us hours. I watched him disappear against the sky.

Mac shook his fist down at the bay. "You son of a bitch," he wheezed, patting his rifle. "I'd like to put one of these below your waterline."

Dick was both crushed and puzzled.

"You coulda had your pick, McCullough," he said. "You coulda laid down here at less than three hundred yards." His eyes were searching. "Now where'd that other one go? We're too close not to check him out."

At times sinking to our waists, we finally reached the arena. The snow was trampled with deep trails and mashed by the falling of the huge bodies. Long, dark hairs and wads of snow scattered all over the surface.

An alder sprang up out of the snow with a whooshing sound. Dick and Mac whirled on it with leveled rifles. My heart almost flew out of my throat.

"Jesus!" Mac exploded. "I'm as jumpy as an old maid in a lumber camp."

"Woke me up, too," grinned Dick. "Just an alder bustin' free."

The tracks of the bear were much longer than my boots and twice as wide. My heart was back in its normal position again, but I felt fluttery all over.

Dick looked down at the *Elizabeth*.

"Boys," he said, "the other one left the country, too. Big John's givin' us the wave off."

Mac lit up a cigarette. "Late for the wedding again," he moaned. "Here I've lived a virtuous, upstanding life. Tried to avoid all excesses. How the hell could this happen to me?"

It was a long way back down the mountain.

Big John greeted us at the beach. "That was a female joyriding in that skiff, Mac."

Mac erupted with a string of curses. "Foul a guy up one way or another," he said.

After supper Dick and I went in to see if we could catch some trout for breakfast. The clear water running over sand and stones seemed barren of fish.

"Hard to figure," muttered Dick. "A few weeks and there'll be a traffic jam here likely."

That night I snuggled into my bag, listening to the wind drive rain against the canvas, and I kept thinking of the two giants I had seen up there in the snow.

~

Fourth Day

"YOU SEE BEAR GO IN SMALL patch," Johnny said. "He don't come out. You look all through brush. You don't find him. Where did he go? He like Dick. Where Dick go this time?"

"He was gone when I woke up," I said, looking at a raft of ducks swimming in smoke. "He'll get lost in this soup."

Johnny shook his head. "He got compass inside," he grinned.

Dick materialized out of the mist. He was standing up facing the bow, rowing the way Johnny did with a pushing of his shoulders.

"Thought I smelled coffee," he greeted. "I got McCullough's bear all staked out. I think we ought to spend the night on that bluff at the head of the bay and surprise that old bruin when he takes his mornin' stroll."

"Don't you ever sleep?" queried Big John, mopping at his glasses.

We spent the day watching the mountains, washing clothes, and eating more than we needed. Mac kept a stubborn vigil with his binoculars and muttered several times about there not being a bear in the whole damn country.

In the evening, when it was still light, Big John rowed us to the head of the bay. "I think you guys are nuts," he said. "You'll be shaking like hounds passing peach pits by morning. You should have brought some gear."

"McCullough don't want it to be easy," Dick said.

"Damn right," agreed Mac. "This ain't no Boy Scout troop."

Big John shook his head. "I'll pick you up for breakfast," he said.

We had foolishly left our sleeping bags aboard and brought along instead the canvas tarp. Dressed in heavy parkas, we figured we could sit on the tarp, wrap it around us, and tough it out until daylight. Another mistake was not wearing our hip boots. To get to the bluff we had to cross a stream that was over our shoepacks. Dick just slipped his off, peeled off his woolen socks, rolled up his pants, and waded across. We did the same thing. The chill stabbed up though the soles of my feet and out the top of my skull.

"Cheese and crackers!" Mac gasped. "I'm with a couple of damn fools."

We walked barefoot over the icy mud. I had to give Mac a lot of credit. He was a tough bird. His veins stood out like blue ropes against his white, skinny legs. He cursed Dick for ever talking him into such nonsense. My feet were so numb, I could hardly feel them, but once I dried them off in the brown grass, pulled the woolens over them, and tugged on the packs, they tingled delightfully under the leather.

We spread out the tarp atop the bluff and lay back looking at the stars.

"More than one way to skin a cat," Dick said. "We can't stalk one up within range so we'll try an ambush."

And there we waited for the dawn, listening to the squalling of the foxes and the splashing of the land otters in the creek that flowed below us.

Several hours passed. Even with the tarp hugged around us and our bodies close together, I had the shakes. I couldn't control the shudders that rippled all through me.

My teeth clicked. I was miserable. If I felt this way, I thought, what about Mac? He just shook beside me and said nothing. He'd gone into a sulk when we said he couldn't have a cigarette.

About three o'clock it began to lighten.

Frost silvered the grass around us and glinted on the canvas. Our breaths steamed. The bay was emptying. Rivulets ran out over the sand past the blocky buttes and trickled into puddles, and then on past the kelp litter and clam shells to catch up with the fast ebbing tide.

With the coming of light, the tidal flat awakened. A few gulls sailed their patrols, while crowds of them waded in the shallow puddles that shimmered among the islands. A shabby fox moped along the beach edge, nosing here and there. Loud whistles shattered the air with a piercing abruptness. A pair of blackish birds, smaller than crows, teetered on a rock pile. Their long red bills and bright red eyes demanded a closer scrutiny. They walked over the rocks as if they wore flapping overshoes. I recognized them as oystercatchers, but I was too chilled to be excited.

I looked again at a margin of brush I had looked at only seconds before. A bear was growing out of it! He moved massively, like a monstrous raised turtle, slinging his forepaws in looping, pigeon-toed strides. His sloping hindquarters shuffled along behind as if they had difficulty keeping up with the rest of him. His shoulders bulged with crawling movements, and he swung his grizzled head from side to side as he came. Now he stopped to turn at a driftwood log with a raking of claws, examined it as if not really interested, and came on tiredly, leaving his crooked trail in the silt.

"Mac. Mac," I whispered, "look. . . . "

The bear was less than two hundred yards away and drawing closer.

"God! God Almighty," breathed Mac.

"Take him," Dick hissed, "take him now."

"I got to—get rid—get rid of these goddamn shakes," quavered Mac. "I got to—"

"Down on your belly and bust 'im."

"I'll miss him. Christ, I'm shaking so much that the rifle's got joints in it." In desperation, Mac crawled back from the bluff edge. He was doing deep-knee bends, swinging his arms across his chest, and jogging his legs up and down.

"C'mon," Dick whispered sharply. "This ain't no gym."

"A little closer," begged Mac. "I don't want to miss. Christ, even my words are shaking." The night chill not only shook his body, it had shaken his confidence. The rifle trembled in his hands as he crawled like an infantryman through the frost to the birch clump.

"Now. *Now*," urged Dick.

I waited for the shot to crash.

It never came. Suddenly the bear swerved and with an incredibly quick motion crashed into the brush. Mac whimpered and cursed. Dick looked at me. He took a deep breath and swelled his cheeks as he blew it out.

"That's one lucky bear," Dick said.

I thought Mac was going to cry.

⌐

Fifth Day

WE SCOUTED ZACHAR BAY. BIG JOHN spotted a bear high in the snow. The sound of our engine must have spooked him, for he moved as if stung, rocked along the alder fringes, scrambled up to the rim, and silhouetted against the sky for an instant before he dropped out of sight.

High-velocity winds blasted us from across the Shelikof. Johnny hunted for a hole until he found one in Uyak Bay. "Glass is down," he said. "Bad weather come."

The rains lashed us. Mac grumbled and chain-smoked cigarettes. "I feel I ought to be out there," he said.

"After last night?" piped Dick. "I could hear your bones rattlin'. Now you want to get soaked in this? You'll catch pneumonia. Take it easy. You're on vacation."

"Vacation, hell. This is strictly a business proposition with me. One of these days Old McCullough will scrunch back in his chair and curl his toes in that long brown hair and think about how he earned him."

Big John looked up from whetting his knife. "Maybe his wife won't allow the hide in the house."

"Wife?" exploded Mac. "You crazy?" He squinted through his smokescreen and uttered a blast of laughter. "Boys," he said, "marriage is a frightful thing. The more I think about it, I'm a mighty fortunate individual."

Late in the afternoon Mac threw his rabbit's foot over the side. "Carried that since the last hunt," he muttered. "Time I deep-sixed the son of a bitch."

"Didn't do the rabbit no good either," Dick observed.

When it was time to turn in, the wind still screamed.

Dick and I decided to sleep in the hold. I thought of how

miserable I had felt on the bluff and how comfortable I was now. What a wonderful sensation to enjoy my private warmth and just lie there listening to the slamming of the wind, the sloshing of the waves, the bumping of the dory, and the creaking of the hoist. I heard Dick's voice getting farther and farther away.

Sixth Day

THE LAND OTTERS CAVORTED AROUND US. They surfaced, holding herring in their forepaws, biting chunks as if from candy bars, and wrinkling their whiskered faces as they chewed. From the shadows beneath the bluff came the tomcat wails of their courtship.

Dick, Big John, and Johnny were making some repairs on the engine of the *Elizabeth*. Mac and I felt we were in the way. We decided to go ashore and follow the creek that emptied into the lagoon.

"Time is money," Mac grumbled. "We can't waste it looking at scenery and listening to this racket."

Dick rowed us into the beach. Schools of herring passed beneath us, resembling moving ribs of sand. Starry flounders, with spurts of sediment, rippled like small rugs away from the bow that slid over them.

"Don't get carried away, McCullough," warned Dick, as the bow grated into the beach and we jumped out.

"I'll push you off," Mac grinned. "I'm wearing Russell moccasin boots."

We walked over the slippery bubble kelp, podded like tiny cucumbers that popped beneath our soles. We passed steep rock bluffs clustered with barnacles and shelved with mussels. The soft sand made sucking noises as our boots lifted. We stopped to examine a battered, red double-ender dory hauled up into a graveyard of grass. The paint was peeling. In white, uneven letters was its name: *STRANGER*.

We crossed bear trails and followed along the creek bank toward the peaks.

It was late afternoon. We were sitting on the trunk of a fallen cottonwood, glassing the slopes when Mac let out a blast of triumph.

"Three of them big bastards up there," he whooped.

Then I spotted a fourth. We watched them for about ten minutes. They hardly moved.

"We know there's four bear up there," I said. "The wind's blowing across the slope. If we work into it, how can we miss?"

"What the hell we waiting for?" barked Mac, jumping up from the log. "We'll surprise that crew of mechanics with a hide."

Charged with enthusiasm, we began the climb. I marked one of the high bluffs in my mind; it had a pile of rubble beneath it. That would be our reference point. The bear were moving slowly away from it in the direction of the lagoon. All the way up, we found fresh bear sign—torn ground where they had rooted for skunk cabbage and wild celery, tracks across the snow patches, and even the strong, lingering smell of their passing.

We reached the rubble beneath the bluff, now veiled with a dense fog slowly sinking and settling around us. The snow was mashed with bear traffic. We followed into the wind like eager, silent hounds. Just ahead a pair of ptarmigan jittered on the snow. They stretched their necks, squatted on their tails, now shrinking their heads close to their bodies, now bobbing and rocking on their breasts. They burst into the air amid snow fragments, croaking a hoarse alarm as they whirred into a swift scaling before us. In the mist they took on huge dimensions and looked like White Holland turkeys.

If ptarmigan looked that big, I thought, *just what the hell would a bear look like?* Any minute I expected a colossus to loom in front of us. On we floundered, following the fresh tracks and straining our eyes into the vapor.

"Mac," I whispered, "can you see in that scope?"

"No, damn it. We got no business trailing these bastards in this stuff. Even you're fading out on me. We better get to hell off this mountain."

In our zeal, we had lost all conception of time. Now we were enveloped in a shroud of fog. No moon. No stars. No flashlight.

Darkness came on like drawn drapes, and we were almost on top of a mountainous ridge. I thought of the alder thickets. They were bad enough in the daylight. Now they'd be hell.

"Stay close, Mac," I said. "Hang on to my shirttail if you have to. I'll take it slow and easy."

"That's my pace."

"We'll follow this brook down."

The brook disappeared into the ground after a time. I just descended with the slope of the land until I heard running water, then moved in its direction to follow it down. We crashed through the alder tangles. We fell down. We joked with each other about getting panicky. We misjudged drops in the darkness, and, miraculously, we kept on going as if made of rubber.

I suggested building a fire and sitting around it until we could see.

"I stop now," Mac moaned, "I'll never get up again."

The slope descended into a black forever.

"Who in hell . . . would think I could miss . . . " Mac panted, " . . . chances at four bear and wind up in these goddamn alders in the middle . . . of the night? I'll chalk this one up . . . to the vicissitudes . . . of life."

I heard the whirring of whistler wings. *We're getting close to the water*, I thought. The slope was getting almost precipitous. Then I dislodged some stones that clattered away from me and after a sickening silence, splashed in water. I didn't move another step.

"Stay put, Mac," I said.

I could see a faint glimmer in the murk. My heart lunged, and I felt a tingling all over. A lantern on the *Elizabeth*! What else could it be? A kindly providence had led two damn fools who had a lot to learn about bear hunting to the steep edge of the lagoon, now brimming with the tide.

"Touch off that cannon, Mac," I said, bracing myself for its roar.

The .300 thundered, and echoes chased each other. Mac cursed, dislodging stones that flurried the water below us. "Caught that one right in the muscle," he groaned. "What a night this is."

I saw a smaller light winking.

"After I count three," I said, "we'll both holler 'Hello, *Elizabeth*' twice. One . . . two . . . three. . . . "

"HALLOOOOO *ELIZABETH* . . . HALLOOOOO *ELIZABETH*!"

We were on our hands and knees. We didn't dare move up or down. Sounds carried to us. I could hear the rattle of oarlocks, and the splashing of the blades . . . nearer and nearer. At intervals I lit one of my wooden matches and let it burn until it got too hot for my fingers. The darkness blossomed as the big light flicked on.

"Stay right where you are," Dick said. "I'll come up after you with the light soon as we find a place to beach."

"We thought you two jumped ship and went over the hill," Big John called. "Keep us up half the night and worry us to death."

Dick worked up to us. "Like a couple of treed coons," he grinned. "Good thing you stopped where you did." He shined the light down. "Not much to hold on to down there."

The water reflected an eeriness that made my stomach crawl.

Back on the *Elizabeth* once more, Johnny shook his head slowly. "Don't see how you get down with no light," he muttered. "You got a friend up there."

"So do them bear," grumbled Mac.

Seventh Day

OUR NIGHT DESCENT OF THE MOUNTAIN must have scared every bear out of the country. We skirted Amook Island and probed deeper into Uyak Bay with no sightings at all. Dick suggested a change of scenery. It was unanimous. We would head back toward Afognak and the spruce.

Mac was cutting his cigarettes in half to make his supply last.

"That old boy's goin' to have a nicotine fit directly," observed Dick.

Mac stayed out on deck, swaying with the roll of the sea, holding the binoculars up to his eyes, and trying to make bear out of the boulders on the mountains.

⌐

Eighth Day

"TEN DOLLARS FOR THE GUY WHO spots a bear that I get a shot at," Mac announced.

"Your money's safe," laughed Big John.

We were anchored in Malina Bay, the Bay of the Berries. On three sides of us were meadows of brown grass looped among stands of spruce. Streams spilled off the slopes from out of the snow and shined silver in the sun. The land twinkled an invitation we couldn't refuse.

We left Mac nestled in the sun against a big granite chunk, where he could glass a broad sweep of country. Dick, Big John, and I went off to explore some beaver ponds. Teal, mallards, and widgeon jumped up straight and sliced off beyond the stark limbs of the drowned trees. We inspected a few beaver dams, took pictures of a lodge, and looked over the cutting operations. No aspen or cottonwood was available here. The animals had settled for spruce. That was all there was.

Dick pointed to some elk droppings. They littered the meadows in piles of pellets about twice the size of jelly beans. I remembered reading about elk being introduced to Afognak Island from the Olympic Peninsula in Washington State years ago.

As we came around a spruce fringe, a grassy clearing opened to us, and in the middle of it posed three elk. One was a big bull. His horns were just sprouting, and he stood there as if ashamed of the little lumps pushing out of his head. His face and neck were a deep mahogany, his flanks a creamy beige, and his rump a blazing white. Slowly we moved toward him, taking pictures. He yelped with a sound I hardly expected. It sounded just like a dog's bark. It was a signal. The alders behind the three elk trembled, and like a band of Indians emerging from ambush, twelve others gathered in a half circle around the bull. Then off they went, the bull taking up the rear, their white rumps jogging and flashing as they moved off through the brush like a pack string.

As we followed along a bear trail in the thick moss beneath the spruce, a succession of waterfalls thundered down a cut to our left. Spruce cones and dry limbs cluttered the hummocks. Above the booming of the water could be heard the high-pitched twitter of birds in the boughs. I felt as though I was walking on sponges. Every clearing we came to was a new adventure, and my eyes flicked greedily for a suspicious shape or movement.

We stopped to look down into a bowl with a pond in it.

The water looked black, and the spruce trees reflected sharply, growing down as well as up.

"What have we got here?" muttered Dick.

A silver fox was trotting along the hillside. I studied him in the lenses. He was hunting mice. He stopped with ears stiffened, squatted, rocking like a cat about to leap and not going through with it. Swiftly he bounced over the ground as if he had coiled springs on his paws. His tail flopped like a squirrel's as he brought both front feet down in a trapping motion. And then I saw him chewing his dinner as if it were sour. *A wild silver fox*, I thought. At one time a pelt like that would have meant five hundred dollars to a trapper, but that was long ago. Fox farmers made them common, and women changed their fur styles.

"You're as beautiful as the country you live in," I said aloud.

We climbed up into the snow where the ptarmigan were crowing. I took pictures of a rooster. He was still in his white plumage. A growth like a scarlet flower showed above his eye. As I crept closer to him, the crust gave way beneath me, and I slammed my knee so hard against a ledge that I felt sick to my stomach. For several moments I just grimaced, waiting for the pain to retreat, wondering if I'd be able to walk. I thought I was going to vomit.

Dick came over to me. My leg was still down in the snow.

"You look peeked," he said. "Think it's busted?"

"I better find out." I pulled my leg out and started to hobble. "Guess it's okay," I grunted. "It doesn't buckle, but it hurts like hell." I sat down on a rock and rolled up my pant leg. The long underwear was red around the kneecap, and there was a small hole through the weave. I pulled up the underwear. Instead of blood there was a pinkish, opaque ooze like a worm casting coming out.

"You drove somethin' into the innards of your kneecap," Dick said. "She might stiffen up on you."

"I can make it back down."

Big John blew out a sigh of relief. "For a minute there I thought me and Dick would be packing you down the mountain."

My leg was throbbing when I reached the beach. I had developed quite a limp.

How one mishap prepares for another! While favoring my leg, I fell heavily on the deck of the *Elizabeth* and badly sprained my right thumb.

Mac groaned. "This is an ill-fated voyage," he said.

"To hell with it. Tomorrow we'll head for home port. Skunked again."

> *Author's journal, May 18, 1953*
>
> *The bear was a very lucky bear. He chose to veer into the brush. I don't think he winded us. I think he just took a notion to leave the beach. Mac cursed himself for not shooting. Five minutes later, I checked my light meter. There was enough light for a picture. I could have easily shot 100 feet of film then. The bear had come at a time when Mac and I were helpless. I guess, as Mac had said on the mountain, "It was just one of those vicissitudes of life."*
>
> *I'm so sleepy now I can't see. We didn't get a bear on the trip. I didn't get any pictures of them, either.*

A YEAR WOULD PASS BEFORE MAC would get another chance to chase his bear. An entire year of enduring the "Bearless" jokes and keeping his quick comebacks at the ready. But time did pass, the seasons did change. And once more our party boarded the *Elizabeth* so Johnny could take us to the mountain.

"B" Day

THROUGH RASPBERRY STRAITS, THE SPRUCE CROWDED either shore, advancing halfway up the slopes to the thickets of alder and brown grass that grew below the snow streaks. Three hair seals trailed us like water moccasins.

Dick was engrossed in glassing the country.

"Elk," he announced, as I stepped out of the cabin. "Thirteen of 'em strung out up there."

"To hell with the elk," growled Mac. He sat on a coil of rope, looking like Rodin's statue, *The Thinker*.

Then I noticed Dick stiffen. He seemed to move into the black cups of his binoculars. "Somethin' movin' up yonder," he said. Then his voice leaked out again, soft but excited. "Movin', sure enough. Might cost you a sawbuck, McCullough."

Mac jumped up, his hands scrabbling for his binoculars. "Where? Where the hell is he?"

"Them alders that look like the letter 'H' up there. Here he comes, out in the open again."

Johnny shut off the engine.

The high slope drew up to me sharply etched. I saw the dark shape of a bear shambling across the whiteness. It stopped, throwing its head up and around, then shuffled on. It grew light in the lenses and shaded dark again.

"God Almighty!" exclaimed Mac. His eyes were bugged into his glasses as if he were studying a chorus girl under a shower. "He's huge."

"Can't tell from down here," Dick grinned.

"Hell, I can't. Look at the head on him. It's big as a bushel."

"You got a right good pair of glasses."

Johnny was studying the bear now in the spotting scope. "Never can be sure how big," he said. "Hide is thick. Not rubbed that I can see."

"Probably a record," exploded Mac. "What the hell we waiting on?"

"Hold on," Dick said. "We'll just watch that old boy for a spell."

"We'll lose him."

"We will if we get panicky."

"No good to climb when bear is moving," Johnny said. "Won't be there. Better to wait. Sun make him lazy. Pretty soon he go to sleep."

"I'll drop the hook," said Dick.

An hour later Mac was pacing the deck, chain-smoking his half-cigarettes. The Model 70 was slung over his parka.

"You suppose that's the same bear from last year?" he asked.

"It's the same place."

"Maybe that's just his fate."

"What's that? One more year." Dick grinned in Mac's direction, then let the binoculars drop against his chest.

"He's pawed himself a bed," he said.

"Let's move out," Mac grunted. "I get him, I'll never swear again."

Big John hauled the dory alongside.

"Just one fly in the ointment," Dick said.

"What's that?" piped Mac, stepping clumsily into the dory, then sitting down abruptly as its rocking tipped him off balance.

"Them elk." Dick nodded at a small herd of brown shapes moving on the mountainside.

"To hell with the elk."

"We spook them elk, we ain't got a prayer. They ain't more than five hundred yards below him." Dick pushed his red hat farther back on his head. "I'll stay and signal. You boys go up after him."

"I'll signal, Dick," I said.

Dick looked at me, surprised.

"Maybe I've been the Jonah," I said.

Dick pointed to the mountain. "We'll follow that ridge that runs just above the bear. We'll circle wide on them elk and watch the wind. You see me stop and squat, you'll know I'm lookin' for a signal. If he moves . . . give us a wave off."

They piled into the dory, and Johnny rowed them into the beach, the gulls churning in a gray-and-white mass around them.

I felt as though my outfit was pulling out into combat and I couldn't go. On the cabin roof, I set up the spotting scope and settled down into the long wait. Next to me was the gaff hook with a big white towel spread out and tacked to it like a flag. I kept my eye on the bear.

Several times he got up, ambled out of the alders, and returned to flop down into his bed once more. I was concerned when I saw the elk trot into a line and pose like statues. The boys were coming into view. Would they spook the elk? I breathed easier when the boys went out of sight again and the elk went back to their grazing.

I saw Dick appear on the ridge and squat for a signal.

I held up the towel to show where the bear was in relation to his position. I looked, but couldn't see the bear anymore. He had to be in the same place. Because I had been checking the area constantly, I was certain the bear hadn't come out. I gave signals more frequently now. I estimated the boys to be within two hundred yards of where the bear lay hidden. They were on a bluff just above and to the left of him. For at least five minutes they never moved. Then all three squatted.

"They know where he is," Johnny said behind me. It was eleven o'clock.

Four hours later my eyes were burning with strain. The boys hadn't moved from their position.

Johnny squinted up at the brightness through the spotting scope. "Bear want to live as long as he can," he said.

The two spaced shots rolling down off the mountain took me by complete surprise. I saw the bear tumbling, and I saw the boys running down from the bluff.

Johnny's big hand glanced off my shoulder.

"Dick make ten dollars," he grinned.

"Yippeeee," I shouted, fluttering the towel happily. "The old bear hunter finally did it! Johnny, I'm going to make a thermos of coffee and some sandwiches and start up toward them."

I was breaking out of the spruce when I saw the boys coming down the mountain. Big John was dragging the hide. Mac spotted me. He held his rifle high and turned loose a rebel yell that echoed along the slope.

"Big" John Yourkowski and Marion G. "Mac" McCullough.

When I saw the hide, I was disappointed at first. According to Dick, it was only average, but it was a beautiful trophy just the same. The claws were unusually long and unbroken. There was not a rubbed place in the hide.

Mac was shaking more than he normally did.

"A hundred different times I wanted to shoot," he said. "The alders kept moving like somebody was pulling at them with strings. I could see the fur, but I couldn't tell which end was which. Drove me crazy. Then the damn wind changed."

"He looked big as a boulder rollin' out of that brush," Dick said. "After that pinwheel second shot, he shrunk to a stone."

Mac was stroking the thick hide. "Just wait until I see them bastards back at the base," he gloated.

"That was a pretty shot," muttered Big John. "You took him through both shoulders."

"What the hell you think I've been practicing all this time for?"

"He ain't exactly a record or a circus elephant," Dick said.

If Mac was disappointed, he never showed it. He sat there hugging the broad head that Dick had left intact. "He's perfect," he grinned. "And I didn't shoot him on no beach. I climbed a mountain to get him. I earned him . . . the hard way. Boys, this little bear's got class. If I was in Seattle now, I'd be right up on top of one of them barber sticks."

Mac's wrinkled face was a boy's again.

~

I SUPPOSE I SHOULD HAVE EXPECTED what happened after our return to the base.

"Too bad he get bear," Johnny had said prophetically. "What he do now?"

Johnny was much wiser than I.

Shortly after Mac had shipped the salted hide and skull in a keg to the Jonas Brothers, he went on a wild, drunken spree in town. He just pulled out all the stops. Just a few months later, he was gone.

September 1, 1954
Dear Dad, Molly, & Mrs. Millett:
. . . Dad, I have to tell you a little story about
Mac. He's an alcoholic and for 2½ years he never
touched a drop. A Kodiak bear was his goal and
whiskey seemed to have been forgotten. Then he got
his bear. Dick went out fishing. John and I moved
into the Quonset hut. Mac was alone in the barracks.
We were the guys he seemed to depend upon to keep
in straight. A Native girl teller must have liked the
figures he deposited in his bank book. She gave him
"bad eye" and Mac forgot about his money, bear
hide and staying sober. He went on a wild spree that
lasted a week. When he finally came out of it, he
was ashamed. He probably would have lost his job
anyway, but he quit and went back to Seattle.
Love to all,
Sam

THE STORIES TRICKLED BACK TO US from the States. Mac was drinking heavily and in a stupor most of the time. One day I received a pathetic letter in a shaky scrawl. He hoped to get back to Kodiak soon. We'd go on another hunt in the spring. It was not to be.

The news reached us of his passing. Dick summed it up best: "Mac thought he done it all up there on the mountain. The rest of the way was all downhill. . . . "

I often wondered what happened to Mac's "world's finest bear rifle," Mac's "bear finder" Bausch & Lomb binoculars, the Leica camera that took all those "masterpieces," and the hide he'd earned, with those beautiful, long claws. I hated to think of him giving them up as the habit consumed him.

Mac was an education. He was a complex study in motivation, determination, and frustration. Above all, he was a lesson, an example of life's turn toward emptiness and bitterness that I hoped mine would never take. Behind his façade of humor was a very lonely man.

One day I saw the big yellow fuel truck go past—the one he used to drive. My eyes filled, and I felt a tear slide down my cheek.

CHAPTER 8

Into the Backcountry

The Valley of Ten Thousand Smokes – Fall 1953

Vince Daly, the pilot, gestured toward the seaplane, a Grumman Goose, on his beach in Kodiak harbor. "Cost you fifty-five bucks a man, with a minimum of six in the party. I can carry nine passengers with gear in the Goose out there." The aircraft was outfitted with boat floats and wheels, so he could land just about anywhere.

"I can take you over to the peninsula early Saturday morning and pick you up Sunday afternoon," he said. "Better take some extra staples along just in case the weather gets ornery and I'm a few days late. You can live on fish forever over there. Make sure you have head nets. You'll need them. Damn mosquitoes and 'white stockings' even drive the animals crazy."

"I'll see if I can round up a crew," I said. "You'll hear from me either way."

"Be in touch," said Vince.

The Alaska Peninsula had enchanted me ever since I saw its peaks floating on the horizon of the Shelikof Straits. Then the stories of fabulous rainbow trout fishing beyond the Valley of the Ten Thousand Smokes fired me even more. Here was my chance to experience it. What a fool I'd be not to take advantage of the opportunity.

Now just hold on there, I thought. *You're spending money like you're printing your own. You just bought a sixteen-millimeter movie camera, a six-inch telephoto lens that cost as much as the camera, a tripod, and all those other gadgets. You got back from a bear hunt a month ago. The cost of that color film is out of sight. When are you going to start saving again?*

I set my lip. *Why the hell did you come to Alaska?* I countered in my thoughts.

"I'm going!" I said aloud.

I was disappointed to learn that Dick couldn't go with us. He'd committed himself for several weekends to a contractor in town, and Dick's word was better than a guarantee. Big John said he could make it. Bob Sowder and his wife, Shirley, were almost as eager as I was. Then I ran into problems. Either those I asked had already planned something else, or in most instances they just raised their eyebrows and whistled when I told them the price.

Finally George Ante, one of my fellow workers, broke down and talked a Navy chief friend of his into going along as well.

I told Vince we were ready to go. With the consent of the group, I bought more grub than I thought we'd need. We could always lug it back with us. Friday night I couldn't sleep. All I could think about was the Valley of the Ten Thousand Smokes and a lake called Nonvianuk.

The next morning we found Vince waiting for us. He was a small, wiry man with eyes that were stony and flecked like a lizard's. Vince was amiable enough, but wise in the ways of a fast dollar.

I sat in the copilot's seat, strapped tight my safety belt, and gawked at the eider ducks we scattered as we taxied out of Kodiak harbor. The motors suddenly filled my ears with their roaring, and every bone in my body took up a shuddering that vibrated wonderfully through the length of me.

Spray hit the windshield and I could no longer see. Vince

116

crouched forward and strained to focus through the slapping wiper. Then there was a lurch, a euphoric lifting, and we were in the air.

I was surprised when we soon slanted down again.

"Another passenger," Vince said.

We landed at Ouzinkie, a quaint fishing village on Spruce Island. By the sound of our grating contact with the water, I thought the bottom of the hull was being torn out. At Ouzinkie, Vince picked up a Russian cannery worker at the pier. The man was en route to the village of King Salmon on the Alaska Peninsula.

Aleut girls in yellow oilskins clustered on the dock and waved to us. A little dark-eyed boy rowed past in a weather-warped dory.

"Any fish yet?" I asked. He grinned shyly. "Plenty red salmon come," he said.

And then we were off again, with the cannery worker tucked in with the rest of us.

After all of my anticipation, the Valley of the Ten Thousand Smokes was disappointing. It was an ugly country of lava flow, dirty white and chalky pink upheavals, and smoking fumaroles, a barren land mottled like a pale batter of marble cake, a desolation gashed with rivers of mud. I looked down at stands of dead spruce spearing out of the crust. The place appeared devoid of life, and I welcomed the sight of green again and living timber as we approached the lake.

We landed on twenty-mile-long Nonvianuk. The Goose crawled out on its wheels up the packed stones of the beach a short distance from where a river funneled out. I saw a trapper's cabin and a cache, looking like a doghouse on stilts. Then I saw the flashing leaps of fish in the water. Everyone was piling out of the side hatch, and gnats and mosquitoes swirled out of the grass fringe to welcome us.

I wasn't really prepared for the mass attack. They hit my face like grains of sand. I almost took a bath in repellent, but the bugs seemed to love it. I lost no time in rigging my head net over my hat and even trapped some of the tiny fiends within its mesh. Insects whirled around us like clouds of soot. I wiped them off the backs of my hands, and saw they had white legs.

"So these are the 'white stockings,'" I muttered. They had a vicious reputation—they didn't sting like mosquitoes. Instead, they just bit out tiny chunks.

I wished I had brought along a pair of cotton gloves.

As the plane took off, I waved to Vince from the heap of gear on the beach. Big John and I took charge of the camp construction while the others went off to fish. We put up a frame of driftwood and tied down the big tarp over it. While we worked, I heard the excited whoops of the others. *First things first*, I told myself. The fish would still be there an hour from now.

I noticed a new structure like a small barracks, and upon investigation found it to be the property of Consolidated Airlines. A padlock was on the door as well as a NO TRESPASSING sign. It seemed out of place in the setting of a trapper's cabin. Even this remote place was showing the first signs of commercialism.

The fishing was too easy. I took some footage of rainbows being brought to the net. The sight of those silver foil sides slashed with grape juice was just too much for me. I soon learned I was a fisherman first and then a photographer. I was casting hardware and whooping right along with the rest. Midway in my first retrieve across the current, I was on to a five-pound trout. He fought deep and I never saw him until he was flashing in surges around my boots. I admired him, released him, and soon had another on. And so it went.

Bob Sowder hooked a heavy fish near the influx of the river. I followed him with my camera whirring. His spinning rod was sharply bent as he leaned back in the fight. He looked straight ahead as he strode in long steps along the bank. Reaching a gravel bar, he staggered back to the grass. The river flurried, and soon a fish was flopping all over the stones. It was a brilliantly hued male of about twelve pounds. A rosy streak gleamed on his side, blazing a path through the black spots, and his gill covers were the color of cooked lobster shells.

Shirley Sowder, in her carnival plaid shirt and head-net veil, waltzed up and down the pebbled bank, stifling squeals as fish tore line from her reel. She was good company. She pitched in with the camp chores and didn't expect any special treatment.

She complained less about the bugs, and her pure enjoyment of the scene rubbed off on all of us. I felt totally at ease with Shirley. Bob was lucky to have found her.

There were times when everyone had a fish on at the same time. Cast from the lakeshore and you hooked a lake trout. It was heavily spotted with lemon drops, had a yellowish cast to its belly, and waved a deeply forked tail. Bob landed one that weighed about fifteen pounds. Move to the river and work its current and you didn't hook the mackinaws anymore. You got into the rainbows.

George caught the only grayling of the trip, a fourteen-inch, dainty-looking fish with a dorsal sail. Black spots were all over his sucker-sheened sides. He had a soft mouth just like the shiner minnows I used for bait back home. His eyes in comparison to his head looked much larger than a trout's.

The Navy chief, a perennial cigar stub clamped in the corner of his mouth, landed a beautiful ten-pound rainbow. He put it on a special stringer. "That's the captain's fish," he said.

I had enough of crowd fishing and the casting rod, so I moved downstream with the little fly rod. Around the bend I stepped into privacy and the bright, sweeping river. The current squeezed at my boots and made noises where it piled on the upstream side of them. I had to brace myself against its strength. Beneath me, as if I were looking through glass, were the stones of the bottom crowded into a handsome mosaic of slate blue, pale green, yellow, purple, and red. The depth was deceptive, and were it not for the hugging against my thighs, I would have thought I was standing in but a foot of water. The chill crept into me through the rubber.

I snaked out the line several times before an eighteen-inch rainbow engulfed the fly. This was more my kind of fishing. Out he came in curving leaps, doubling himself, straightening, and spanking down on the flow. He was worth more to me than the much larger specimens I had taken on the hardware.

While I battled and released trout, a black-headed gull sat on a spire of spruce and jeered noisily at me. Arctic terns sliced back and forth above me. A sudden commotion and I looked across to see a cow moose. Ungainly and high-shouldered, she trotted into the brush and was gone before I could slosh into the gravel bar for my movie camera.

I went back to join the others. Big John was enjoying his role as camp engineer and keeper of the fish. He had a long safety-pin stringer chain anchored to a rock in the river. When he retrieved the chain, he made me think of a dog handler with several spirited dogs on a single leash.

The water thrashed silver, crimson, and lemon as he showed me the fish so far selected for the trip back to Kodiak.

We had a fish fry. I liked the rainbow better than the mackinaw. The gnats and mosquitoes kept us constantly in motion, and I'm sure the pieces of fish we tucked in beneath the head nets were well seasoned with insects before reaching our mouths.

A Consolidated Airlines amphibious Goose landed and beached where Vince had. Two men came toward us. They appeared friendly, yet there was an irritation in their glances as if they resented us being here. One smoked a stubby pipe. Finally without introducing himself, and motioning toward the building, he said, "You can bunk in the camp tonight. Cost you ten bucks a head."

"No, thanks," I said quickly. I was thinking about the fifty-five dollars the trip already had cost.

The man shrugged. "Suit yourself. But you'll be sorry."

We watched them walk to the plane. There were others in it.

"They got a fishing party," observed the cigar-chewing chief. "This is one of their hot spots. Now they'll drop them off to another one of their camps. They got several over here. They advertise exclusive fishing, and us being here don't make it that exclusive."

Big John glanced at the building. "Must be a first-rate hotel," he grunted.

It turned out the man knew what he was talking about. We put in a miserable night. I slept with all my clothes on, my pants tucked into my woolen socks. I listened to a symphony of whining thousands and even shared the interior of my sleeping bag with the pests as I covered up inside it.

All night long we slapped, scratched, and twitched. Even the fumes of the chief's cigar failed to ward off the attackers. By morning, Shirley's face was swollen. Bob looked haggard. "Might have been worth the ten bucks at that," he said.

Down by the river, the chief let out a mournful howl. On checking the stringer, he had lifted just the head of the captain's fish from the water. Big John's chain of fish in deeper water had not been touched.

"Probably otter," I said. "There's lots of signs around."

I learned once again that things that come too easily are not appreciated. We were in the midst of too much plenty. Here were big rainbows and even bigger mackinaws to be taken with a deep retrieve of flashing hardware, but here I was spending my time flicking a tiny black gnat in an effort to catch a grayling. The grayling was something I wanted and couldn't have. I enjoyed the rainbows I caught instead, but the grayling remained the enticing phantom I knew was there and couldn't tempt. I was to learn later that it was still early for them. In July and August they fed greedily.

The weathered trapper's cabin fascinated me. It was badly in need of repair and I didn't go inside. I looked up at his little house on the gray poles. That was probably where he kept his furs and grub supply. I found an overturned dogsled and several cubby pens where he must have kept his dogs. There was also a crude smokehouse and some rotted mesh along a lead line to evidence he had netted fish in the river.

Probably to feed the dogs, I thought. Then I looked up at a tiny house atop a slender pole. Tree swallows were swooping around it. The trapper must have liked it here for more than what he took from the land and water.

"I can imagine Dick in a place like this," I said.

"So can I," agreed Big John, "but he wouldn't take to the airline traffic much."

The weather held, and Vince returned.

"Looks like you been through the 'Battle of the Bite'," he said, smiling as he glanced around at us. "Sure is a buggy country. But it takes bugs to make good fishing. I guess you just can't have it both ways."

~

Kizhuyak Bay – September 2, 1953

I HAD PUT IN MORE THAN twenty hours overtime for the week. I remembered how jubilant I felt yesterday evening to learn there would be no work the next day. I was going to crawl into the bunk and stay there until I got bedsores.

That was until I saw Dick in the cafeteria. He was going to be on the other side of the island and fishing for red salmon. That was the routine these days. We worked hard and played even harder.

At a day-bright three in the morning, the sixteen-foot boat was bouncing on its trailer cradle behind Dick's red pickup on the rough track into Anton Larsen Bay. At three-thirty, the boat was in the water. The 25 horse Evinrude whirred into its song, and we skimmed over the bay, scattering the seabirds before us. I looked back at Dick in the stern. He was squinting into the wind and licking the salt spray off his lips. The brim of Big John's hat was going flop . . . flop . . . flop, and he beamed.

We passed an island that humped like a huge, green loaf of bread. Bright orange spots were sprinkled throughout the grass near its top. The spots moved toward us like oncoming golf balls and magically changed into the bills of sea parrots. The birds braked their black bodies out of their swoops and splashed into the shimmer before us. Far out in the Shelikof I saw the spouts of whales. They made me think of ghostly elm trees on the horizon.

About 5:00, we beached at Barabara Cove in Kizhuyak Bay. I heard the roaring of Red Salmon Creek, and I saw the tossing mane of its falls above the green grass.

They were red salmon. They were squirting out of the white water, thrusting their silver bodies against the torrent that rushed down over the boulders to the bay.

"Come on, Sam," pleaded Big John. "I got the fire going. Where's the fish?"

"You better drag out the three-fifty-seven, John," Dick teased, "and shoot one afore we starve to death."

I waved at the gnats that whirled before my eyes and crawled over my hands, set my lip, and flicked the fly out again. It bounced on past over the spume. Salmon heaved like small porpoises all around it. They weren't interested.

My reputation was waning fast.

Now it was after 6:00. The artificial flies just weren't going to do it. An overdue breakfast demanded other methods.

I tied a large hook on to a stout leader and squeezed on a split shot a few inches above the shank. Second cast and I was on to a big Red. I had snagged him just forward of the tail. He leaped several times in succession, then headed for the sea with me dancing over the rocks in pursuit. I lost him in the middle of a jump, and Big John groaned. He and Dick weren't addicted to fishing as I was. They preferred their fish in the pan.

Minutes later I was on to another, and after a spirited aerial display he was flopping in the tender grass much to Big John's delight. What a beautiful fish! He lay there gasping, a streamlined four pounds, his bluish back accentuating his sides of mercury. Dick quickly ended his spawning run. He laid him over a driftwood chunk, and I watched his knife expose the fillets of deep orange. Soon the strips were sizzling in the pan, and before long we were squatted around the coals, our cheeks bulging with savory salmon fresh from the sea.

I caught several more while Dick recorded the action on film. As soon as the steel stung a fish, out he came as if the water was too hot to enter again, just touching it as he splashed and hurling back into the air. The ferrules of the fly rod rattled, and my wrist ached.

"That little willer wand squirms like a snake," Dick said.

The banks of the stream were a new leaf green. Scattered throughout were the blue spikes of lupine, the brown blossoms of squaw lilies, and the dark pink blooms of salmonberry with their golden centers. The clear water leaped and frolicked with a wild and thrilling music. *Red salmon*, I thought, *I don't blame you for coming home to a place like this.*

Big John was loaded down with artillery. He had a .30-06 slung on his shoulder and the .357 Magnum belted on his waist, gunslinger style.

Sam proudly displays his catch.

"I won't bother a bear if he don't bother me," he said. "I just want to have something along so's I can argue on more even terms."

We came to a falls. I just had to sit on a ledge and watch the traffic. Dick started off with his gold pan and Big John followed. "We'll poke around for a spell up in the hills," Dick said. "Meet you at the lake around noon."

Salmon spurted out of the foam into the onrushing apron.

They drove frantically with their tails until they were flung backwards. I gasped as some vaulted to the brink of the falls and miraculously kept on going. They were a lesson in persistence. I had no way of knowing how many times a particular fish attempted the hurdle. Fascinated, I watched the constant vying of bodies against the flowing force. I took some footage of the leapers. Then I noticed a very strange thing. Just below me was a natural fish ladder. The salmon would land in a rock basin and then bypass the falls by swimming up the steps of the chute that raced less violently beside it.

I don't know how long I sat there entranced in the thunder and the spray. Thoughts tumbled in my mind. The salmon became people struggling. There were those who kept beating

124

their brains out in the face of others making it. There were those who "bellied up" and went down the drain. And here were the others that found the easy way around the competition. Was it just luck that some discovered the rock basin and others never did? Where did I fit in? I didn't think I had reached the falls yet, but I was headed upstream . . . headed somewhere.

I dallied along the bank until I saw the lake. Then my pace quickened. Near the outlet of the stream that flowed like molten glass through an overhang of alders, I saw the trout banquet. Fish were whirling and slurping greedily into the insect clouds. I tied on a light leader and a tiny fly that bristled with hackle. It bounced on the surface, and I floated it down the slot. *Splash!* My wrist quivered. Even though coated with repellent, the insects crawled into my ears, my nose, and over my face. I kept making nodding motions of annoyance as if my collar were too tight, and I steered the scrappy ten-inch rainbow to a landing place. Just right for the pan. I caught enough for our lunch. When I was dressing out the last one, a bear grunt whirled me upright out of my trance. Instead of a bear, Big John stood there, grinning.

"Find the Mother Lode?" I greeted, recovering.

"Not even a grandchild." Big John shook his head, smiling. Once the fish were cooked, we dined on the lakeshore.

"Last year," Dick said, "I was here in late July. Man, them reds were here in the lake and flashin' around like fire engines. They looked nothin' like they do now. There was lots of bear sign, too, but maybe the bear don't expect the fish yet."

We cleared our camp so that no one would ever know we had been there and trailed back to the beach. I caught more red salmon. Dick and Big John dressed out six. Skunk Bear had promised to show us how to smoke salmon in green alder smoke.

We cruised deeper into Kizhuyak Bay toward the mountains that appeared crowned with wood ashes. A young fellow hailed to us from in front of a tent that was pitched back from the beach. Dick shut off the motor.

"Have a cup?" he greeted happily. He had a scraggly growth of beard and wore a duck hunter's hat of camouflaged canvas.

We sat around sipping coffee he had perked on the Coleman

stove. He was a college student, getting summer credit as a stream guard for the Fish and Wildlife Service. He was full of chatter.

"I've been here since June first," he said. "Almost three weeks now. Sure gets lonesome. Yeah, those reds arrived a few days ago. Most of them will spawn along the shoreline of the lake. Reds generally pick a stream to run that comes out of a lake."

He just kept talking—you could tell he hadn't talked to anybody in a while.

"Other day I saw a bear just disappear under a waterfall and come out shaking himself like a big dog. No, I haven't started talking to any seagulls yet, but I sing songs to them with my guitar. When the pinks come, I imagine the commercial fishermen will give me more company than I want. As long as they stay out of the creek mouths, I'll be happy."

His face fell when we announced it was time to get going again.

"Glad you fellows dropped by," he said. "You made my day."

He looked pitifully alone waving to us as we planed away from his beach.

"He must be crossing off the days," Big John said. "That's what I'd be doing."

It was late in the afternoon when Dick shouted over the roar of the Evinrude, "Nothin' to do now but head back for all that overtime."

I was thinking about the stream guard. *I'd like to try that sometime.*

―

Destination: Danger Bay – September 19–20, 1953

BIG JOHN JOINED US ON A trip to Larsen Bay in the boat. On our way, we passed a lone figure in a skiff. He waved to us and strained his arm upwards. A halibut of perhaps forty or fifty pounds came into view, cave-mouthed, white as a grub on the one side, and a dirty, mottled brown on the other. Dick waved back, and after we passed, he throttled down the motor.

"That's Happy George," he said. "Nothin' he likes better than halibut fishin'. I seen him bring in hundred-pounders and better. You notice them gallon cans floatin' around him? He has them hitched to heavy line and lead and hooks baited with Dolly Vardens. He just lies back with his hands folded across his big belly . . . nurses a beer now and then, and don't care if he gets a bite or not."

Thunder began to rumble as we put the boat on its trailer. Then lightning suddenly made great bright cracks in the sky.

"I never seen thunder and lightnin' here before," Dick told us. "Appears like the birds ain't, either."

The birds wheeled high against the leaden sky like leaves caught in an updraft. There were thousands of them: sea parrots, gulls, cormorants, and terns, mewing and rasping their lost and lonesome calls. They milled like frightened children, and even though Dick and Big John were next to me, I felt strangely alone as the sky purpled and the rains came.

Suddenly, to the side of us, about one hundred feet away, the sea bulged and burst as a black, cylindrical "island" rolled into view, like locomotives awash.

"They ain't blackfish," yelped Dick, throttling down the outboard.

"Cripes," Big John grunted. "Don't argue with them."

My eyes bugged. A snorting bellow, a spurt of vapor, the gleam of an eye, and the endless curving of the great shapes. I waited for the flukes, but they did not appear.

Whales were surfacing on both sides of us. They were in three groups, three or four in each, moving away. Perhaps the sixteen-foot boat made them appear much more monstrous than they were. How easily they could have overturned us or smashed our planks to splinters! As I crouched in awe of their vapor jets, their hulks rising out of the swells, I thought of a harpooner tensing to drive his iron home.

Suddenly panic struck the group closest to us. They dove with a flailing and a crashing of their flukes that rocked the sea in successive underwater explosions. Then all was quiet. We gazed upon a shrinking and swelling emptiness.

The bow of the boat sent spray in a lather that spilled over the surface like soap suds running over a polished floor. Headed out across the straits to Afognak Island in the late afternoon, we were about two hours away from our destination at Danger Bay. Porpoises rolled along the kelp beds. I did my best to make killer whales out of them, but the high dorsal fins I so hungrily wanted to see never materialized.

On the horizon, the mountains dimmed. The sky shaded into a dismal gray, and the blue went out of the ocean.

"We won't be gettin' off the water any too soon," Dick shouted.

Danger Bay was margined in dense spruce. Eagles, perched in the snags, watched us as we drifted into the beach.

Once on the shore, we worked steadily with the axes to beat the rain. Dick trimmed two spruce saplings that grew about ten feet apart and slashed out the site. Big John and I cut several poles and stockpiled the boughs. Then we helped Dick with the lean-to frame. We lashed a pole near its one end as high as we could reach to each sapling and braced its other end into the moss. Across these jutting high ends we placed another pole and lashed it down. To complete the lean-to skeleton, we slanted poles on and down from the frontal crosspiece and thatched over them with spruce boughs. The big tarp overall completed our shelter, and soon the interior was pungent with crushed spruce needles and mattressed with boughs beneath our sleeping bags.

Dick made a fire within a firebox he'd built of green logs. Big John cut a supply of wood from a seasoned snag. I packed water from a brook that chuckled through the moss, readied the coffee, and packed in wood. When there was a glowing bed of coals and the coffee brewed in its pail on the end of the green alder crane, Dick broke out the camp grate from the gear and rested it on his firebox to heat through.

"Can't call this livin' off the country," he said, as he threw three T-bone steaks on the fire with hissing sounds.

"Wonder I haven't sprouted fins this summer from all the fish I've eaten," Big John said. "We deserve a change."

When the steaks were almost done, Dick raked in a smoldering log which drifted smoke over them, and knifed out a butter chunk to top each one before he speared it and tossed it on a tin plate.

We tore into the charred red meat like savages as we hunched beneath our shelter and listened to the fire hiss at the first drops of rain.

I lay there warm and dry in a dripping forest. I looked up at the firelight flickering on the slanted poles. The fire wheezed tiredly in front of its reflector logs, and the wind tossed the heavy boughs. I listened to the rhythmic rushing of waves along the beach, and watched the thin blue smoke ascending to the weird branches, grotesque with moss. "Thump, thump," said the rain on the canvas above us. With my shirt, pants, and woolen socks rolled up into a pillow, I fell deliciously asleep, thinking about the whales and wondering how Danger Bay got its name.

The storm passed in the night, and the mist was lifting to unveil the slopes by the time we emerged from our shelter in the morning.

At low tide on the clean beach of pulverized shells and sand, we looked for butter clams. I dug a hole about a foot and a half deep, stepped down into it, and lifted the tines of the fork up through the slopes of the widening crater. The clams were so ridged in fat that their shells wouldn't come together. We selected them from silver dollar size to about twice as large as that, for steaming and for frying. Some of the larger ones we saved for chowder. While we worked, a pair of oystercatchers scolded us, ratcheting loudly from different points of the compass, trotting swiftly and scrambling into the air with their loud calls as if to alert the entire bay of our claim jumping activities. We kept the clams in a bucket of water and tossed in a few fistfuls of cornmeal so that they could purge themselves of sand.

The day was a leisurely one. Big John tinkered with the motor because it didn't sound just right to him, and he puttered around the campsite making improvements on the quarters. Dick made a plaster cast of a bear track, then went off by his lonesome with the gold pan. I watched some beaver, then scouted the creek for the silver salmon we hoped to take back with us the next day. They were there in force. As I came on one pool, they bolted like frightened cattle. Their backs came out of the water as they churned up through a riffle as if their tails were motorized. They were fresh arrivals from the sea, and bright as new dimes. It would have been no problem to wade out to intercept them and kick them out on to the gravel. Bear sign was all over the place, but I saw none of the shaggy fishermen.

That evening we had a clam orgy. We steamed half a bucketful, drank some of the juice and saved the rest, peeled the skins from the necks and dropped them butter-drenched into our gullets. We fried them in batter. I don't know which way I liked them better, but I ate until the sight of them sickened me, and if it was possible, I felt like a sated seagull.

Now it was time to make chowder. I fried some cubes of salt pork, tossed in several sliced onions, and dropped in the minced sections of the larger clams. Next I added the clam juice, some powdered milk, and chunks of raw potato. The whole mess simmered until the potatoes were done. Then we dug a hole in the moss, and placed the chowder pot into it to let the flavors marry until the next day. We rolled a boulder on top of it just in case some animal arrived, wanting to sample it before we did.

There's something about a campfire that invites open talk and bares the soul. Far into the night we talked with the light from the flames playing over our faces.

"The dream keeps comin' back," Dick said, "and someday I'll do it. It won't be on Kodiak. Another year or so and I'll have her about panned out. I'm goin' way back in beyond the peaks, find me a lake that's got fish aplenty, and in late summer I'll cut my cabin logs. Peel 'em and leave 'em to season durin' the winter. Then in the late spring I'll come back to build my cabin the way I thought about it over and over all these years. I'll build it with hand tools and stay the winter. You boys can visit me."

"That hermit life's not for me," said Big John, shaking his head. The firelight danced over his glasses. "No, thanks. When I get my stake, it's back home to Washington. If that little gal's willing, I'll build a house and get a family started. My mom's been wondering what's taking me so long."

Dick leaned forward, playing the end of a stick in the embers. "What's your plans, Sam? You been in this country better than a year now. Think you'll stay?"

"Haven't made up my mind yet. There's lots to see up here and lots to do I haven't done. May be a while yet before I go back east. When I do, I'd like to be straightened out in my mind just where it is I want to head. I hate to admit it, but I'm still turned around. I'm still searching."

"Done that all my life," mused Dick.

"Me, too," Big John chimed in. "I guess the search ends when they lay you out in the box."

A large beetle was scuttling over a moss-covered log.

"Look at him," I said. "I don't think he knows where he's going or what he's looking for, but he sure acts like he does. That's more than I can say."

"I think the whole answer," said Big John, "is finding somebody you think more of than you do yourself. Then you spend the rest of your life doing for her. If she feels the same way about you, then you got it made."

"No woman's goin' to put up with my wanderin's and where I want to be," Dick said.

Big John laughed. "There's a nut for every bolt."

"Dick," I said, "you arrived in the wrong century. You should have been a mountain man in the high country of the Blackfoot."

For all of our kidding, I had made the decision to stay in Alaska for at least one more winter, but I wasn't making any announcements today. Beyond that, I couldn't say.

The next day we caught the silvers. They were larger and more powerful than the reds. They leaped explosively and made long, reel-screeching runs. The slopes rang with our whoops as we splashed up and down the creek chasing salmon on our fishing leashes. We kept six that ranged from twelve to fifteen pounds. They would be enough for the square dancing wives to pickle. We didn't take advantage of the helpless fish in the riffles. We earned each one we caught.

The weather soured in the afternoon. At slack tide, we headed back for Anton Larsen Bay. The waves shattered against us, whipping the salt spray into our reddened faces and making our slickers glisten. Now the bow rode upwards and all support fell away until it dropped thuddingly, to send the water spewing.

Now we pitched into a valley between the swells, the motor popping strangely as it lost its bite in the sea . . . then that lifting, shoving thrust in a dizzy ascent and the dipping, dying sink as we settled again. Halfway across we struck the rain, and we were very small on a wild, gray sea.

It was late when we got back to the base. One fellow who knew where we'd been asked, "What the hell would you damn fools done if the weather socked you in or you swamped?"

"Well," Dick said, "I guess we'd been late for work."

~

On Sharatin Mountain – June 1954

"IT SURE IS A PRETTY LAST day of July," said Dick, as he sat down at my cafeteria table for breakfast. "I'm headed for a little lake that sits right up there behind Sharatin Mountain. We flew over it one time. Bluest water I ever seen anyplace. S'pose there's fish in it?"

"You son of a gun," I said. I kept right on eating, but I was thinking about the lake. Pretty soon I glanced at Dick again. "It's bad for a guy to get too money hungry, isn't it? I wonder if the foreman would blow his top if. . . . "

"Man, them fish would be pretty out of that blue water."

I nodded. "Hold up until eight or so and I'll see if the foreman will let me off the hook."

"Figured you'd come around," Dick grinned.

The foreman told me if a big enough crew showed up for the paving it wouldn't make any difference if I took the day off.

"Can't figure you out, Keith," he said. "You can make yourself thirty dollars extra. All gravy and you want to go off climbing some mountain. That don't make sense to me. Wish I could borrow some of your philosophy."

"Better keep yours," I said. "That's why you're a wheel and I'm just a spoke."

"Get the hell out of here," he grunted, feigning anger.

Dick was sitting in the red pickup with the boat in tow. He was all smiles when he saw me approaching with the gear.

"Sharatin Bay, here we come," he said. "What'd you tell the old boy?"

"I just told him I had more important things to do than make money."

"Bet you lost him there."

"Guess I did."

Dick started the engine.

As we topped the hump and descended into Anton Larsen's, I saw the fog rolling in from the sea. It came thick and tumbling, swallowing up the land. It was hard to believe my eyes. Here the sun was shining out of a cloudless sky, and spread below us, a dense vapor erased everything.

"I'll be damned," I exploded. "I'm being punished by the Puritan Ethic."

"Don't get shook," Dick said. "We'll climb the mountain and get above that soup."

We launched the boat. Very dimly we could make out the islands. Dick only advanced the throttle partway, and we moved off through the damp veil. Dick was smiling broadly beneath the fluttering of his hat brim. He made me feel good in spite of the elements. I felt his pleasure as well as my own in every breath of charged air, in every bird that scrambled before us, in every blackfish that arced lazily in the sea and sank into it again.

We idled into the mouth of Elbow Creek at the head of Sharatin Bay, startling a ginger-colored fox that looked at us for a moment over his shoulder, then trotted off beneath the low limbs of a spruce. Dick cut the motor. We pulled our boots up high, snapped the straps around our belts, and I stepped out to tie the painter to a partially buried driftwood chunk. The boat swung in close to the tall grass.

"We'd best eat here," Dick said. "Then we can travel lighter. I'll get a fire goin' and start the bacon. You fetch somethin' to go with it. That hardware on the end of my fishin' stick will scatter everythin' in the crick."

While I strung up the fly rod, I watched Dick break up some spruce twigs matted with dry, beardy moss, stack them tepee fashion, light his candle, and hold the flame to the base until it climbed and crackled up though the sticks.

"And away she goes," he murmured, half to himself.

I wandered off through the fog tendrils and into the chest-high grass. I raised up on tiptoe to glance into the current for fish. They were there. In the clear water grouped along the bottom were the shadowlike forms of the Dolly Vardens, holding their positions against the sweep of the flow. They whirled their white-margined pectoral and ventral fins and waved their tails.

The first pattern brought no results. A trout wagged up behind it, and sank again as if it was something he had too much of recently. Not so with a bright Royal Coachman. I worked it deep with a series of twitches. A trout nailed it, then flashed his sides like a heliograph as he wiped his snout at the gravel to rid himself of the mouthful that was fighting back. I worked him into the shallows until he ran out of water and freckled himself with black sand. Then I bent his head over to touch his backbone and tossed him shimmering into the grass.

Three more pan-sized companions followed him. "That should do it," I said. While I dressed them out, I could smell the bacon cooking back at the campfire. I could see Dick moving like a ghost around it beneath the big spruce.

Sometime later, Dick sat with his back against a spruce trunk. He was working on a large mouthful of fish and studying a mosquito on his shirt sleeve. The insect was probing down through the cloth.

"How's he know he's goin' to strike blood?" he mused.

"Maybe he don't," I said. "How's a bee know that pollen makes honey? I guess insects are somehow just programmed. They aren't handicapped by too much thinking."

I wet down the coals and naturalized the site while Dick used spruce cones to scrape the brown crust that scaled the bottom of the skillet.

We were ready for the climb.

Dick went on ahead with his packsack and the "fishing stick" swinging on the end of his arm. I trailed him in my canvas coat and gear through the fog-shrouded spruce timber. The moss was hummocked and pillowy. Ferns and spruce seedlings grew out of it. We skirted a beaver pond and walked past snags bleached white on the stump like skeletons.

We avoided the devil's club. The plants appeared as if in prayer, their giant maple-like leaves outflung from thorny stalks. Even the ribs of the leaves had thorns on them. I knew only too well from past experience how those thorns could fester in the flesh, but to a bear, devil's club was candy. We climbed steeply through alder and salmonberry canes, heavy with berries.

"Dessert," Dick announced, poking a salmonberry as round as a quarter into his mouth. They made me think of large raspberries but had a texture more like blackberries. After eating a few fistfuls, we moved on.

As we climbed, it was interesting to notice the progression of things. Salmonberries in fruit at one level were just blooming higher up. Spikes of fireweed in bloom to the tips down below were just showing color around their bases at the present level.

An amazing transformation was taking place before my eyes. We were well above the timber and had just clambered up through a brushy stretch when I saw the short grass above me in sunlight. We were emerging from a gloomy February into a sunny June. I looked down on a land buried in fog feathers. It was as if a huge pillow had been ripped open and the earth below strewn deep with its contents.

"Almost make a man believe in the Hereafter," Dick observed.

The slope was generous with its lip-numbing trickles, and I often sprawled on my belly to savor the liquid frost that spilled from the snow.

Dick figured the snow-splashed summit to be about 3,000 feet above sea level. It beckoned against the sky above us. Dick kept his tireless pace, ascending almost vertically, and I stubbornly stayed at his heels. It was like Marine boot camp at Parris Island all over again.

"If you can, I can," I muttered at the ground. "I'm younger than you are." I drove my legs without stopping. Suddenly charley horses knotted in both of my thighs. The muscles froze up on me. I was ashamed of myself, but I called to Dick to hold up for a spell.

"Too much of that flat land on the base," he said.

After a few minutes, the muscles responded again and we moved on.

I saw the lake first, or perhaps Dick just waited for me to notice it. It was in a deep bowl off to one side of us, brimming the rich, exaggerated blue of a movie. The snow along its far edge was shadowed in indigo.

"Beautiful," I whispered to it, as we began the treacherous descent toward the lake.

I was close behind Dick when it happened. We were feeling our way down the outcroppings. Suddenly Dick flung himself back into me, as if he had stepped on a rattlesnake. A large piece of rock toppled away from his feet, bounding and flinging itself into the air, crashing into the brush far below. I felt a chill in the pit of my stomach. Dick could have gone along with it.

"Didn't feel right." Unbelievably, he was smiling. Nothing bothered Dick very much.

We worked the rest of the way down to the lake, and dropped down on to a green bench with flower gardens growing into each other. Wild rhododendrons, Indian paintbrush, tiny asters, stunted lupine, and pincushions of moss campions. I half closed my eyes. The greenery glittered with scatterings of prismatic gems.

"Couldn't be better for a picnic," Dick said.

"Why not?" I reached into my canvas coat and pulled out a parcel wrapped in wax paper. We sat cross-legged and chewed on chunks of smoked salmon that Skunk Bear had cured for three days in green alder smoke.

The majesty of the lake held our tongues. We were lost in silence. The beauty was felt and needed no expression; an emanation from its setting oozed a spell over us. Pale turquoise along its edges, the lake shaded to a deep, scary blue at its center. A thin waterfall curtained the precipitous rock on its far side and spattered the only sound we could hear. Off to our right was a miniature glacier.

We walked its straight-cut edge and looked down twenty feet to the eerie blue of anchor ice beneath the surface.

Dick cast his red-and-white daredevil lure and retrieved it at different depths. I did the same with flies of different patterns and sizes. Neither one of us got a bite. Not even a follow-up. Not a weed. Not an insect. Not a hint of aquatic life at all.

We had climbed to a barren lake.

We sprawled in the lupines that grew back from a stretch of meadow edge and studied our surroundings.

"Never seen a place like it," Dick said. "A man dreams about a spot like this. Just look at it. I can imagine fish rings all over it, but there it is just grinnin' at us like a swimming pool."

"In a place like this," I said, "you don't have to catch fish. Being here's enough. This will stay in my mind forever. . . ." Before I realized it I was saying more than I had intended. " . . . like the girl I knew in high school," I said, my eyes on the waterfall and the rock face, as if I could see her there. "She made me quiver. Between classes I used to take different routes through the corridors until I found the one I passed her on. She was as pretty as this little lake and it turned out, just as cold. The guys flocked to her, but she never dated the same one twice. One guy said she was a pretty package with nothing in it, but I never got that close to find out. . . ."

"If pretty's all," Dick said, "it ain't enough."

"I guess a lot of damn fools find that out every day."

Dick sat up. "I got an idea," he said with a smile of mischief.

"What's that?"

"We'll keep our little secret. Others want to find out, let 'em climb up here like we did. They wouldn't lose a thing and probably gain a lot. I got a name all picked out."

"You have?"

"Fightin' Rainbow Lake."

CHAPTER 9

Kenai Moose Hunt

From the window of the Pacific Northern Airlines plane, I looked out on the sharp peaks of Afognak Island. Beyond them was ocean, but it appeared a shimmering lonesomeness through which long, slender clouds sailed. To the west loomed the high white ranges of the Alaska Peninsula. At first you would think they were clouds, but when you looked long enough, you knew they were mountains.

The wheels touched down on the gravel strip at Homer, and the land rushed past. In the distance I glimpsed a glacier, pale blue in the sun, like a mountain torrent stopped with a fast film. Jess Willard, the camp owner, was waiting for Vard, Bob, Tom, Reynold, and me to arrive.

Jess was long, lean, and blue-eyed. His face was bronzed and weather-lined. He wore a bushy moustache with waxed ends and made me think of a high-collared dandy on a tintype or a Confederate cavalry officer.

Johnny Klingbiel, the Bush pilot, had just finished a busy season spotting salmon for commercial fishermen. The tiny floatplane could only carry one passenger at a time, and Johnny singled me out to make the first trip with him into Caribou Lake. I guess I looked the most big-eyed of the group.

I climbed aboard the tiny floatplane with my gear, and we taxied out for takeoff. As we sped over the water and lurched into the air, a boyish delight must have spread all over my face, because Johnny looked at me and grinned. I waved to the others as we shot over them. Some ducks flying below us cast their shadows on the bay so that it looked like two flocks instead of one. Soon we were moving over brown meadows that pockmarked the spruce timber. In one of them I spotted the first moose and jabbed my arm at him excitedly. It was a big bull. He tossed his antlers at us.

"Pretty safe there," Johnny shouted. "No lakes close and a man's a damn fool or awful hungry to pack meat that far out of the muskeg without horses or a tractor."

We saw several cows, some with calves.

"Three blackies," yelled Johnny, nudging my arm and gesturing. Sure enough, poking through the willow brush was a large black bear followed by two smaller ones. With the sun on them they rippled like black velvet.

About twenty-five minutes out and there was Caribou Lake before us. I looked down on a great raft of lily pads on the one end, their edges upturned by the wind. I noticed several beaver houses, and then I saw the peeled log cabins that Jess had built. It was like a small settlement on the edge of a wilderness.

We landed, the beach hurtling toward us until Johnny throttled down. At the float I met Jess's wife, Alice, a large woman beaming with warmth. When she laughed she really meant it, and her entire torso shook. She introduced me to their sixteen-year-old daughter, Jo, who promised to show me some trout fishing. Jo exuded all the wholesomeness of one advertising a breakfast cereal. The smells drifting from the Willard kitchen made me sorry we had brought our own grub along.

I lugged my gear to a guest cabin. Huge, bleached moose antlers welcomed me over the doorway.

Fireweed seed drifted in the air like feathers. Clusters of red berries bloodied the forest floor. My first trip to the outhouse acquainted me with a flock of spruce hens that whirred from the moss and sat clucking on the limbs while I sat studying them and enjoying the picture view.

One by one the others were delivered from the sky. Moose season did not open until September first, so we had the next day for a council of war. We studied maps of the area, sighted in our rifles, checked over our gear, set up housekeeping, and swapped stories.

Tom pulled up his undershirt, exposing his white belly. "Enough slack here," he said, "to grab a handful and blow my nose on it."

"This country won't stand for that long," drawled Vard.

The thought of fresh fish for supper and Jo volunteering to act as guide lured us in the afternoon across a squishy meadow of wire grass and moss. We passed heaps of moose dung, like jumbles of short, fat oval cigars, and I noticed the recent trails that betrayed the traffic of the big animals.

The dark stream boiled with trout that were too easy to catch. They were brilliantly colored with bellies and fins of orange sherbet and red spots on their sides as big as buckshot. Jess figured them to be a cross between Dolly Vardens and the landlocked red salmon of the lake.

We all had fish on at the same time. The smaller ones we saved for the pan. Reynold waded in one feeder stream, stampeding trout that panicked out of the water and flopped until they tumbled back into the brook again. The fish were on the verge of spawning. They were mushy-fleshed and strong-tasting, and the fry we so looked forward to brought no compliments to the chef.

Across the lake was a country of willow brush that made up most of the moose's browse when he was not wading for water lilies, a country of narrow spruce trees that grew halfway up the slopes of the Box Car Range, so named because, notched with passes, the great ridge resembled a stalled freight train. In another direction gleamed the glaciers between peaks that appeared swirled into points of whipped cream.

"Boy," I whispered, "this is Alaska. . . . "

JO SKIPPERED THE OUTBOARD THAT FERRIED Vard and me across the lake to look for moose. She squinted into the wind with the curls beating against her face. Her cheeks glowed with the blush of peaches. *Not many like her*, I thought. I almost wished she were older . . . or me, younger.

Vard and I hunted together. We climbed the slope of a range called the Box Cars. Blueberries grew on top of the moss. We sat amid the ground junipers to glass the meadow islands in the spruce below. Cows and calves were there, but no bulls.

"If I get my moose early," Vard said, "we can spend our time taking pictures."

Vard went on ahead with his rifle shouldered. I tagged along behind like an odds-and-ends traveling salesman, my movie camera and tripod in one hand, a gadget bag with accessories for it, plus my still camera and binoculars looped on my neck, a packboard with butchering tools, and my slung .348 Winchester. As I jounced over the hummocks, I sampled the dried apricots and pears I had stashed in the pockets of my sleeveless canvas coat.

I began to feel weak and very sick. The more water I drank, the sicker I became. I didn't think of it at the time, but the water must have been swelling up the dried fruit inside of me. Too stubborn to mention anything to Vard, I tottered along in his wake. Now and then he turned to scold me with his eyes when I raked the packboard against a limb or stepped on a dry stick.

We dropped down off the Box Cars ridge in the late afternoon. As we rounded a peninsula of spruce that jutted into a sea of yellow grass, there in the open was a young bull. The sight of him revived me for the moment. I slammed the tripod down and fumbled at the camera adjustments. Vard's rifle crashed wickedly. The bull didn't even flinch and trotted in a bouncing gait toward the spruce. All that I could see was that he was getting away. I deserted the camera. The .348 was suddenly in my hands. I jacked a cartridge into the chamber, swung on to the moose, and fired, my shot blending with Vard's.

Moose hunt at Far Camp.

The bull collapsed on his forelegs. His rump sank, and he rolled over on his back, his hooves making slow, bicycling motions.

"You get all that?" shouted Vard, not realizing that I had shot. Then he saw the rifle in my hands. "You shoot, too?"

I was ashamed to admit I had. "I thought he was going to make it into the timber," I said.

"No harm done. I fouled up on that first one. How was you to know I wouldn't do it again? Shot right over his back. I took my time on the second one. Too bad you didn't get that action on film."

"From now on the rifle stays in camp," I said.

Vard's .270 slug would have been enough. It had shattered the spine near the hump. Mine had torn through the lungs. At least I hadn't spoiled any meat, but I felt I had tainted Vard's kill just the same. He didn't seem to feel that way at all. He kept remarking about all that tender meat for his freezer.

The bull's antlers were still sheathed in velvet. The blood had not yet dropped out of the horns. Flies collected in places where they bled through the sheath.

I was feeling so sick I almost wanted to join the moose. Just as we began to dress out the bull, the others arrived.

They had been on their way to the lake when they heard the shots. I hacked the brisket open, and Vard chopped through the pelvic bone to make the hind legs spread apart. Then Vard cut the windpipe free in the throat, and we began rolling the entrails out. Still feeling nauseous, the sight of the well of blood in the chest cavity and the smell of internal organs were more than I could take. I flung away and vomited into the moss. I retched until I got rid of it all, and I started to feel better. I took deep breaths and welcomed the chill creeping into the air.

Vard shoved a stick crosswise between the rib cage so that the chest cavity would stay open.

"He'll cool down tonight," drawled Vard. "We'll peel the hide off in the morning and pack the meat to the lake. Can't be over half a mile."

"What about animals?" I asked.

"They won't bother him the first night with our scent all over the place. They come poking around, there's the insides to keep 'em happy."

I didn't eat any supper. I just crawled into the bunk and died until morning.

At breakfast I made up for the supper I had missed.

I was relieved to find the bull undisturbed in the frost. We skinned him out, cut off the head, halved him at the third rib, and cut each section down the spine with the meat saw.

After the misery of yesterday, I felt like Superman. I carried the first quarter to the lake, my feet sinking into the muskeg and making slurping sounds as I withdrew them. I soon learned that I was with a crew that went through the motions, but had neither the strength nor the endurance for the rugged job of packing out the meat. I kept thinking about Dick, back in Kodiak. He would have loved it here.

Vard threw his back out, but gamely tried to hold up his end. Tom and Bob carried a quarter stretcher-fashion, lashed to two spruce poles, and stopped often. Reynold, the youngest and chubbiest of the group, had a definite opinion about the entire operation.

"Hard work is for horses," he said, "and even they turn their asses to it."

Anyway, I shamed him into using his muscles and drove him to limits he never suspected he could reach.

Once we got to the lake's edge, Tom looked down at the meat pile and groaned, "That's the roughest meat market I ever picked up an order at." We ferried the meat to camp and cheese-clothed the sections. They were ready for Johnny to fly into Homer. One down and three to go.

After that, I left the rifle in camp.

Instead, I took pictures of a cow moose with twin calves, spruce hens parading on spruce boughs, and some whistlers mirroring their reflections on a beaver pond. The bulls had disappeared. At least we couldn't find them.

"They're back beyond the Box Cars," Jess said. "We'll go to the Far Camp. We'll find the bulls back in the Caribou Hills."

Far Camp was about eight miles back in from the lake. Jess's plan was for us to use packhorses.

We topped a rise and there below us in a hollow of the surrounding hills was a white canvas shelter. Horses grazed in the meadows around it, and a stream sparkled out of sight into the willow brush. Through a green saddle jagged with spruce tops, I could see the blue of Tustumena Lake and the glacier at its head.

Already at camp was Bruce, Jess's eighteen-year-old son. I liked him at once. He had the energy and enthusiasm I admired, and I wished secretly I could spend the entire season with him. He was thick-armed. His blue eyes twinkled from beneath a shock of yellowish hair. He was wise beyond his years in the ways of the country and his horses.

"Any bulls back here?" Tom asked.

"Lots of 'em," said Bruce, running his fingers through his hair. "Big brownies, too."

"To hell with the brownies," Tom grunted. "I come for meat . . . not a hide."

That afternoon, Bruce and Jess steered Tom and Reynold to a stand of cottonwoods where a bull moose convention was being held. Tom downed a bull with a massive spread of shovels just under sixty inches, and Reynolds dropped a younger one. What interested me was the efficiency of the butchering operation. In the time it had taken us to quarter Vard's bull, Jess and Bruce had two ready for the meat tree.

"Warm for the season," Jess said, wiping his forehead with a red bandanna. "Weather like this, you get the hide off fast so's the meat has a chance to cool. Then hang it high so's it will get a crust all over it. If the flies blow it, you can just brush the eggs off."

In a gnarled spruce snag we hung the red sections of meat. Several Canada jays planed in from the spruce shadows, steering their gray bodies to a landing on the grayed branch ends. They looked like large, whiskered, frosty-faced chickadees as they picked at the fat.

"Looks like Christmas for them," Jess grinned.

Bruce lashed the horns of the old bull to his packboard, shouldered it, and off he went into the spruce. Tom's eyes followed him.

"Damned if I don't see an Alaskan angel," he said.

~

ON THE KENAI, I LEARNED A new respect for wildlife photographers.

Bruce was leading the pack string from the kills of yesterday, now and then turning in his saddle to cluck at the animals with the crusted meat slung on their flanks. I was taking pictures of the train winding up the rise. Suddenly Bruce gestured for me to get up to where he was.

"A brownie with three cubs," he whispered. "Just ahead over the hump."

I hurried forward, brandishing the camera with its telephoto mounted on the head of the tripod. Just as I peered above the grass there they were, the old sow throwing her muzzle into the wind, and the three little guys waltzing around her on their hind legs. What a picture! I jammed the legs of the tripod down. One leg sank farther into the moss than the others. I fumbled at the lens opening and distance settings. Before I could get into action, the sow looked at me, grunted a deep WOOF, swung off with the cubs rolling behind her, and dropped out of sight. I cursed and stumbled forward, falling down, and scrambled to my feet again.

On the brow of the hill, I slammed the tripod down and pressed the trigger. In the viewfinder I saw them crashing through the willow brush and scattering ptarmigan into the air. The sow kept stopping, rearing to look back at what had startled her into flight.

"How'd you do?" asked Bruce.

"Damn it all," I growled. "I missed the close-up."

A short time later, I was bellying up a ridge to where a black bear was feeding. For several minutes I couldn't see him. I guessed that when I reached the ridgeline the bear would be about 150 feet away, so I set my telephoto distance accordingly. I also took a light reading with my meter and set the lens opening. I was fully prepared. How could anything go wrong? When I peered above the grass, I was looking into the face of a black bear less than 20 feet away.

I never even got the camera going. All I saw was whirling of black as a huge furry bowling ball crashed away into the alders.

For a while after, I kept seeing his startled face. Only he would be able to testify how scared mine was.

I found out just how uncooperative wildlife could be, and at times I really strained my vocabulary. Now I understood why wildlife photographers crouched for hours in blinds with preset lenses and calculated distances. The trick was to let the subject come to you.

~

ONE MORNING, BRUCE, BOB, REYNOLD, AND I were perched on a bald ridge, glassing the country for Bob's moose. Jess, Vard, and Tom had gone off for some ptarmigan.

"Now there's a big blackie," Bruce grunted, breaking the long silence, and motioning toward the pink top of one of the Caribou Hills, "and I mean big."

I found him, and studied him through the glasses. Perhaps a mile and a half away, he looked the shade of night against the strawberry-colored background.

"I'm going up after him," I said. "Maybe I'll get my bear close-up after all. I'll find you boys later on."

"We'll be here," said Bruce, "unless we spot a bull."

It was a long climb over mossy hummocks, steep in places, and I grabbed fistfuls of brush to pull myself up the slope. Sweat soaked me. It ran into my eyes and burned. Finally I broke out of the high grass and it was easier going. Then I lost sight of the bear. When he moved into view again, I put the glasses on him. My heart flopped like a beached salmon. No wonder he was such a big blackie! In the changing light I saw the gleam of his brown flank and the hump on his back. I was in the presence of a massive grizzly.

But I wasn't going to waste all that climbing for nothing.

My palm was slippery on the folded legs of the tripod. I guess I felt more excitement than I did fear. Danger always made me more alive. As I got closer, I moved slower. I kept whistling tonelessly the same tune over and over. I didn't even know what tune it was.

I came to a bench in the slope and lost sight of the bear again. As near as I could tell, he was just above me. I extended the tripod legs, took a light reading, and set the telephoto lens. I was ready, but I didn't feel as brave now as I had farther down the slope. Sweat boiled out of me as I crept up the gully. My heart was thudding in my ears. I couldn't see the bear. I could feel him. Then above some fine, wind-tossed yellow grass, I saw the shaggy line of his back.

I got down on my belly. I was close—too close. I crawled forward and raised my head. Through the tasseled screen, I saw the great hulk looming about fifty feet away. He looked as ominous as a growing thunderhead. If he were a dinosaur, he wouldn't have looked any bigger.

"God," I whispered, "look at him!"

He moved a forepaw in slow swipes at the ground, and I could hear the gluttonous sounds of his grazing as his jaws scooped up leaves as well as blueberries. I sank on my arms, almost afraid to breathe, my blood squirming, and my heart thumping against the earth.

I couldn't spread or adjust the tripod legs so that they rested evenly. Instead I bunched them together and pressed them into the moss. I moved in inches. Perhaps the normal lens would have been better, but I didn't dare to switch it now with the telephoto all secured. Now the snout of the lens was at grass top level. I trembled up on the balls of my feet, peered into the viewfinder like a child watching an electric storm, and pressed the trigger. The camera whirred. In the stillness, it sounded like a rattlesnake.

The bear looked up sleepily. I could just about get him in the viewfinder. He stared right at me with his little pig eyes, then swung the great basket of his head, dropping it to the moss, and pushing with his nose the way a dog does at something he is not sure of eating. The wind blew at his long fur. His shoulders bulged with a rippling every time he moved. I could feel the sweat spilling down my cheeks and the middle of my back. There was not the slightest doubt that he was an old boar.

Twice the camera's drive spring ran down, and twice I wound it tight again. I was trembling. Several times now the bear's broad head had lifted to stare toward me as if he felt a presence beyond the screen of grass. I kept blowing a soft wheezy tune through my teeth. Suddenly the whirring of the camera changed in tone, and I knew the magazine had expended. I don't know why I didn't think of the slide camera. All I could think of was more movie footage.

Fumblingly, I opened the side of the camera to remove the exposed magazine and replace it with another . . . CLICK. . . .

The bear pulled up. The sluggishness vanished. He plumed to an awesome height, flinging a forepaw above his head as if he were going to hurl part of hilltop at me. He shrugged toward me, swaying and teetering and throwing his muzzle at the wind. Then he dropped to all fours. In a rumbling bunch he hurled right at me.

I was terrified. I don't remember slamming the camera shut,

but I must have done it. I did the only thing I could do.

I ran.

I ran as if catapulted. Panic drove me down over the hummocks, gadget bag thudding against my hip, binoculars bumping my chest, the camera and tripod clutched in my hand.

I looked back once. He was breaking over the rise like an oncoming train.

HE'S GOING TO CATCH ME. HE'S GOING TO CATCH ME.

There wasn't a tree. I thought foolishly about the knife in my pocket. I thought of the camera on the panning head of the tripod. Could I swing it like a baseball bat right into his nose? I didn't dare to look back again.

Faster and faster I drove my legs, in a growing momentum down the slope. How I kept from tumbling on my face I'll never know. I wondered when the smash of the paw was going to come, when the half-ton avalanche would overwhelm me. My feet exploded from the hummocks in a speed I could no longer control.

I threw a frightened face back over my shoulder. The bear was gone! Still I kept running. I couldn't stop. When I finally did, I babbled out loud to no one. My voice shook.

"Holy Jesus . . . where did he go? Did you ever see such a bear? Oh, Mac, you should have seen him. There was your circus elephant! I thought he had me. . . ."

I kept seeing that one illuminated moment of the bear dropping down on his forepaws and coming on as if no bullet in the world could stop him.

Finally I made it to the ridge where Bruce, Bob, and Reynold were sprawled. They looked up at me with tight faces.

"Boys," I panted, "you see before you a mighty religious man."

That broke the tension and they rolled with laughter. I looked at Bruce. "Blackie? That sure as hell wasn't a blackie!" I said. "You bastard."

That brought another gale of howls and watery eyes. Then they told me how it had looked through the binoculars.

"I thought there'd be guts all over the hill," said Bruce. "But, honest—I didn't know it was a brownie."

"You know when you're at a circus and you see a guy miss the trapeze?" Bob said. "That's just how helpless I felt."

"He chased you a ways," Reynold said. "He was going so fast it looked like he was scratching his ears with his hind legs. But damned if you didn't pull away from him. He just gave up and turned off."

"Wonder that slope ain't smoking."

"I think he all of a sudden whiffed something ripe," grinned Bob, "and couldn't stand it."

"I haven't checked yet," I said. I began to laugh. It was funny . . . now.

THE NEXT DAY BOB SHOT HIS moose, a fork-horned bull. Jess said that one would be the best eating of the lot. While we dressed him out, the Canada jays magically appeared. The ravens were whooping.

"Hear 'em?" said Bob. "Guts, guts, that's what they're talking about."

We cooked some moose liver and onions for supper. It was tender but strong and peculiar tasting.

"I don't know if it's the liver or me," drawled Vard, "but every time I belch I think I swallowed an aluminum cup."

"The damnedest taste in my mouth," Tom said. "Just like a buzzard's been roosting on my nose all day."

There was that air of the frontier again as I followed the pack string loaded down with the meat of one of the bulls. As the horses trailed toward a rugged scene, I whirred off some movie footage.

"I heard that brownies will come roaring out of the timber and tear meat right off the pack saddles," said Bruce. "That ain't happened to me yet."

Jess grinned. "Lots of things ain't happened to you yet," he said.

The boys decided to leave the next day. There were still two moose to be brought in from Far Camp. I volunteered to stay and

Bruce and Jess Willard skinning out young bull.

help Bruce pack them in. He and Jess quickly agreed that would be a good idea.

Bob summed up the end of the hunt when he swung a long leg up on the sawhorse and looked wistfully across the lake at the Box Cars. "You know," he said, "the man who invented work was just too damn lazy to hunt and fish."

⌐

DURING THE NEXT FEW DAYS, BRUCE showed me a flock of sandhill cranes settling in a moose meadow. Some of them almost somersaulted as they landed. I filmed them as they took to the air again. They had an ethereal presence as they rose, wheeling above us like vapors clouding, spreading, thinning, and coming together again. They made a whooping, purring racket that descended upon us.

"I hear they taste like turkey," Bruce said. "But they're protected now."

Atop the Box Cars, we looked down to see two horsemen moving along the valley and watched them through the glasses.

Bruce didn't recognize them. A black bear lumbered out of the other side of some spruce before them, doubled back, and sat behind a blowdown to watch them pass.

"They don't know he's there," Bruce said. "I wonder how many things watch us the same way?"

We saw two great horned owls perched in a snag, black against a red evening sky. I watched a huge bull do a fade-out. He kept his head down as he tiptoed along the meadow edge like a brown ghost. I never identified one with such stealth before. Bruce pointed to what looked to be a grayed limb sticking out of the grass ahead of us. The limb changed into antlers as a bull got up out of his bunk and moved off.

I looked down into a valley with a banner of cloud hovering as if a locomotive had just huffed through it.

Bruce told me he was finding more and more evidence of planes landing beyond Far Camp.

"They drop hunters right into prime country, and it shouldn't be," he said. "They enjoy the fire, but they didn't cut the wood to make it. They even land in the high sheep pastures and the glaciers, too. This country was never meant to be opened up like that."

"The beginning of the end," I said.

When it was time to leave, I said to Jess, "What do I owe you for the extra days?"

His face wrinkled into a grin. "No charge," he said. "Paid in full. You been a big help to us. Wouldn't surprise me one bit if we could make an Alaskan out of you."

That made me feel real good.

When Johnny took off and buzzed the cabins, there were the Willards, all four of them, waving. They had shown me another dimension of Alaska—its open heart and hospitality.

⌒

As I stepped out of the *Pacific Northern* at Kodiak, I spotted the red pickup waiting for me. *Good old Dick*, I thought.

"Been meetin' the afternoon plane these past days," he greeted.

"Thought you had a mind to homestead that country." Then that look of mischief spread over his face.

"There's talk around that you can run mighty fast."

CHAPTER 10

Comings and Goings

My close-up of the big brown bear, although slightly blurred by the waving yellow grass, became a conversation piece, and all through the winter my films of the Kenai hunt were a ticket to home-cooked suppers.

Dick became swamped with repair work for contractors in town, and Big John and I didn't see him very often on the weekends.

"I don't know what's happened to that boy," Big John said. "All of a sudden money's worth more than our company."

"He's in demand," I said, "and he can't say no. He's worth two or three men the way he works and the contractors know it. They won't let go easy. And besides . . . maybe he's working toward early retirement."

Big John got a buy on a 1942 military jeep. For weeks he was a doctor treating an only patient, and finally the pampered retread was released from his surgical tinkering and pronounced mechanically perfect.

"As good as when she came off the line," Big John said with loving appraisal. That little powerhouse responded to the caress of his big hands. I always felt it resented me. It was definitely a one-man vehicle, as I was to learn later on.

In several of his letters Dad had asked me to get him a Kodiak bear skull. So when the word came to us on a Friday afternoon that Tom Felton, a cattle rancher at Middle Bay, had shot a marauding bear—"the biggest since '41," Big John suggested we go out the next morning and put in a request for the bruin's headpiece.

At Tom's place we were met with two surprises. First, he hadn't found the bear's body yet, and, second, we weren't the only ones who had heard the news. A small army had gathered.

Off we went through the snow . . . up . . . up . . . up through the alder tangles, the devil's club, and the salmonberry canes. I wasn't surprised to look back and see that the army had dwindled to a few straggling squads strung out in our wake.

We hit the blood trail. You'd think someone had saturated a giant mop in gore and dragged it in a swath through the snow.

"He's packing a lot of lead," Tom said.

On and on snaked the red path, always keeping to where the brush was thickest. We found where the bear had dug a hole a foot deep and three feet wide in earth frozen so hard that a pick wouldn't have dented it.

"Jumped him here yesterday," said Tom. "Starting to get dark, so I give up on him."

About a mile farther on the bear ran out of blood. We found him on his back, a huge mound in the snow, foreclaws long and whitened at his chest, and his toe pads as big as silver dollars turned up at the sky. He showed yellowed teeth in a final grimace. His thick, dark hide was full of devil's club thorns.

"Big Jasper," Tom said. "That's the end of his beef diet."

It started to snow. The flakes collected on the fur as we slashed into the white fat and pulled the hide away from the carcass. I was disappointed to learn that someone else had already claimed the skull, but Big John and I dragged the hide down the slope anyway as a favor to Tom. The claws kept snagging the brush. Sometimes we'd get a momentum going and couldn't stop with the heavy hide tobogganing behind us.

I realized Tom had lost cattle to this shaggy giant, but I marveled at the animal's tremendous vitality and endurance. He had found the cattle easy prey in his old age and left them to stew in his burial mounds. Perhaps it was his way of trying to reclaim his territory. Tom had to make a living, but the bear didn't understand. He was a slave to his appetite.

December 10, 1953
Dear Dad, Molly, & Mrs. Millett:
. . . Now for the last bit of news on the program this week, something that very definitely worries me. I am not going to kid anybody. I haven't been doing the writing I should be doing up here. I've done some, yes, but not nearly enough. I've collected several rejection slips. I've taken a lot of notes. I try to make the excuse that I work all day and am just too damn tired at night to do anything other than write letters, wash clothes and see a movie now and then. But that's not good! My ambition should be such that this would be no obstacle at all. On weekends I choose to ramble about the countryside, instead of planting myself firmly behind a typewriter.

I once told you, Dad, that I could make a million dollars at anything and if it wasn't at writing, then I would never be satisfied with myself. I still mean that. Perhaps throughout life this will be one of my main frustrations, a frustration very similar to the one you must feel when you get your check every week at the Bay State and look sadly at your palette in your studio upstairs.

I swear I will never stop writing, scattered though the attempts might be. Now a very serious distraction rears its siren head, glitters its promise of gold and casts a shadow over my typewriter.

The other day my foreman, or leading man as he is called in the lingo of Civil Service, called me aside. I have always given him a day's work every day I've been here, so I was really not too surprised at what he said.

"Keith," he asked, "How would you like to take over my job?"

"What are you going to do?" I answered.

"I think I'm going into the front office. A Quarterman's rate," he said.

"Let me sleep on it. I'll let you know in the morning."

"Here's the deal," he said. "I'm going to make you Snapper (a sort of straw boss—13 cents more per hour), then break you into my job so you'll be ready for it when my job comes through. You'll be a leading man. It's as simple as that."

So that evening at quitting time, I walked alone, trailing the others, and my mind was busy. Do I really want the job? I thought. It seems as though I've been dodging responsibility all my life. Maybe it's about time I took some. Maybe I ought to test myself.

Now wait a minute. What about home? Is that what you want, to be away from home all your life? You know it's a damn lie. Right now you'd like to be back there, wouldn't you? You're not kidding anybody. And your writing, what about that? You just going to forget it? You're going to be busier than hell if you take this job, and you'll probably sprout a few gray hairs too. You've worked with all the men.

*You know the ones that work, the ones that don't
work, and the ones who will try to take advantage
of you. One hundred and thirty bucks a week for a
straight forty hours, $3.25 an hour. That's a lot of
dough. Now just what the hell are you going to do?*

*There it is. I went in the next morning and said,
"I'll take you up on that offer."*

*If I get the leading man rate, it won't be until
summer. If I get it and like it, I'll take leave and go
home for about a month and come back north again.
If I don't like it, if I fail at this test of myself, then I'll
be home anyway.*

*What would you have done, Dad? I miss all of
you. It is not natural to stay away from those you
love. I came up here with the idea that one year
would be my limit. It has stretched to longer than
that. What lies ahead? Well, when more materializes
on this business, I'll let you know. I suddenly seem
to find myself more serious than I have ever been
before, almost as if I have realized that at last I have
tossed aside my short pants and fishing pole.*

So long, love to all,

Sam

I TOOK ON A JOB WITH greater responsibility, and in the weeks
that followed, the men cooperated. If I had something to say, I
said it to them and not to others about them. I tried my damnedest
not to play any favorites.

Any reasonable gripe, I gave attention to. Even if it seemed
relatively unimportant to me, I tried to understand that it had to
be important to the one who made it. I was busy with paperwork,
and I lost my precious weekends that came and went all too fast.

"You don't laugh like you used to," one of the men said. "You're different. You're like a traffic cop now that holds up his white glove and it says, 'That's close enough.'"

What I gained in my paycheck I was losing in my physical condition. I was putting on weight again. Where I had been burning up calories before, now I was chauffeuring others around to burn up their calories instead, telling them what to do, and hardly ever getting involved in the actual doing of it. *What the hell's the matter with you?* I thought. *You better yourself and you don't appreciate it. You want to be a laborer all your life?*

"Not a laborer," I said to the mountains, "nor a boss either."

THE COURTSHIP PERFORMANCES OF THE AMERICAN goldeneyes or whistlers in the bay amused me. There they were, three drakes drifting around a hen. One of them would suddenly rock forward, throwing his head back until it appeared that his bill touched the middle of his back. You'd think he was enjoying a hearty laugh. Then the others would join in with broken neck advances. The hen swam unconcerned. What damn fools men can make of themselves in front of a woman!

Women. I still had no idea when I would find the right one, and guessed that my father was disappointed in regard to grandchildren. In one of my letters home, I wrote him, "I know I should have married long ago. I'm getting older, but dammit all, I don't feel any different than I did ten years ago. I've got another few years left before I have to get desperate."

I did, didn't I?

THE KING CRAB BOATS WERE IN. They were dirty looking and badly in need of paint. Native fishermen slung the long-legged crabs out of the holds and flopped them to the decks where others waited to snatch them up and pile them in the weighing baskets. The crabs were white-bellied and brownish-purple on top with barnacles plastered to the shells. They looked like huge warty spiders. My skin crawled as I watched their movements.

Crab-laden dories were sculled to the foot of a conveyor belt that clanked and groaned monotonously. The belt disappeared into a dark hole in the side of a squat building on the pilings. Men stabbed at the crabs with gaff hooks and swung them aloft to ride up and into the hole.

As the crabs toppled free, butchers grabbed them. Chop . . . chop . . . chop . . . long blades lifted and fell. The severed sections rode down a long table to where women, wearing yellow rubber aprons and colored scarves wrapped about their heads, shelled the pieces and fingered them into cans. Machines did the rest. All refuse was washed down a chute that emptied beneath the pier. Here the gulls swam and pirouetted by the hundreds, fighting over the bits that tumbled into them. Their mewing pleas of greed mingled with the clank and the thud of the conveyor. Some of the women glanced at me, muttered, and laughed among themselves. Fog tendrilled in from the sea, and the air was heavy with the sweet stink of crabs cooking.

"I guess I can cross off a cannery as a career," I said to the gulls.

I saw Dick just before he left on the *Elizabeth* to go commercial fishing with Johnny Malutin.

"We're headed for Chignik," he said. "Never seen the country that far to the west. Johnny says that's where the red salmon hold a big convention."

I wished I was going with him. I felt as though he were moving off into combat and I was left behind to mind the store.

Vard Smith was leaving, too, but he was going Outside. He asked Big John and me to move into his Quonset hut on the base while he and his family were away. He said he'd feel better knowing the place was lived in and being looked after. We thought it would be a change in the barracks routine, so we accepted the offer. "Help yourself to the deep freeze," Vard said. "There's moose and ducks that should be eaten."

With a refrigerator, an automatic washer, and a dryer at our disposal, we had suddenly moved to a level of luxury. We became finicky old maids. We took the responsibility of the household much too seriously and went to extremes not to abuse the place. I suppose we didn't want Vard's wife to think a couple of pigs had been rooting in the carpets. After work we showered at the barracks before going to the hut to cook supper. I did the cooking. Big John did most of the cleaning.

"After this," he said, "take your shoes off before you come in the house."

Usually it was about eight o'clock before we finished with the dishes and tidied the place up to our strict standards.

Big John suggested we ought to entertain, so one evening we invited six to dinner. Big John busied himself with the vacuum cleaner as if he were running a D-8 Caterpillar over the rugs and into the corners while I sweated out the preparations in the kitchen.

The company straggled in. Big John took care of the drinks and served the cheese and crackers while I prayed that the Swiss steaks and all the trimmings would be ready at the same time. I bustled around talking to myself, wondering if I remembered everything. Did I have enough mushrooms in the sauce? Did I salt the potato water?

I didn't enjoy the meal at all. I was too involved in the others enjoying theirs. When they left finally, I felt all wrung out.

It was long after midnight when Big John and I finished the enormous stack of dishes, got the place back in order once more, and aired out the cigarette smoke.

"If I ever have a wife," I said, "I'm going to really appreciate her."

"Me, too," said Big John. Then he grinned. "And go easy on the company."

Everything was going along fine until Big John got his orders to report to a National Guard camp. He left me with his old rattletrap jeep to provide transportation to and from the job. He gave me specific instructions on coaxing the motor to start, and I almost felt the jeep was listening and plotting fiendishly as he went over the checklist.

Machines have always plagued me. Be it cars or outboard motors, I have never had the golden touch. My presence just seemed to stop engines. Each unpleasant experience added to my persecution complex. I had no confidence in them at all.

My arms, my legs, a canoe paddle? I had faith in them. If Big John's balky brat could talk, and I almost suspected it could to Big John, then our friendship would have been in jeopardy.

I became convinced the heap was endowed with human qualities. The headlights were baleful eyes that resented me. I could imagine its instrument panel frowning and sulking as soon as my weight settled behind the wheel.

"Pull the choke out about a sixteenth," Big John had said. "No more than that.

"Shove it back in at the first cough and she'll purr like a kitten. You don't catch her just right she'll flood."

I must have deluged her. I ground away at her innards, fiddled with the choke, and all she did was bray like a jackass. It was not the master's hand. The spoiled brat went into a shell and gave me the silent treatment. Finally I pushed her to a hill and started her that way. "I hope you're satisfied, you damned hussy," I said.

The second day she greeted me with a flat tire. The spare was soft, and when I went to inflate it with the hand pump, I found the pump wouldn't work. No compression at all.

I was ashamed of what I called Big John and his hand pump in the presence of hungry gnats prospecting along my hairline.

After a downhill start one Saturday, I went to the base gas station to fill the tank. I merged on the end of a long winding line. A sign in big red letters above the pumps made me shudder: ALL VEHICLES WILL BE SECURED WHILE BEING SERVICED.

Once I turned off the ignition I knew the jeep would squat like a whipped mule and refuse to budge. That's exactly what happened. I held up the line as the attendant's expression spoke volumes about my driving ability.

At that moment trumpets blared and drums pounded. Down the road marched a company of marines to the strains of *The Marine's Hymn*. The music sent tingles down my back, and I hoped it would also stir the jeep out of her stupor. No such luck. As the boys gave a send-off to General Lemuel C. Shepherd, Jr., I contributed the discord notes of the starter. To add to my complete humiliation, I had to ask some sailors who were roundly booing my former buddies to give me a push.

I found myself pleading with this "creature" every time I opened her canvas door.

"Please start," I mumbled. "There's no need of us fighting all the time. Come on, old girl, don't let me down." Choke out a sixteenth . . . I tried to be as precise and as gentle as possible until the inevitable happened. Then I hurled myself out from behind the wheel. "You miserable old son of a bitch!" I shouted, and resigned myself to look for a push, or the nearest hill.

My stay at Vard's place showed me once again that I was a slave to my conscience. I had a household all to myself. I could have raised hell. Shyness held me on a leash. I was a hopeless square. I have often thought when I hear men say, "If I only knew then what I know now, things would be a whole lot different," that if given the chance, they would probably do all over again what they had done previously. It is very difficult to be different than you are, to turn your back on the real you.

～

I HAD LOOKED ON THE MOUNTAINS for more than two years now. If any woman had a wardrobe to match the subtle color combinations the mountains wore throughout the seasons, she would be the absolute envy of all.

～

DICK'S RETURN WAS AS IF I had a visit from the horizon. He was bronzed and smelled of salt air. We sat on an overturned dory atop the pier, and while we talked, Dick spliced an eye in a rope with his fid. Before us clustered the fishing boats, swinging on their anchor lines, their windshields catching the sun and flashing. The shadows of the gulls slid over us back and forth. Dick told me of the bear he had seen along the peninsula, how bright the red salmon looked amid the sea lettuce, the shooting of a caribou for fresh meat, and the outlaw tactics of fishermen.

Dick with a "humpback."

"We pulled into Agripina Bay, Johnny's old stampin' grounds. Man, there's traps hangin' in some of them cabins. They been there so long they're all stuck together, rusted in one big chunk. And stretcher boards—the three-piece kind—two pieces held together at the top with rawhide and the third one like a wedge you fit in between to make the skin tight. Pull out the middle stick later on and off comes the pelt slick as grease. Smooth. Man, I never felt anything as smooth as them boards was.

"Dollar apiece for the reds. We figured to get more than we did. It was the pinks that saved the day. Thirty-seven cents apiece for them, but they made the money for us. Them tally boys on the tenders know their fish. Reds, pinks, chums, silvers, kings . . . they just look silver and all alike to a greenhorn, but not to them guys.

"If some I seen out there can make a livin' with a boat, why can't two hardworkin' boys do it? Maybe we ought to think on it. Spring and fall bear hunts. Seinin' salmon in between. Trappin' in winter. Maybe some crabs. I bet we could do real well." It was tempting, but. . . .

Big John said he planned to take his jeep down the Alcan next fall. I made up my mind to go with him. By then, it'd be better than three years that I'd been away. It would be good to see everyone back home again, but I had a feeling I wouldn't be staying long.

Boomerang Alaskan

PRE-HOLIDAY PARTY

Samuel Keith was the honor guest at a pre-holiday family party held at the Copeland Street home of Mr. and Mrs. Merle V. Keith. Sam has been enjoying a few weeks' vacation with his father and family, but leaves today or Wednesday by plane for Seattle, Wash. He will then transfer to Kodiak, Alaska, where he will continue his duties in a civilian capacity with the navy.

The piece-de-resistance of the dinner were two geese, raised by the Keiths, and declared excellent eating by the family.

—*The Brockton Enterprise*
Brockton, Massachusetts

After six weeks of leave with my family and friends in Massachusetts, I returned to Alaska. Anchorage had a few inches of snow, and it was chilly when I stepped off the plane. I thought I might stay over a few days, but I changed my mind when I saw there was a plane leaving for Kodiak within the hour. I figured I might as well get back when I could.

It was hard to leave the family in Boston, but once Seattle was behind me, I experienced a wonderful release. It was almost as if I was about to leap over a prison wall. As nice as everybody had been to me, I just had to get away.

I was back in the barracks, back on the job, but I wasn't doing very much I hadn't already done before. It was time for a change.

August 10, 1954

Dad, I'm up a tree. To be absolutely frank with you, I don't know what the hell to do. Some days I am so damn sick of this job, I could start swimming for Seattle. Then there are other days when it doesn't seem so bad after all. I've made a lot of friends up here. I'm in love with the country. But on the other hand, I want to go home for a while.

Anna sent me some pictures today, and it made me want to go home all the more. God, those kids have grown. I have twenty days' leave. That won't be hardly enough. This new regime that has taken over frowns on leave without pay, so it looks to me like I'll just terminate, put in a faithful winter back east writing, and head back up this way with the geese next spring.

So long,

Sam

I YEARNED FOR HOME, AND YET Alaska wasn't ready to let me go. I spent another winter working in Kodiak.

One day while in town, I went into the Fish and Wildlife Office and talked over employment possibilities for the coming spring and summer. When I came out, I had a smile on my face. Perhaps I was doing a very foolish thing. Fish and Wildlife could only promise me temporary employment working on construction. I didn't even ask about the pay. I just told Jim Branson, the enforcement agent, to put me in the wildest, most remote area he had under his jurisdiction, and I gave my thirty-day notice at the base.

I passed up an offer to stay on at a considerable boost in salary, and another one to work at a desk in the front office.

"You're always welcome back here," a quarterman said.

All kinds of thoughts tumbled in my mind. Was I running away from responsibility again? *You damn fool*, I thought, *you're like a man on a boat steering past all these coves that keep opening up to you. When are you going to head in and drop anchor?*

At quitting time on my last day, I plodded up the shack steps.

"You got some mail," one of the boys greeted.

I saw a large box on the table by the mail rack, bound with string. An envelope was tucked under its strings, and my name was on it.

I opened it. There was a bon voyage card with names scrawled all over it.

"Well . . . look in the box, damn it!" someone shouted.

I cut the strings. Hands helped me tear off the wrapping. There was an expensive down sleeping bag, an air mattress, a keen-edged hunting knife, a red woolen shirt, a hot patch kit, and fifty dollars' worth of movie film.

My eyes filled. My throat closed up on me, and the words didn't come out the way I wanted them to.

I bunked aboard the Fish and Wildlife boat, the *Shearwater Two*. This would be home until we helped an old carpenter rough out some sleeping quarters on the second floor of the warehouse.

I worked with Jim Mellin from California. He was nineteen with adventure shining from his face. He was up here to see the country before he started college in the fall. As eager as I was for the arrival of the *Kittiwake*, he was a companion that not only made the hours pleasant but shared my love of fishing as well.

One day after work we were practice casting with the fly rods from the pier. Two small Native boys were watching with what I took to be amazement at how the lines smoothly shot forth. Finally one of them lit a cigarette and said out of the side of his mouth, "Why don't you quit fartin' around and put a hook on?"

Jim and I helped Old Charlie stud off a section of the

warehouse, plywood it, hang a door, and build several bunk beds. We helped with the plumbing, too, and soon moved into quarters that boasted a flush toilet and sink.

We spent our time doing various odd jobs. While we were driving oakum into the seams of a dory with caulking irons one morning, I noticed the *Elizabeth* sliding past and moving out into the channel. Dick was on deck. I jumped up and hollered. He was off on another spring bear hunt. "Bring me back a bear skull," I shouted, "a big one!"

"Thought you'd left," he yelled through his cupped hands. "We'll see what we can do."

Jim and I thought we should have left, too. We were doing all kinds of odd jobs we never expected to be doing. We were getting itchy. What was holding up the *Kittiwake* down in Southeast? Carpentry, plumbing, caulking dories, and painting them didn't exactly fit the romantic life we had envisioned. What kept our imaginations fired were the bull sessions in the evenings.

May 22, 1955
Dear Dad, Molly, & Mrs. Millet:
    We are getting a little peeved with the outfit so far. We were supposed to leave the first week of May, and here it is the 22nd, and still in Kodiak. They say we leave tomorrow, but I will believe it when I feel the heave of the sea beneath me. We've done all kinds of jobs here. If I don't get the area I want, I'm going to do a little squawking.
    For all the crap Jim and I have had to put up with, we deserve that choice, at least. We've had bad weather. Poor Dick must have had a miserable week on the bear hunt. I've been keeping an eye for his boat coming into the channel. No sign yet.
    Love to all,
    Sam

ROY LINDSLEY, FISHERY MANAGEMENT BIOLOGIST, AND Jim Branson briefed us on past tactics of commercial fishing outlaws. Some worked in relays in close to the creek markers, keeping the stream guard awake until he finally had to give in to sleep.

Then they slipped inside the markers and stole his fish. Sometimes they set submarine gill nets in the creek mouths. Since no cork lines were visible, they were difficult to locate.

There had been instances where sugar had been put into the fuel tanks of outboard motors, and others much more serious where stream guards' boats had actually been swamped as fishermen ran them down. Black smoke was often blasted out to screen illegal seining operations, and bluestone was put into the creeks to make the salmon dash back to salt water and into the meshes that intercepted them.

The night operations of the Fish and Wildlife boat Coho intrigued me. It maneuvered into the bays with no running lights to surprise fishermen in the middle of an illegal set. It made me think of P.T. boats that used to hunt for Japanese barges at night in the Solomon Islands.

"You've got to remember," summed up Roy, "we're a threat to a livelihood. Most of the fishermen are square shooters, but it's like everything else. The bad ones spoil it for the rest and bring on more regulations than should be necessary."

He continued, "We found that fines did little to discourage violations. Now we suspend violators for periods of time during the peak of the run. That hits them where they live."

"YOU AIN'T LEFT YET?"

Dick was back. Yes, they'd brought back a hide, too. It measured ten feet, two inches by nine feet, six inches. Dick never mentioned the skull, so I took it for granted that the fellow who shot the bear wanted the skull for his mount.

"I wish I was goin' out to mark them creeks with you."

"Look at that good money you're making out to the base," I grinned. "You wouldn't even make half as much here."

"Money?" he said. "You said there was things more important . . . remember? Same old routine on the base. One day's like another, twistin' wrenches and bustin' knuckles. Here, you know you're goin' someplace. That *Kittiwake* ain't got here yet, but you know she's comin'. Even if she sits at the pier a spell, you know she's bound to pull out directly. The base don't go anywhere."

Several evenings later I was surprised to see the red pickup and Dick step out of it with a bear skull swinging on the end of a wire. He was whistling, and that old trademark of a red bandanna was trailing from his back pocket.

"That son of a gun," I said.

"Clean forgot to tell you about this," he grinned. "I gave strict orders not to shoot the old boy in the head. Then I did some scrapin' and scratchin.' She's cleaned up pretty good and ready to ship off to your dad."

"Boy, he'll appreciate it, Dick."

DOWN AT THE SHOP, DICK HAD rasped some brass into coarse grains. He'd bought some gold paint in town and painted them up, then poured his "nuggets" into a little poke of buckskin. The stage was set.

At supper time we sat with Oasis, who had come to the Yukon back in 1918 from his homeland in Syria. Dick finally produced his poke, slammed it down on the table, and loosened the drawstrings.

"My summer's take," he said.

Oasis trickled some of the grains into his hand.

"That's a high grade you get there," he grinned. "Where you get this high grade? Long Creek? Poorman?"

"Kodiak."

"Look for gold on Kodiak, you starve to death. How much to the pan, this brass?"

June 1, 1955

Dear Dad, Molly, & Mrs. Millet:

. . . I'll try to get the skull in the mail tomorrow. I warn you, before you open it, that it will not smell like a high school girl going to a prom. I could have cleaned the brain cavity better, but being lazy, I merely poured sawdust into it. It has hung in salt water and sea lice have nibbled at it; it has hung from an alder, and raven and magpies have pecked and torn at it. If it doesn't cost too much, I'll ship it air mail. The bear was shot in Uganik Bay, Kodiak Island.

Take care of yourselves,

Sam

THE NEXT MORNING I CHECKED OUT the skull at the Fish and Wildlife Office and sent it off. When I arrived back at the warehouse, the *Kittiwake* was tying up to the pier.

Jim and I bunked in the forecastle. The skipper, mate, engineer, cook, and two deckhands made eight of us aboard the seventy-two-foot converted army tug. We were finally off to mark the streams. Every ten days or so we'd be coming into Kodiak harbor until the job was done. Then in late June, Jim and I would be the last stream guards dropped off.

Our district included Kodiak Island, Afognak Island, and a stretch of the Alaska Peninsula. Our job was to check the positions of the creek markers in accordance with the charts and to replace them if necessary. These large signs were placed five hundred yards on each side of the creek mouth from the mean low tide point. It was illegal for a fisherman to make a set inside these markers. This was the vital area where salmon milled for days before making the final journey into fresh water. In such numbers they were too vulnerable to the seines, and, unfortunately, too tempting for some of the fishermen to resist.

We chained off the distances carefully. The positions of some of the signs were decided by latitude and longitude, and Hank, the skipper, critically studied the lines on his detailed maps and signaled us as to their beach coordinates.

I enjoyed the vigorous exercise. I used my personal axe, kept its edge sheathed when not using it, and didn't allow others to use it at all. Let them dull their own edges, but not the one I had honed so fine. We cut green spruce for posts when we had spruce, used driftwood of which there was always plenty, nailed planks to twisted alder trunks, and spiked the signs to them. Sometimes we towed posts in and hauled them up to prominent bluffs. We dug deep holes, tamped in the posts, and braced the signs against the winds.

We put these warnings: NO FISHING BEYOND THIS POINT, to stay until the wood rotted. To see those white markers gleaming when we got back aboard in no way indicated the trouble it was to place them there.

Jim and I tried fishing a stream that poured into Uganik Passage. After an hour of flailing the clear flow, Jim said, "Even Ted Trueblood couldn't catch one here." The fish hadn't arrived yet. While on the beach, we heard a whale blow, and the sound of it off the cliffs was like a lion's roar.

A bridle was attached to our working dory, which was lowered into the sea by the boom and winch. Whenever we got underway again, the dory was brought aboard the same way.

In Zachar Bay we found a marker on one side of a creek that had been moved in toward the mouth about two hundred yards. Hank checked a course line on his chart, ran it, and we found the nails in a tree where the sign had been originally.

We marked bays that I had been in before, but most of them were strange to me. Each one was the next page in an exciting book, and my eyes were alight with wonder and anticipation.

I enjoyed the *Kittiwake*'s galley with its red-and-white checkered tablecloth. Boards were screwed to the edges of the cabinet shelves so that you had to reach over and behind them to get at the dishes, one indication of impending rough weather. Another was that the cook, out of habit, only filled the coffee cups and the soup bowls halfway.

One day the big-bellied engineer said to me, "I never saw a guy who enjoys eating the way you do."

"I come to the table hungry," I said, smiling. "Three meals a day . . . that's all I eat. You eat one all day long." He bluffed a rush at me as if he were going to throw me over the side.

~

THE MENU ABOARD THE *KITTIWAKE* WAS varied. Once, when we tied up next to some halibut boats, the cook on the *Laredo* tossed us a fresh "chicken" halibut, big enough to go around, but not so big that it would overwhelm the galley.

Another time, I was watching a seal rearing curiously off our stern early one morning.

"Don't move," whispered the cook, shouldering his rifle. The seal sank.

"Damn it," the cook whispered. He lowered the rifle. The head eased into view again, even closer this time.

The rifle spat viciously. I heard the whuck of the lead and saw the water spurt just beyond. The seal wallowed in a widening red slick.

"Get him before he sinks," yelled the cook.

Jim appeared magically and helped me put the skiff over the side. The water rippled around a small part of the seal still above the surface. What a job to haul him aboard! We almost tipped over the skiff. He resembled a long sausage with an end tied off into flippers. We muscled him aboard the *Kittiwake*, where the cook waited with a knife, its blade glistening and upward swooped. The seal's brisket burst open at the swipe of the steel. Steam rose from the cavity. The blade nicked the heart or an artery and blood jetted the deck into a red slippery mess. Finally the cook lifted the liver free. Then he peeled off the scalp for bounty. The eyes looked as large as golf balls embedded in the skull. We tossed the carcass over the side. As I watched it slowly sink and wondered what would attack it first, the skipper's voice startled me.

"What the hell is this, a slaughterhouse?" he bellowed. "Get that slop hosed off. Don't ever do that on my deck again."

I never tasted better liver and onions in my life.

June 12, 1955
Dear Dad, Molly, & Mrs. Millet:
I was glad to hear the bear skull reached you.
I was afraid to send it parcel post. And I was afraid,
too, that the skull would stink its way right out of
its wrapping.

I SLEPT IN A TOP BUNK, which was hard to squirm into at night. Thank God for portholes. I would have either sweltered or suffocated were it not for the one beside me. I cracked it open, and there in the darkness, with the gentle rolling of the ship at anchor, I stretched out to feel the cool sea wind brushing my face and pouring into my lungs. It gave me all the pleasure of a frosty drink in midsummer.

ATOP ONE BLUFF WHERE WE PLACED a marker was an eagle's nest, a depression in the brown grass with two white eggs in it and tufts of fur and fish bones along its circumference. One of the eggs had a quarter-inch hole in it. I could hear a peeping inside the shell. The parent birds squeaked and shrilled as they soared above us. We had to move on before the eaglet saw the world.

While we were underway, I often sat with Hank in the wheelhouse. His eyes were squinted from the glare of the sun on sea and ice, his face seamed and leathered, his shoulders hunched from long hours at the wheel. He wore a red baseball cap. Beneath its peak bushed his eyebrows, gray and tufted like the ears of a lynx. His smoky eyes indicated he was a man who made no excuses for his decisions. He smiled by his radio while the wheel on automatic pilot turned back and forth as if nudged by an invisible helmsman.

"These Scandahoovians tickle me," he said. "All the time complaining about the weather and how bad the fishing is. And there they are, sitting on their quotas."

The radio crackled.

"It blow last night and the water smoke yust like sandstorm. We bane yogging."

"Tied up to a buoy," Hank explained. "They run their long lines from these buoys. Bamboo pole on the buoy has a metal cap that gives off a signal they can take a bearing to find. They fish their spread of lines until they fill their quotas and head in."

Then a short while later we heard the angry voice of the *Arctic Maid*'s skipper, talking to a Japanese boat.

"We just got about a mile of your tangle gear inside our buoys, up in our drag. You better take a radar bearing on us. It'll be in a wad, right on the bottom."

"Tangle gear is used for king crab," Hank explained again. "These Japs are crowding us right off our grounds. They're damn good fishermen, but they ain't tomorrow-minded at all. We won the war, but it appears to me there's another one shaping up over these waters."

When I wasn't in the wheelhouse, I liked to lie on my belly in the prow, my chin resting on my folded arms, and watch the dolphins frolic below me. They scattered in a fan as the bow bore down upon them, cleaving the water like knives through syrup. I watched the shearwaters vibrating from side to side as they trotted and pattered over the swells before they lifted and sailed. Hank called them "whale birds."

I marveled at a kittiwake as it stepped daintily on the wind, tiptoed on the sea, dipped with its bill, and drifted like something gliding in a dream. Once I saw a herd of fur seals porpoising, their hind flippers appearing like whirling propellers as they arced. The sharp triangles of their heads resembled the fins of sharks. And how would I ever forget the sight of the great whales thrusting unbelievably at the sky until they balanced on their flukes and toppled like falling trees.

POOR JIM! HE WASN'T GOING ON the southern trip with us. He took his change of assignment like a man, and I felt an emptiness as I watched him carry his gear back into the warehouse. He had outboards to tune and more dories to ready.

"He made his mistake," observed Johnny, the mate, "when he showed he understood motors."

We delivered the first four stream guards of the season.

The stern deck of the *Kittiwake* was stacked with lashed fuel drums on end and overturned dories. Provisions were stored in the hold, the cartons labeled with their destinations.

At each assigned bay, we followed the stream guard in with his gear, helped him unload his provisions and the two fifty-gallon fuel drums on the beach, helped him with his tent, and left him with the gulls. The last one we dropped off at Red River. He really concerned me. He was too jittery. He couldn't get his rifle loaded fast enough. He wasn't in prime bear country, but the stories he had heard were working on him.

"You'll get a preview of Christmas," I said, attempting to make light of his uneasiness. "This is where they introduced the reindeer."

"So long as it's reindeer," he said.

As we pushed off into the surf, I glimpsed the fright on his face. I didn't like the look at all.

＝

"RIGHT THROUGH THE HOLE IN THE wall," said Johnny, as we entered the Olga Bay Narrows.

"See that white marker there?" pointed Hank. "See that one over across? You line up your stern on this one and aim your bow at that one. Natives marked it. Local knowledge gets you up this damn gut. See that slick spot? That's a rock. See them others? They're rocks, too."

Johnny watched the flashes on the fathometer screen and tolled off the readings. "Four . . . three . . . two. . . ."

Hank nudged at the wheel. "Every time we go through this damn place," he muttered, "I got both feet drawed up, waiting for the crunch."

The shape of inlets and bays on Kodiak's rugged coastline created tidal shifts that varied greatly from place to place, even between bodies that were just miles apart. I learned that at high tide, Olga Bay was four feet above sea level, and the tidal changes arrived four hours later than at Moser Bay, even though the two bays were connected by a narrows. At times the current through the narrows was as swift as a torrent.

"One time I came through here in front of the *Dennis Wynn*," Hank said. "Pop followed too close. He was right on my ass and I mean on my ass. His boat was heavier and he was gaining all the time. Finally I run the *Kittiwake* as close to shore as I dared and let Pop go by. He was wiping at his face. Later on all he said was, 'Whatta you say two damn fools have a drink?'"

THE COOK ASSIGNED ME THE JOB of catching a feed of rainbows out of Akalura Creek.

"The bugs are murder," warned the engineer. "They chased me back to the beach before I got the line wet. Better take along one of Tex's rotten socks to wrap around your neck. That'll panic the bugs."

"No, thanks," I grinned. The deckhand's feet were another reason I fervently thanked the Lord for the inventor of the porthole.

Many rocks jutted from the fast, clear stream, and cowslips grew in lush clumps along its edges. The pussies were bursting on the willows. Gnats whirled around my head net. I found the trout in the eddies behind the boulders, and when they tumbled into the swift current, they were hard to hold.

I dropped them into the burlap bag I had brought along, dowsing it now and then, and dragging it behind as I moved on. My insect threshold was high as long as the fishing was good.

When I came back aboard, I had about twenty black-spotted, lavender-hued beauties all dressed out and just right for the pan, but to my belly-sinking dismay I couldn't find my sheepskin fishing tackle wallet that bulged with flies and light lures. I went back to retrace my steps. I couldn't find it. All those old friends were gone.

My loss spoiled the taste of the crisp trout.

"The glass is going down, Skipper," said Johnny, looking at the barometer.

"Batten down the hatches and check them lashings on the fuel drums just in case," Hank ordered.

We slid the boards into the fastening irons and drove in hardwood wedges against them. We tightened the ropes half-hitched around the drums and snugged them to the cleats.

The skies brooded in tones of gray, but the sea shimmered like glass. When we lifted anchor in Three Saints Bay, it looked like an easy trip into Kodiak.

I was wrong. The swells hit us as we passed Ugak Island. Then off Cape Chiniak the sea went into a frenzy. The *Kittiwake* pitched violently. Showers of spray sloshed the windshield and poured over the top of the wheelhouse. On each side of the cabin the water rushed like seething rivers, piled in the stern, and squirmed out the scuppers.

The drums lurched and strained against their lashings. The dories winced and thumped as the boom rigging shrilled in the wind. It seemed as though we were moving incredibly fast. On either side of us swept great waves, like moving mountains with the snow whipping from their peaks. We were hurling into each other and slamming against the bulkheads.

We braced ourselves against the rocking and held on to what we could.

I could hear the Skipper shouting. He was shouting for water and that seemed ridiculous, until we saw that smoke was coming from the wheelhouse. Soot was ablaze in the stovepipe. We made a chain, passing water buckets along, staggering and fighting the heaving and the plunging of the deck until the emergency had passed. We sat around the table in the galley bracing our backs against the bulkheads, gripping the bolted down benches. The dishes clattered. It was like being on a wild ride that we couldn't get off. We kidded each other, but inwardly I was afraid the ship would break apart.

I had never been seasick in my life. While others had suffered on the troopship during the war, I had been spared. Now I fought down the feeling as if it were a welling shame. Then the cook lit his foul-smelling pipe. I was trapped in the corner, slanting this way and that with the steep pitching of the ship, inhaling the nauseating stink of the pipe smoke until I knew I had to break away fast. I lunged over the others for the doorway. On deck the frosty spray of the ocean showered me. I wrapped my arm around a guy wire, retching as the wind and the sea slapped my hair all over my face. I almost felt like letting go and toppling into the fury that screamed around me.

I just didn't care. I heard the engineer shout, "You think you're going to die, but you won't."

"There's always a first time for everything," the cook said later on. "Now you know what it's like to shake hands with a sixty-mile-an-hour northwester."

Kodiak never looked so good.

June 22, 1955

Dear Dad, Molly & Mrs. Millet:

This will probably be my last letter for a long time. I don't really know when I'll be able to get off another one. Tomorrow I leave on the trip that will carry me to Wide Bay on the Alaska Peninsula. I've got grub for two months. I'll be pretty well isolated. I look upon this venture as a test of myself. I should get some good pictures.

They tell me I have an old cabin to establish headquarters in.

We had a little bear cub here for two days. He had a white collar. Boy! he was an onery little cuss. He'd lunge at you with a blow of air and a stamp of his front paw, then wag his head and watch you, and roll his eyes to the side. He was in a heavily slatted cage and I couldn't get a picture of him. What a smell came from his cage!

Well, I've some last-minute preparations to make.
Hoping all is well.
Take care of yourselves.
Love to all,
Sam

HANK PUFFED HIS PIPE AND SQUINTED out at the channel, watching fishing boats pass.

"Like a grandstand seat," he said, "watching a parade. They've been leaving steady all day. The fever's got hold of 'em as well as a living."

I studied the boats, storing their names in my mind: *SWALLOW, MELODY, WESTWARD, RELIANCE, GLACIER, NORTHERN PRINCESS.* Perhaps I'd see some of them later on. We were going out with the last bunch of stream guards, and this trip I would be left off, too, in a place I'd never seen before: Wide Bay on the Alaska Peninsula.

I had ordered more grub than I really needed, but I wasn't lugging it on my back, so I could afford to be generous. If anything was left over, it wouldn't be wasted. I had half a ham and a side of bacon, some canned meats, plenty of flour and tins of butter, and a variety of canned fruits and vegetables. On all my cartons I crayoned WIDE BAY, put my mark on a twenty-foot dory and a 25 horse Evinrude, and carefully stowed my gear into the old seabag that was moving out once again.

Dories, skiffs, motors, and provisions were loaded. Ropes strained and blocks squealed as drums of gasoline were swung aboard on the boom. The winch stuttered as it lifted and growled as it released.

The engine rumbled and a shudder pulsed through the deck. Hank leaned from the wheelhouse and tossed his hand upward. Off came the bow and stern lines. The deckhands hauled them aboard and coiled them neatly beside the cleats. Sluggishly the *Kittiwake* moved away from the float, then swung into the running tide of the channel. Her blue and white Fish and Wildlife pennant with the goose and salmon on it snapped in the wind.

"So long, Kodiak," I said.

We passed through Raspberry Straits, and I looked up at the mountain where Mac had had his moment. "I miss you, you old rascal," I whispered.

One of the stream guards on board was a schoolteacher from Moose Pass named Fleming Clemson. His stature wasn't impressive, but his words were.

"Did you ever think of teaching?" he asked, his eyes following a whale bird that soared, quivered, and dipped into the swells.

"Not really."

"You should. You'd make a good one. You'd have great rapport with the kids. There's no thrill in the world like the light of understanding you see in a little face that looks up at you as if you were God Almighty. Better than a sunrise. That's the biggest part of your pay. There's too many in the profession who come to the classroom fresh from a teacher's college. You could give them so much more than just your subject. You'll even enjoy going to work on Monday."

We dropped Fleming off in Paramanoff Bay, rigged an outhaul line for his skiff, and helped him set up his camp. He waved as we pushed off, and his words came to me above the splash of the surf.

"Think about teaching," he shouted. "That could be the anchorage you're looking for."

I told him I would.

⌐

NOW IT WAS MY TURN TO be dropped off at the most remote outpost.

We headed across the Shelikof toward the white peaks that floated on the sea.

"Damn this stretch of water," Hank growled. "Worst son of a bitch in Alaska. I'll be glad to be off it again." He pointed at the mountains, "Pretty, ain't they? Scary's a better word. They make my belly crawl. They spawn winds that'll blow your head off and whirl this Shelikof like batter in a mixing bowl. You picked a hell of a place to spend the summer."

I couldn't take my eyes from the mountains. They swooped right up into the clouds, and the closer we approached the more ethereal they appeared, looming specter-like beyond the blue water. There was just something about them that made me feel I wasn't as important as I thought I was. And when they drew up close, the ship shrank in their massive presence. We neared my drop-off point.

"See you in August, Sam," Hank said, "maybe before." He looked at the high clouds that drifted like solid ovals of smoke, and spoke to Johnny. "Don't spend too much time in there on the beach. Them windbags up there are telling me to get to the hell out of here."

CHAPTER 12

The Bay of the Winds

Johnny had been into Wide Bay before. He and Tex, the deckhand, led the way with some of my gear and provisions. I followed in the twenty-foot dory, loaded down with three drums of outboard fuel, six five-gallon cans of white gas for my Coleman stove and lantern, and the rest of my gear and food cartons covered with a tarp.

The prow of the dory aimed like a shark's snout at the slope of a green, buff, and snow-spidered mountain. Spray leaped over the bow, wetting the canvas, and numbing my face. I rounded Coal Point, then trailed Johnny along the low, grassy-topped cliffs where the sea had hollowed out caves in the brownish black rock of their foundations.

Johnny was headed for a stretch of beach where dunes humped above the wash of the breakers. Tumbles of driftwood were strewn high on the sand like heaps of bleached, deformed skeletons. A churning mass of gulls betrayed the entrance of Big Creek.

From the top of one of the dunes slanted a tall, stark pole. A raven with blowing feathers was perched on it. Johnny was zeroed in on him. The raven dropped awkwardly into the wind and sagged away along the beach. I cut the motor. The dory slid with a grating upon the sand. Johnny with a rifle slung on his skinny shoulder was already disappearing over the dune by the time I stepped out into the slosh. Hardly had he disappeared than there he was again striding back over the rise.

"Shack's in good shape," he said, eying the sky. "Roof needs some work. One creek marker's down. We'll give you a hand with the drums and we got to shove off."

He acted as if he knew something about the place that I didn't. He pointed to a bear track in the damp sand. "Look at the size of that son of a bitch," he said.

We tumbled the drums over the side of the dory and rolled them high on the beach against the bank. Then Johnny and Tex unloaded their boat, placing the gear and provisions in a pile above the clutter of weed and kelp ribbons, and left me with mine and the transportation of all of it.

"Like to give you a hand with this stuff to the shack," offered Tex lamely.

"No time," barked Johnny, glancing at the sky. "You wanted

Bear track.

185

isolation, Sam? Brother, you got it. I'd shoot myself if I had to stay in here for even a day. You got what's left of an antenna pole and no radio. Until the fishermen get here, you're shut off from the world." He started up the motor as Tex shoved the boat out of the wash and hopped aboard the prow on his knees. They waved, and I watched them plane away.

I looked at my faint shadow on the sand. I glanced at the gulls circling higher. I stared after the shrinking boat until it became a speck, until it went out of sight around Coal Point. Then the heap of supplies shocked me out of my trance.

I had a lot of work to do.

THE SHACK WAS AN EIGHT-BY-TEN-FOOT STRUCTURE with a slanting roof of red asphalt strips. Its boards were split and grayed. Cables fastened to rafters were guyed on either side to "deadmen" buried in the sand. A crude window with a crack in one of its panes shone out of its easterly side. From its roof jutted a stovepipe with a dunce cap top. I bounded up the single step to the porch, looked at the wood piled in the closet-like shed, and hesitated, sweeping the view, before going inside.

A brook came out of the alders, tracing a dark, crooked furrow through the grass and fireweed, and chuckling past over the gravel about fifty feet away. Beyond the brook, the alder-choked hills wrinkled away to slopes of willow and sharp white peaks that glared against the sky. I swung the pivot board door latch upward and stepped inside.

A bunk was built against the far wall. There were tiers of shelves in one corner, a table beneath the window, and a small rusty-topped stove with an oven next to its firebox. Sand and dormant flies were all over the floor. From the dark stains in the planks, I suspected Johnny was right about the roof. I picked up a tobacco tin from the stove, opened its lid, and saw several dry wooden matches within. The stove was ready to light. There was a can of beans next to a pot with flies and mouse droppings in it.

I talked out loud as if the shack were another person. "First thing is to get you cleaned up. Then I better get things lugged up here undercover before the weather changes. I'll pull the dory up high and dry. First chance I get, I'll look for an anchorage in the creek. Getting settled is what's important right now, and the sooner, the better."

I brushed off the table and the shelves with a rag. Then I grabbed the worn broom and swept everything out the door, and the wind swept the porch.

The tide had ebbed enough to leave the dory cast up sideways on the beach. I slewed one end, then the other until I had it above the tide litter. Next I covered the outboard with a canvas hood, dug the anchor into the sand, ran another line from the bow and secured it to a driftwood chunk imbedded in the banking. That should keep it there.

I shouldered a box of canned goods and began the first of many heavy-footed slogging trips over the sand, up, and down, and back over the dune again. As I worked, the wind blustered from the mountains, stronger and stronger.

"Just hold off a little longer," I said to the scary purple sky.

My luck held. It took me longer than I thought it would to get everything up from the beach. I was pooped. The ominous glowering of the sky had demanded too fast a pace.

I placed my spring box in the riffles of the brook.

A piece of one-inch diameter copper tubing passed through the box about two inches above its bottom. The box rested just deep enough so that water flowed through the tubing. I laid flat stones inside, then placed on top of them the butter tins, eggs, and the slab of bacon which I had cut in half. I clamped down the lid. On top of it I set a boulder almost as big as I could lift. If the level of the brook rose, its waters wouldn't overturn the box or carry it off, and if some animal became curious of the contents, it would be discouraged about breaking and entering. But if a bear had a notion, that boulder might just as well be a pebble.

I packed the canned goods on the shelves and stowed my gear away from the stained places in the floor. From the spikes partially driven into the walls I hung my rain outfit, boots, pants, and shirts. Then I unrolled my sleeping bag on the bunk, and even though I was weary enough to fall into it, I passed up the temptation. There would be all night to sleep. I set up the Coleman stove, hung the lantern from a nail in one of the roof rafters, and organized my pots, pans, and other hardware.

The big stove I would use for heat when I needed it, or for baking beans, bread, and biscuits. Right now something simple and quick was in order. I was more tired than hungry.

As the can of Dinty Moore beef stew simmered and coffee began to slurp sluggishly in the little percolator, I watched the purple shroud settling and erasing the mountains. "Whatever it's going to do," I said, "I wish it would get it over with. It's worse than watching somebody hold his breath."

My eyes traveled over the wildly tossing grass to the gray piles of driftwood jackstrawed along the edges of the slough. In the slough itself were islands of grass that rippled silkily and pale green amid the silt. A movement riveted my attention.

The spot faded and grew bright again. I focused the binoculars on it. A straw-colored bear and a cub were crossing the creek. As the sow emerged on the gravel, she shook her loose hide, making the water fly. Then on she came across the flat, her sides bulging like a cask. She tractored over the driftwood in crawling strides, now hanging her head to pull at the grass, now lifting her muzzle and swinging it into the wind.

The bear lay down ponderously, extending her head between her outstretched forepaws, watching the cub that dallied in the greenery. When the cub ranged too far, she rose tiredly and moved after him, appearing as an animated haystack closing in with a smaller one.

"I'll call that the Bear Pasture," I said.

As I absently sopped a piece of frying-pan bannock into my stew, I spotted a red fox trotting over the driftwood piles. He was carrying something in his mouth, and he kept stopping to look behind him. He acted as though he had stolen something. On he came, the fur bouncing along his back, and his tail streaming out like a banner. Through the lenses I could make out that his jaws held the head and shoulder section of a rabbit. I moved to the doorway and hooked it open. The fox stopped again to watch his back-trail, then jogged on to halt abruptly about fifty feet from me. He looked up with a most comical expression, dropped his mouthful, and shot off through the grass. Then he put on the brakes, hesitating as if wondering whether or not to go back and snatch up what he had lost.

I noticed something else, a dark shape humping over the bone white litter of logs. It was stocky and thick-necked, like a small bear with a bushy tail. It was rocking along, scuffling its nose on the track of the fox. My heart almost stopped. A wolverine! It had to be! He huddled and rippled closer. A pale orange streak flanked his brown hide. As squat as he appeared, he had all the nervous mannerisms of a mink.

The fox crouched, bellying down in the grass. About fifty feet from him, the wolverine froze. He glared, squirmed back on his brush, and hunkered down on his forefeet. Suddenly he swung about as if a force had struck him. Off he loped. The fox tossed several squalls after him, then vanished into the grass.

"I've seen a wolverine," I shouted, "an honest-to-God wolverine! Dad, if only you could have been here." I was ecstatic—then furious. "You nut, why the hell didn't you get a picture of him?" My answer came in the buffeting sounds the wind made, and the wailing of the gulls above the dunes.

It was time for me to retreat to my shelter. The wind came on now with a rush, heaving against the shack, volleying it with sand, wheezing through the cracks, and rattling the window in its casing. The purple sky had reached its limit and couldn't hold back any longer. I thought the shack would be torn up in the explosion of its breath and tumbled on before it over the dune and into the bay. With each savage blast, the shack just swayed and groaned and held as if it had a taproot into the ground.

Monday afternoon
July 27, 1955
Dear Dad, Molly & Mrs. Millet:
I guess for the first time in my life I am really
isolated. I'm in an 8' x 10' shack located on Big

*Creek, Wide Bay, Alaska Peninsula. I came ashore
early yesterday morning and with my sea dory
riding low, heavily laden. . . . Last night I was so
tired from slogging my supplies from the sandy beach
to my cabin that I couldn't sleep. My bones ached. . . .*

*I forgot to tell you while going after the wolverine,
I started to go over a rise and there, 75 feet below
were the brown sow and cub. I changed my course.*

*So after my first day at Big Creek, it's no wonder
I couldn't go to sleep. With all the things I mentioned
there are still even others. The bank swallows along
the sand hills, the black, yellow and chestnut colored
Alaska longspurs, the semi-palmated plover, the
solitary sandpipers. (I looked these last three species
up in my bird book.)*

*Friday, July 1st the salmon season opens here
in my area. I hope there's an honest bunch of
fishermen. I'd hate like hell to have to arrest one.*

Hoping all is well. Take care of yourselves.

Love to all,

Sam

I LAY IN MY SLEEPING BAG listening to the slamming and
shuddering of the gale, the flailing of sand. I could hear the
measured gnashing of the surf. At times the wind lulled to the low
growling of a cat crouched over its prey, and then it crescendoed
to the yowling of monstrous toms tearing into each other. I could
imagine fiends pounding for entrance against the boards. And
then came still another sound: the pellets of rain hitting the
window like charges of shot.

I finally had to get up after midnight, light the lantern, and
survey the interior of the shack. At least there were no leaks over
the bunk. I set out a washtub, some buckets, and a few large pans

to catch the heavy drops that were causing minor flooding into my gear. After I turned out the lantern and crawled into my warm bag, I listened to a symphony of liquid voices.

Plink? . . . Plank? . . . Plunk-plunk?

I awakened to the sound of rain driven against the boards. I put on the rain gear and pushed my shoulder against the door. It yielded stubbornly, then slammed like a sprung trap a second after I had wedged through it. With each step I walked, I planted my heels firmly to keep the wind from driving me uncontrollably along.

The bay was smeared in long white streaks. The creek ran mud into it. Uprooted alders and willows milled in the yellow brown slick spreading from the mouth. I couldn't see the mountains. High on the beach slewed into the kelp litter was the dory with several inches of water in it. Overhead the gulls hurled like white boomerangs, scaling, rising steeply, and returning. I walked as if planning each step, bracing one foot before advancing the other. Outside projects were definitely off for now. I was a prisoner of the wind.

I had to make the most of my confinement. Alaska had taught me to do that. I scribbled a long list of things that had to be done. Then I started on the things I could do. I sharpened the heavy-duty crosscut saw, honed my axe, and whetted my knives. I made a canvas scabbard which I intended to nail on the inside of the dory and protect the Winchester from the salt. I made a pot of beans, cooked the half a ham, baked bread, and wrote letters that would have a long wait for mailing.

I only ventured outside when I really had to. The slamming wind not only threatened my balance, but scoured my eyeballs and whipped water from them. It was difficult to breathe, as if the air were being snatched away when I inhaled. Although the rain had stopped, the wind rushed with such velocity I felt as though I were wading against an invisible torrent. It was hard to adjust to the constant force. It made easy tasks difficult.

I gave up my first attempt to repair the roof. I needed more hands than I had to hold the asphalt strip down and keep myself braced at the same time. Finally the winds abated to a level where

I was able to get the job done. Hank knew what he was talking about when he said to bring some roofing along with me.

I replaced the creek marker. I dug a rubbish pit. I built up a wood supply. There was certainly no shortage of wood. Although the country was alder and willow brush, past storms had cast acres of driftwood along the beach, beyond the dunes, and along the edges of the slough. I wondered where it had all come from and marveled at the power that had tossed it there.

The dory had been on my mind. I didn't like the idea of it being on the open beach. I wanted it in a sheltered place where it would always be afloat and I could count on it for immediate use. On a scout along Big Creek I found just the place, a narrow cove in the slough, not far from the sweep of the current. The problem was to get the dory there.

I could see that another storm was coming. I decided to try to beat it. An offshore wind was already blasting. I bailed out the dory, wrestled it one end at a time from the kelp, swinging and straining until whiskers of light danced before my eyes. Dust particles seemed to twinkle all around me. Twice I worked the dory into the surf, and twice it was slammed hard sideways by a roller. I waited until a breaker started to recede. With all my strength I launched the dory and leaped into it. Grabbing the oars, I was able to keep her headed out and ride the next big one before it broke. Then the wind pounced on me from over the dune and hurled me away from the beach. I was fast sweeping over a dark and heaving bay. The acceleration was frightening.

I pumped some fuel into the sediment bowl and checked methodically to see if the shift lever was in neutral. I yanked on the starting cord. Nothing. Again. Nothing. Roiled patches of kelp rushed past me. A loon rolled on the ugly swells, stretching its neck and lowering its head to mew the most lonesome sound I ever heard . . . over and over again. I was being blown out to sea. It was scary, yet I was strangely calm. I was express training toward a bluish purple, white-smeared expanse. The shrilling of the wind mingled with the loon's cry and hissing of the dory's passage.

Strangely I thought of the stubborn jeep. Here it was all over again, but even worse. I thought of missing Kodiak altogether and winding up in the Hawaiian Islands, foolish thoughts as I pulled and prayed. The oars would be of little help. Then a miracle occurred. The Evinrude shuddered with life. It coughed into a wonderful spasm. I just let her idle until she warmed, and I slipped her into gear and quartered the bow into the steep-sided swells. I headed for the creek entrance, now and then grinning back at the wake that bubbled away toward the storm.

The gulls stood in silent ranks along the spit, all facing the wind. Breakers were creaming in and tumbling crazily in the current pouring out to meet them. Slowly I approached. I glimpsed a swell suddenly looming off the stern as if it would engulf me. I gave the throttle a quick twist and shot ahead with a burst that thrilled me, beating the wave and knifing into the flow of fresh water. Then I was veering into my sheltered place in the slough.

As I pulled the canvas hood over the motor, I patted it affectionately. "Good girl," I said. I lashed the canvas down, secured the dory with slackened bow and stern lines, and ran the anchor line above the water mark.

I had performed no great feat, yet I felt I had. No one had been there to see me win my round against the wind and sea. I felt a tremendous inner satisfaction. A job had to be done and I had done it.

"Now," I shouted at the ominous sky, "go ahead and storm all you want to."

And that night it did.

Wednesday afternoon
July 6, 1955
Dear Dad, Molly & Mrs. Millet:
    I have decided to number letters so that you will read them in the proper sequence. The last letter I wrote to you, along with one to Anna and one to Dick, still wait here patiently to be mailed. Today makes my 11th day here at Wide Bay. I haven't seen

*a soul except for a small plane that passed overhead
one day. I've got plenty of grub. I'm not really too
worried when the Fish & Wildlife plane will stop in
here to check on me. I do miss the mail though. I'd
like to hear what is going on at home.*

*My half a ham lasted me ten days. Now I have a
split pea soup simmering on my little Coleman stove,
and in this flavorful brew, I have given the ham
bones a proper burial. . . .*

Hoping all is well. Take care of yourselves.

Love to all,

Sam

I WAS ADAPTING TO MY NEW way of life. To enjoy my isolation, I had to keep busy. I found myself thinking ahead to the next project, planning the next day, and doing my chores with an exaggerated thoroughness.

What I was very proud of was the driftwood shelter I had constructed over my latrine. No door on it at all. Just a comfortable seat on a knoll . . . wide open to the rippling grasses and the great notch in the mountains. The wild vista always made me stay much longer than was necessary and made physiological functions pure pleasure. I often thought I had built this necessity more from an aesthetic point of view than a practical one, for it was at least fifty yards from the shack.

One morning Nature called with such urgency that I dashed to my relief station without the rifle. As I sat there lost in the panorama, a huge, furry shape bloomed above the grass tips and grew into a grazing brown bear. He was about forty yards away, eating his way slowly toward me. The wind was gusting from him to me, blowing light patches in his dark hide. I wasn't sure what to do. If I bolted for the shack, would he come bounding after me? If he did, my handicap wouldn't be enough. With a growing uneasiness I watched him turn over a driftwood log with a cuff of his broad forepaw. Could I just ease away while he was so intent upon his foraging?

There I sat trying to decide. He was about twenty-five yards away now. Just as I was about to panic, haul up my pants, and make a run for it, he swayed up on his hind legs, teetering there before me, throwing his nose into the wind as if analyzing what it brought to him. His eyes glinted, peering at me as if feeling instead of seeing. His forepaws drooped. The claws were whitened and curved like sickles. He winced as a sandpiper quivered in the air within inches of his muzzle. Any other time I would have laughed out loud.

Suddenly he collapsed to all fours, and with a fluid motion he swung about, shambled a few steps, looked back at me, then rocked in a sweeping motion over the driftwood piles as if a great weight were seesawing from one end of his body to the other.

My bowel movement more complete than usual, I made not only a beeline for the shack but also a solemn promise that the rifle would be a companion in all future meditations.

DURING ONE BREAKFAST AS I WAS attacking a stack of pancakes and bacon slices, I suddenly realized what had made the morning seem so strange to me. Not a breath of wind was stirring. It was almost eerie. I went outside to investigate the phenomenon. Mosquitoes ascended and descended all over me. They crawled over each other's backs as they piled up on my woolen shirt. They whined in my ears and clouded before me like sawdust whirled from a planer. I made an arm-waving retreat. Hereafter I would be more kind with the language I hurled at the wind. It was a relief when I finally saw the grass in motion again.

As many problems as the almost continuous wind caused, it afforded me delights as well. I loved to wash the flannel sheet liner I used in my sleeping bag, hang it out to flap like a loose sail and absorb the sweet smells that came down from the mountains or in from the sea. Then there were those days when I took my sponge bath. I took complete advantage of my wild freedom and raced naked over the dunes to dry in the wind that toweled all over me like silk.

Sunday evening
July 17, 1955
Dear Dad, Molly, & Mrs. Millet:

I've been here three weeks now and still no word from Kodiak. They either think I'm a damn good man or else they've forgotten about me. The Enforcement Agent from the Chignik district dropped in here about a week ago, and I gave him my letters to mail. I don't really care too much if Kodiak shows up, but I would like to get my mail. Even though my bread is all moldy and my bacon is about gone, I am not hunting a bit. I've got flour and corn meal and cans of SPAM and I've got a perfectly good rifle to get meat with if I have to.

Perhaps I told you in my last letter about "Sneaky the Seal." During high water, he used to sneak into my creek and slaughter what few salmon were showing at the time. He'd just bite off the heads and let the rest of the bright carcasses float down the current and out to sea. I began to think of him as a wily U boat commander on prowl after the ships that were my salmon, and I, myself, began to feel as a destroyer who was out to erase this raider. . . . Each time I saw a headless salmon, I fumed and swore a terrible vengeance. . . .

Well, I better sign off. Hoping all is well. Take care of yourselves.

Love to all,
Sam

I EXPLORED THE UPPER REACHES OF the creek, plodding over a pillowy terrain and skirting the edges of alders now misted with the green of new leaves. Ground squirrels sat upright and whistled at me with pumps of their tails. Not a fish did I see. Bear droppings were in piles like green ovals of horse manure or black braids of rope. They evidenced no fish diet yet. No gulls waded the creek edges.

"Hew! Hew! Hew!" greeted a greater yellowlegs as I came over a rise of horsetails and tough grass. He bobbed up and down on his spindly bright legs, then lifted away to knife over the puddles in the silt and show off his white rump patch.

I walked the beach. Minnows trapped in tidal pools winced as I approached and stirred the bottoms into dirty clouds of panic. A flock of sanderlings rose in unison from a spit, veered into invisibility, then appeared again in a precision of rising steeply and tipping down to land as one and pace once more along the lather edges. I walked over the crinkled kelp pieces of pink, yellow, and brown. The surf washed into it and bounced it as if it were loose feathers. An army of flies crawled over the damp sand left by the retreating tide, thousands on the move. I stepped over the stranded jellyfish that gleamed like upturned saucers of gelatin. Ahead of me scampered a young plover. He brought to mind an urchin running away with no pants on.

In the lee of a high dune I came upon an assembly of bank swallows. Hundreds of them were sitting on the sand. Did the wind even make them tired, too? Knowing the flies were there on the sand, I suspected the swallows were feeding, but watching them through the binoculars I could see no evidence of dining at all. They rose softly in groups, skimmed back and forth along the sand slope, lifted into the flow of the wind, and dropped again. Such a quiet fluttering of wings all around me! I thought of bats emerging from a cave at twilight and setting the sky into motion.

Although the weather had been mostly bad, I still took the dory for a run whenever I could, cruising past a rocky structure that reared out of the bay. I named it "Battleship Island." Its boulder slabs were piled like pagodas, and when the seas smashed over its blocky turrets it appeared as a Japanese battlewagon underway. Cormorants perched on the shelves of its superstructure, snaking their necks like feathered cobras as I passed, some lumbering into the air, losing altitude until they slowly regained it. It was understandable why the Natives called them "double-enders," for their outstretched necks in flight were replicas of their long tails.

I investigated a long arm of the bay that wound like a gleaming corridor between kelp beds to its head where a shallow stream came out of the willows and rushed over colored stones to greet me. A jagged peak provided a backdrop for the scene materializing in my mind. I could see prospectors squatted in the riffles and swirling their gold pans.

On my return to the creek anchorage one afternoon, the motor acted strangely. Once I shut it off, I couldn't start it again.

"So what's new?" I muttered in disgust. Perhaps I'd have more patience later on.

July 23, 1955
Big Creek Hermitage
Dear Dad, Molly, & Mrs. Millet:
    As Anna probably told you, I got 10 letters all at once. I had one written to you and sealed. Because of my shortage of envelopes (I have two left now), I decided to send it off while the opportunity was at hand. First I want to tell you that I read and reread your letters, enjoyed and then enjoyed all over again. . . .
    I don't think [my] letters are polished up enough for publication. I didn't write them with that in mind at all, but merely to try and pass on to you some of the incidents in my lonely life. I've been taking a lot of notes. No too many pictures yet. I have tried to be at least thorough. For example, I took a slide of a

generous heap of bear dung with flies on it. I think
it might have surrealistic possibilities for the next
art show in Boston. I shall entitle it, "Critics at a
seminar."

    Take care of yourselves.

    Love to all,

    Sam

AFTER SUPPER I FELT THE FIRST knife thrust of pain, and I did my best to ignore it. Probably pulled a groin muscle, I thought. I had just wrestled more driftwood logs than I should have or cut more wood than I had to. The twinge would work itself out.

As tired and as miserable as I felt, I decided I had better attempt to start the outboard again. I slung my rifle and swished through the grass to the slough. To the limits of my knowledge I checked over the Evinrude. I kept pulling on the starting rope. Not even a cough. My patience was ebbing fast. With each pull I cursed for emphasis. Then the knife in the right side of my groin returned and worked itself deeper in. To hell with the motor. I wasn't punching a clock. Let it wait until morning.

Back in the shack once more, I lay in my sleeping bag. The wood fire crackled and wheezed. I pressed over the painful area. It was tender, and warm to the touch. Was this an appendicitis attack?

Suddenly I remembered the fellow who had left the base soon after I had come. He had saved his money and was going to homestead on the mainland. Shortly after he had left, the news reached us that he had been found adrift in a small boat, with gulls all over him. His appendix had burst. All those muscles and all that drive, but he never made it to the help he needed. If it could happen to him. . . .

Suppose it is your appendix. What are you going to do about it?

I thought over my options.

Operate on myself? Ridiculous. If I didn't bleed to death after the incision, just what the hell did an appendix look like anyway?

And even if I found it, what did its removal entail? What about infection? You're no surgeon. Forget it.

Why didn't I have a transmitter? My presence, they said, would be enough to keep most fishermen honest. How would they know whether or not I had contact with headquarters? And, besides, I was rugged and self-sufficient, they said. What a laugh that was.

I could build a bonfire on the beach and hope the glow would arouse the curiosity of someone somewhere. As of yesterday the commercial season had opened in my district, but I hadn't seen a salmon yet, let alone a boat.

I could take the dory and extra gas and head into the Shelikof, perhaps hail a fishing boat or be spotted by a plane. Or make it to the Native village of Kanatak. But could I start the motor? As for rowing against this wind. . . .

I cursed my body. It was betraying me. What a dirty trick! This happened to old men. A physical peak one moment, a time bomb ticking inside of me the next. I couldn't get at it to turn it off.

The pain stabbed even more sharply. Cold sweat popped on my forehead. I was shivery one moment and warm the next. Was imagination making the pain worse than it really was?

This pain was not imagination. Was this the way it was going to be? Was I going out this way? I always wondered how it would be. Mauled to death by a bear, or going under in the white water . . . I could understand that. But this? How long did it take an appendix to burst? How long did you have after that? I thought I'd be older.

"Hold on there," I said, "don't get all shook. You're not a corpse yet. You don't even know for sure this is appendicitis."

The walls heaved and creaked from the volleys of the wind. A searing twinge made me groan and clutch at my side until the spasm was over.

"Lord," I said, "I need help. I can't handle this. I don't even go to church. You've got others to look after who do, but I'm asking . . . please . . . please. . . ."

Dad always said if the Lord helped those who helped themselves, then do something. Anything. Anything is better than nothing.

I went out into the wind to the brook and grabbed up a large can of peaches that I had submerged in an eddy. Then I went inside again, peeled off its label, lay down, and slowly rolled the icy metal cylinder back and forth above the pain. Back and forth, back and forth. The numbness soothed me. *I guess I can tough it out*, I thought.

Groggily I sat upright. I had been asleep. Had it all been a dream? The can against my abdomen brought me back again. To my amazement the knife in my groin had been withdrawn. As quickly as the pain had come, it had vanished. I grinned in the darkness.

"Yaaaaa . . . whooooooo," I whooped. The cold can had done it. I was back in control again. Once more I was tough. Self-sufficient. A real Alaskan. I didn't need anyone but myself. My cockiness holding sway, I fell back into a deep sleep.

The next morning I was a dynamo. I did my wash, double-clothespinned it on the line and left it whipping in the strong wind while I went down to the slough. Confidently I unbuttoned the head of the motor. That was my trouble yesterday. No confidence. I scraped the carbon from the plugs, wiped out the sediment bowl, checked the fuel lines, and worked a wire into the water intake. Then I pumped gas from the can until the plunger squeaked. To show the power of my positive thinking, I stowed the anchor and pushed the dory out into the grab of the current. I pulled out the choke and hauled back smoothly on the starting rope. Nothing. Another pull. A feeble stuttering, and I pushed in the choke. The engine purred evenly and roared as I advanced the throttle.

"Anybody got an outboard to fix?" I shouted into the wind. I took the dory for a short run, then idled back into my anchorage to secure it for the day.

Across the creek mouth the gulls were gathered on the spit facing into the wind, making clean lines of gray and white against the dark litter. Now and then a flurrying, a wheeling about and landing again as if to dress up their ranks. Some dangled their feet and hung in suspension, rocking gently above the formation, dropping to feel for the sand, touching it, and settling their wings in close to their bodies. I could imagine the rising and falling set to music.

I leaned into the wind as I plodded toward the dunes, and cursed it. Why must it blow so hard all the time?

Within a few feet of my face a tiny sandpiper quivered on set wings. It was examining me. Its bright eyes held an accusing glitter, probing as they attempted communication. Strangely I felt ashamed that I didn't understand.

Then something very ordinary happened. I had seen it many times before. An Alaskan longspur, a sparrow-like bird, rose out of the tough grass, struggled upwards to perhaps thirty feet, stiffened its wings, and floated. Its song rained joyously. It was its flight song to its hidden mate, but it transcended her. It touched the very core of my being.

It had begun in the eyes of the sandpiper, and now it flooded into understanding in the song of the longspur.

How had I forgotten so easily? How could I have been so arrogant?

I faced the slamming wind and hung my head. My hair flailed my face, and my heart beat all over my body.

"It was more than the can of peaches," I said. "I'm sorry. I only think of You when I'm hurting." My words seemed snatched away and hurled along with the flying pieces of kelp. "Thanks for Your help with the motor, too."

I looked down at the clumps of grass in the buff-colored sand, each clump with perfect arcs and semicircles traced around their bases by their sharp tips and the artistry of the gale.

"And thanks for this strong wind that dries my wash and keeps the insects down."

THE WEATHER FURTHER DETERIORATED INTO DRIVING rain and maniacal blasts that whipped the bay into a froth. I could actually lie on the wind. If I braced my feet atop the dune and leaned off balance into the blast, it held me from falling on my face. I was living in a wind tunnel, and Nature's blowers were turned up all the way.

I didn't venture too far from the shack. Now and then I fought the elements just to get out, but the screaming winds soon drove me back inside again. I was thankful I had a hole to crawl into. My outgoing mail grew into a stack. I was lonesome for the sun.

My color film needed more light for the colors to reproduce well. I passed up pictures of bear grazing in my pasture beneath leaden skies and amid tossing grass. I was hoarding my film for sunshine. I watched one old boar, head down in the seething greenery, his shoulders humped like a bull buffalo's, slowly drifting along the slough edge. Banners of rain whipped past him. He had to be soaking wet, but if he was uncomfortable, he gave no indication of it. I admired his apparent stoic philosophy. I should complain less and just accept what I couldn't do much about anyway.

What tremendous growth the dune grass made! The brown blades of last year had given way to the eager new spikes of thrusting green.

Frequently I checked the dory to bail it out and check its lines. Straight-sided slabs of sand toppled from the bank into a swollen, discolored creek. Ripped pieces of kelp rode on the winds far into the grass. Hank was right. I picked a hell of a place to spend the summer.

⌐

THE COMMERCIAL SALMON SEASON HAD BEEN open for nine days now in my district. I had seen neither a fish nor a fishing boat. The rain finally stopped. An overcast ascended the slopes of the mountains like a window shade inching up on its roller.

The flash at the edge of the kelp bed heliographed a change in my routine. Then another winked as a bright fish quivered into the air and landed with a sharp spank on the bay. At last the pinks had arrived.

I heard a plane. It must have been a spotter plane for the fishermen. It cruised back and forth, then went off. In the late afternoon the boats came. Uncanny. They were right on the tails of the fish.

No fish except Dolly Varden had shown in the creek yet. Perhaps the salmon were already at the mouth, milling by the thousands as if deliberating the final assault on the fresh water of their birth. From now on, I had to be on the alert. Granted, the fishermen had to make a living, but I was determined they weren't going to rob my creek to do it.

I slid the dory out of its lair and advertised my presence to the fishermen. I warned the boats that drifted in too close to the prohibited area and pointed to the signs that stood out like beacons. I cautioned crews about setting too close to a set from another boat just being completed. I walked along the spit at the creek mouth like a sentry on watch. At night I even strolled there with my Coleman lantern, catching a few winks, and then going back again. Sometimes when I wasn't cruising in the dory, I sat on a bluff to glass the busy scene. To get some needed sleep, I sometimes left the vantage point guarded by a shirt-and-pants dummy stuffed with grass.

The round-haul set was fascinating to observe. To see the boat suddenly move out, seine spilling from its stern until the run to the anchored skiff was completed, leaving the bright floats in a wide ring upon the surface. To watch the crew, backs bent, arms endlessly pulling the cork and lead lines aboard until the ring shrank to an arc of floats alongside that surged with the rushes of salmon against the mesh. To see fish squirting into the air and leaping the barrier to freedom. To watch the boom swing out over the bagged seine, the brailing net plummeting into it, then lifting as the winch ratcheted. To see the mesh bulging and twisting and dripping as the boom swung inward over the hold. To watch the bottom open and the silver pour out—that was eye-stopping.

One skipper invited me aboard to take pictures of the operation. It was a thrill to look down into the bagged seine and see the pale green multitude of shapes, the flashing of their sides, the yawning of their mouths as they bit the mesh, lunged against it, and made the corks buck. When released from the brailing net, they slapped against the boards and against each other with the sound of torrential rain. Scales flew all over the place.

Another skipper asked me to go up in the little spotter plane with him. As much as I wanted to, I declined. Up there with him, my creek was left unguarded. As much as I wanted to trust everybody, I couldn't. I felt a strong responsibility. Wide Bay's fish were my fish. If outlaws were going to rob my creek, then they were going to have to work at it.

High water was due at midnight. I thought there might be some activity at the creek mouth and it wouldn't be seals.

DURING HIGH WATER I HAD SEEN a seal in the creek several times. I was tired of discovering bright salmon carcasses floating down the current and out into the bay. I became alarmed. I could excuse the whole fish being eaten, but when just the head was sheared off . . . that was too wasteful. I became madder with each headless salmon I saw. Was the same seal responsible? I decided it was.

Because he was so elusive, I called him "Old Sneaky." Each time I saw the shining periscope of his dome in the current, it always sank before I could get a shot off. I began to think of him as a wary U-boat raiding the ships that were my salmon. I was the destroyer commander dedicated to end the career of this raider.

One day, I sat cross-legged on the spit watching a phalarope. Its dainty bill darted nervously as its buoyant body pirouetted amid the flotsam. Out of the corner of my eye I saw a suspicious spot upstream. Old Sneaky was returning from a fresh water foray. When he submerged, I lay on my belly in the iodine-smelling kelp litter, cocked the hammer of the .348, and waited over the barrel. The gray head eased into view, then swiveled its neck to survey the creek mouth. As he rode upwards on a swell, I saw the gold dot of my front sight shine against his grayness. I squeezed the trigger. The spreading stain that resulted gave me the satisfaction of the man on the bridge watching the oil slick of a submarine gushing up to form a tombstone on the sea.

A few hours later I found his black-spotted body shrouded in the kelp that had washed in with the tide. I removed his liver,

Old Sneaky and the .348

then dragged his five-foot length high on the beach. Something else could have the rest of him.

I WAS PATROLLING AMONG THE BOATS when the orange-and-black Fish and Wildlife plane, the *Goose*, landed in front of my beach. Roy Lindsley leaned out of the hatch.

"Fresh meat and vegetables," he hollered. "You've got a good escapement already. You can ease up a bit and read your mail." He handed me a packet tied with a string. "And something else. Jim's got a moose assignment on the Kenai. He'd like to have you give him a hand after you get through here. He can probably use you well into September. Interested?"

"Sounds good," I said. That would fit in with Big John's plans to go down the Alcan.

Roy was in a hurry. He had other stops to make. I hightailed it to the shack and brought back my stack of outgoing mail for him to send.

"See you sometime in August," Roy waved.

That evening I made a pig of myself on lettuce and tomato salad and fried pork chops. I read my mail several times. Everyone was fine. The world hadn't changed very much.

I had my first uninterrupted sleep in days.

FROM THE BLUFF I SPOTTED AN old friend out among the fishing boats. It was the *Elizabeth*. I went back to the shack, headed for the slough, and leaped into my dory to plane out for a visit. I had a present for him.

"Hello, you old creek robber," I greeted Johnny Malutin.

"What you doing here?" asked Johnny, really surprised.

"Supposed to watch guys like you."

Johnny introduced me to his wife who stood beside him in her rain gear and a big smile.

"Thought you might like some seal liver," I said. "Fresh since a few hours ago, I got more than I can eat."

Johnny's wife beamed. "We'll have that for supper," she said. "We love it."

"Too bad Dick not with me," Johnny mused. "Good man. I ask him after bear hunt but he say he do something else. He like to be alone, that feller. I think he go to other part of Alaska soon. He give you bear skull?"

"Sure did."

Johnny grinned. "He sit out in rain scraping meat out. Then he hang it over the side. Treat that skull like gold."

"There's fish showing. I don't want to hold you up," I said. Johnny tossed his arms. "Not hold me up at all. The boys mend seine and work on kicker. We do pretty good so far." He pointed. "Pink salmon jump all excited, like he enjoy himself. Chum come out like old man and fall over."

"Only a few days left in this district, Johnny. You better get them while you can."

"Learn to take my time long ago," he said. "You feel alone in this place?"

I nodded. "I guess I need people more than Dick does," I grinned.

"That feller do anything." He eyed the crewman tinkering with the kicker. "I wish he here right now."

"So do I," I said.

✂

BIG CREEK WAS ALIVE WITH FISH from its mouth to its upper reaches. The riffles splashed with spawning activity, and the gulls waited for the salmon to grow older.

If I wanted a salmon, I caught him in the salt water where he was bright and a few sea lice clung to him like flattened tadpoles. A salmon was really more fish than I needed, and after having the pale orange flesh boiled, baked, and fried, I tired of too much of it. I ignored the Dolly Varden. My choice was the sand dabs of flounders that scatter-rugged the bay. They struck readily at a small spinner twitched over the bottom. I caught just enough for a meal, and their fillets were the sweetest treat of all.

✂

FROM WHAT I SAW OF THE operation, I decided I didn't want any part of commercial fishing. In the month the season had been open in my district, perhaps eight or ten days had been utilized. The weather and weekend closures had taken the lion's share of the thirty days.

Wide Bay had fish, but they didn't come easy. They were safe when the winds screamed and boats could do nothing else but strain on their anchors. The crews could do nothing but catch up on sleep and curse. When the weather finally broke, they worked feverishly to make up for the time lost, wearing their hands raw pulling seine and stinging them on the jellyfish that stuck in the meshes. They reaped the silver harvest while they could. In a few short months some made a year's wages, but for most of them, the weather and Lady Luck wielded a strict censorship on the season's take.

Friday morning
August 5, 1955
Big Creek, Wide Bay
Dear Dad, Molly, & Mrs. Millet:

The fishermen left here on the evening of July 29, that date being the closure here in my district. The run of pink salmon was extremely heavy. I would estimate that somewhere in the neighborhood of 500,000 fish were taken from the bay alone. Most of the fishermen left in high spirits. This bay had made the season for them. The remaining few weeks in the other districts would all be gravy. And so the fleet left. The next morning the bay was empty, and standing on the high dune, I saw my shadow flung against the sand, and for a moment I was almost lonesome. There were only a few empty beer cans in the litter of kelp that marked the high water line during the night. And of course, the ever-present, complaining sea gulls. . . .

I don't think this country will ever really be settled, unless like Japan, we become so terribly crowded that we move into such places out of necessity. I think the bears will be safe here until the big-game guides deplete the other areas. This is the last place the guides will turn to. Why? Because this Peninsula country has the most vicious weather I have ever seen. Winds that make even the sunny days miserable, slamming winds that you must crouch into to walk, winds that gust with the jolt of a great hammer and heave my shack and make my lantern, hanging inside, swing on its nail. For ten days now I have listened to the bluster of a northwest blow. It is not the soft sighing wind that lifts at pine boughs, the kind that poets write about, but the merciless, roaring kind, like a wild beast enraged, that preys on a man's mind in much the same manner as a drop of water continuously hitting the forehead. I never saw such winds. I hardly dared to open my door. I don't know how many names I called it.

One morning I think I was on the verge of "flipping my lid," for I climbed to the dune, braced myself, and with my hair slipping and slapping at my face, I yelled into it.

"Blow, you @*#(%*," I yelled. "Blow my shack down if you want to." It just seemed as though I had to have a release, and this was all I could think of for the moment. . . .

Before I left Kodiak I took the precaution of purchasing several bottles of deodorant. A few generous sprinklings once or twice a week works wonders. Do you realize all the time that is wasted in a lifetime beneath the shower or in a bathtub? What we need in this world today is not the banishment of bodily aromas, but the cultivation and accumulation of them. I'll bet the bear are beginning to feel like kindred spirits toward me. "You know that guy in the shack," they'll be saying, "he smells like one of the boys." . . .

I better sign off. Hoping all is well. Take care of yourselves.

Love to all,
"Aromatic" Sam

FROM WHAT I COULD OBSERVE IN the creek, I had done the job expected of me. Barring any natural catastrophe, the escapement of salmon should insure a big run two years hence.

In the weeks remaining I decided to concentrate on taking pictures. I shot six or seven seals to aid my film production. Old Sneaky's demise had not halted raids into the creek, and I made the marauders pay dearly for their selective appetites. Ravens and gulls poked holes into the bloated shapes and dragged out the intestines. Bear dragged off the carcasses and raked them into burial mounds to stew. I noticed their droppings were runny now, like puddles of cow dung. Was it the seal meat or the fish diet that brought about the change?

I decided not to shoot any more seals. They couldn't help their instincts. For thousands of years they had done this butchering of salmon. This was their way. What they didn't eat of a kill, something else did. Who was I to stand in judgment? No longer was I going to pass sentence on them with a squeeze of the trigger.

For days the wolverine had not shown himself. The morning after shooting the last seal, I noticed his tracks paralleling mine along the edge of the slough. I found them all around the shack, too. While I slept, he had probably sniffed at me through the cracks in the boards. I wondered why he hadn't raided the cooler box.

I came upon the phantom unexpectedly. Crouching into a wind that blew water from my eyes, I headed toward the creek. As I approached the latest seal carcass, I glimpsed what appeared to be a fat woodchuck squatting on its haunches observing me. I strained my eyes into the wind. The animal dropped to all fours and rolled off. When I saw the light-colored band on his sides coming together at the rump, I knew my guest of honor had at last accepted an invitation to the banquet table.

The next morning, instead of the seal carcass, I saw through the binoculars a conical mound like an anthill. I went to investigate. There were the wolverine's tracks in the silt leading toward the mound, then veering away from it. From what I could see, he had circled before moving in to bury the seal. An area perhaps ten feet in diameter had been scooped toward the corpse to a height of about two feet. It was topped with roots and tidal grass. One flipper protruded.

I kept a watch on the place.

One morning the contour of the mound had changed. Curious, I moved in for a closer look. To my amazement I found the seal exposed and neatly skinned, the gray hide clinging to a hind flipper, the red carcass slashed with tooth and claw.

Both wolverine and bear tracks were all over the area, so it was difficult to determine who the expert was that had peeled the pelt from the seal.

I spotted the wolverine in the early afternoon. There he was huddling toward the seal in that sloppy, shambling lope. He was about 400 yards away. Here was my chance to get some pictures of him with the big lens. I had some beans in the oven, so I loaded up the firebox with wood just in case I would be away for a few hours. Off I went in the guise of a wildlife photographer.

It was easy to cover the first hundred yards by keeping a hump of grass between us. After that the available cover petered out. I parted the grass stems and studied him through the binoculars. My star boarder was gluttonously tearing at the seal. He was at least 250 yards away. I could see a lot of the weasel in him now. It was in the head and the neck that kept snaking upright, the quick movements, and the nervous alertness. He shook pieces from the carcass, darting his head up from his feeding to glare right at me.

I wanted to get closer, but the way he was acting I didn't think I could. After taking some footage to salvage something of the scene, I wriggled forward. I never made another ten feet. Suddenly he bolted off, making the water fly to both sides of him as he parted a puddle, and scuttled over the driftwood. He had known I was there all the time and just waited for me to make my move.

The sun was bright. I dallied along the slough edge whirring off film at sandpipers, longspurs, and wildflowers. I came upon bear tracks mashed in the mud. They were the biggest I had ever seen. The hind foot track measured more than sixteen inches long.

When I finally arrived back at the shack, I found I had paid a price for my wanderings. My evening meal had dried up on me. Instead of a pot of beans waiting for me, I had a pot of buckshot.

I saw the wolverine several other times, but I could never get close to him. I suspect he had always seen me first. Heavy-bodied with neck and head tapering out in front of him, he sometimes made me think of an anteater. He gave me plenty of room, and I always experienced a special thrill whenever I saw him.

After supper I enjoyed sitting atop the dune just watching and listening behind a wind barricade of driftwood. It stayed light until eleven. The wind kept the insects down, and it was a pleasant way to spend the hours.

A bull moose spotted me the moment I saw him. His antlers were in the velvet. He stopped long enough to stare at me through a thin screen of willows, then like a dark pacer going into the stretch, he strode off into the scrub. He was the only bull I saw at Wide Bay.

In the midst of my many pleasures, more and more frequently as my gaze swept over the teeming creek, the twilight glow on the mountains, and the effervescence of the surf, a feeling haunted me. At times it was terrifying. I was the only human left in the world. What I was seeing, only I would know about. There were no sharers, no listeners, no exclamations of delight to join with mine. I made my comments out loud and turned to someone who was never there.

SURPRISE!

I saw the orange-and-black amphibian plane cut across the bay and follow the windings of the creek. Soon it returned, slanted down smoothly until her boat-shaped hull and the floats on her wings spewed white trails against the blue water. It turned, wallowed on the swells, then taxied to my beach, and crawled out on the sand. One motor revved louder than the other. The plane pivoted to face the bay.

Roy waved as he stepped out.

"Your job's done here," he said. "The creek's crammed with fish. Jim can use you over on the Kenai. Still interested?"

"Still sounds good," I grinned.

"Let's get your gear aboard. Secure the dory. The *Kittiwake* will pick it up before the week's out."

I hadn't expected any visitors for another week or more. I packed hurriedly.

"Just your personal gear," Roy said, his eyes roving over the shack's interior. "The boys will get the rest later. You've got this place looking just like home."

As Roy disappeared with the last load over the dune, I trailed behind for a last look around. I glanced at my "Bear Pasture" with its rippling grass. I looked at "Battleship Island" with the swells washing its rocky turrets. I looked at the mountains, as impressive and as lordly as ever.

"Thanks," I whispered. "You sure taught me a lot about myself."

~

HANK HAILED ME FROM THE WHEELHOUSE of the *Kittiwake* and motioned me to come aboard.

"Why in hell didn't you pack in the dory?" he grinned. "You mean I got to make another trip into that damn place?"

"I thought you boys were coming to visit."

Hank shook his head. "Too busy," he said, scratching behind his ear and making his baseball cap move. "Never saw such a season. You know that bird we dropped off at Red River? He told a tender he wanted to be picked up a few days after we put him in there. It was weeks before we got to him. I blew the whistle four times. He never showed, so I sent Johnny and Tex in to get him. They had to push in the door. They found that coot sitting on his bed with his rifle off safety. A wonder he didn't blast the boys.

"'You saved my life,' he says. He'd wounded a bear that was trailing some reindeer. He locked himself in his cabin afraid that bear was waiting for him. Just stayed in there eating canned milk and candy bars and pulling whiskers out of his face one at a time to keep awake. Damnedest thing I ever heard of. He wanted Tex to stand guard with the rifle while they packed the gear. All the way in all he did was babble a lot of nonsense about the bear."

"They were my company," I said.

"Had to pick up Jim Mellin, too."

"Jim?"

"A telegram came that his father passed away."

I hated to hear that. I'd been looking forward to seeing him again.

The warehouse bunkroom was jammed. The returning stream guards were full of chatter and reminded me of combat veterans jabbering in a rest leave area. I met Hal Waugh, the Alaskan guide. He was ruddy-faced, amber-eyed, and smoked a curved stem pipe. I liked the hair-seal rifle case he carried. He kept us interested with his tales about his camps at Rainy Pass on the mainland and Deadman's Bay on Kodiak. Out of $11,000 he grossed last year, $5,200 had gone for plane charters. Yes, he knew Wide Bay. I told him about the monstrous bear track. The way he looked, I wouldn't be surprised if he thought about flying a client in there this fall.

I had planned to visit with Dick and Big John the next day, but found myself on a flight to Kenai instead. What I had to share with them would have to wait.

Thursday noon
August 11, 1955
Dear Dad, Molly, & Mrs. Millet:
   The son of a guns picked me up yesterday with the Fish & Wildlife plane. Just when I had the bear coming around fine. Well, I've got some pretty good pictures, I hope.
   Got letters from you and Anna. I enjoyed them even more than usual. Now I'm just in one helluva rush.
   I wanted to get this off to you. I could write several

215

pages, but I will have to wait until I get settled.

I'm going over to the Kenai to work the moose season until Sept. 20th. I could have stayed longer, but I decided that this was what I wanted. I just didn't want to miss that Maine hunt with you, Dad. Can you go? Can we line up a trip for November? Let me know.

Maybe you better wait until you get my new address at Kenai before you write. I should be home in early October.

This is a helluva letter. I've got so many things to tell you. Tonight I want to go out to the naval base and see Dick.

Hoping all is well. Take care of yourselves.

Love to all,

Sam

CHAPTER 13

Enforcement Patrolman

I was coming up in the world.

As a stream guard, my annual salary had been $2,950. Now as an Enforcement Patrolman, I would be paid at a rate based on an annual salary of $4,857.50. I understood perfectly that my employment was short-term. That was the way I wanted it. In late September I would be going down the Alcan with Big John.

I fidgeted in the Fish and Wildlife Office at Kenai. My eyes still smarted from the dusty trip over the Homer Road with Fleming Clemson. He had worked on me some more about teaching school and told me to drop in on him at Moose Pass if I had the opportunity. Jim Branson tapped at the typewriter while I strolled past the sprawled maps of the Kenai Peninsula, lingered to inspect a musk-ox skull from Nunivak Island, and brushed at two confiscated wolverine pelts that emanated an aura of solitary places. Jim snatched the papers from his typewriter.

"There's your muscle," he said, handing them to me. "You got some homework to do."

I scanned them. "Enforcement authority is granted to enforce the provisions of the Alaska Game Law, Migratory Bird Act, and amendments thereto," it read. "I see what you mean," I muttered. "I better know a lot more about these laws than I do now."

"We got some odds and ends that need tending to besides," said Jim. "Most resident hunters are after caribou up around Eureka. They'll hunt moose later on when the bulls start moving down out of high places toward the lakes and roads. They're not going to work harder for their meat than they have to. What I intend to do later is put you in at the Kasilof and have you go upriver into Tustumena. From the lake you can hit some of the hunting camps along the different drainages."

Monday evening
August 15, 1955
Dear Dad, Molly, & Mrs. Millet:
Well, here I am in the small town of Kenai and the moose season is only five days off. All I seem to have time (or is it ambition?) for these days is short letters. I have to study the game laws. I am now an Enforcement Patrolman. Just think of an outlaw like me trying to keep these moose hunters in line! I guess I'll be doing a lot of traveling until Sept. 20th. This date will terminate my duties and I will decide upon which route to take on the long trip home. . . .
I am sitting here in the Game Office at Kenai. There is a musk ox skull and two wolverine pelts on the shelf. The pelts were confiscated last spring.
I really don't feel like writing a letter. This is just to give you my new address. It looks as though this next month is going to be an extremely busy one.
Hoping all is well. Take care of yourselves.
Love to all,
Sam

I GUESS MOST OUTFITS ADHERE TO a policy of "Hurry up and wait." It was the warehouse deal in Kodiak all over again, but instead of a warehouse to make ready, it was a very dirty trailer. Two of the agents intended to use it as living quarters at a roadblock junction later on. My job was temporarily that of housekeeper and maintenance man.

Every now and then I gazed at Mount Iliamna and Mount Redoubt across Cook Inlet, sighed noisily, and went back to my scrubbing. I guess pride has a way of shining through the most menial of tasks, for in the next few days I felt a satisfaction in changing a hovel into an efficient apartment. It was like the transformation of the ugly duckling.

In the evenings I studied the game laws. Jim often quizzed me on their contents.

Finally, I went on car patrol with Jim.

At Cooper's Landing we stopped at a cabin. From a high pole hung a black bear cub by its hind legs. A man came waddling out, squinting into the sunshine. Jim was tight-lipped as he checked over a license that had taken a long time to be produced. I saw a beautiful set of mountain goat horns almost spoiled by a head shot and a full curl Dall ram skull out to the weather.

"We'll have to issue you a special long license," said Jim, "so there'll be room to tally all the game you kill."

The man scratched his stubble and took it as a compliment. "There's plenty game in this country," he said. "I manage to get my share."

"Yeah," muttered Jim. "I see it all over the yard."

"Never seen such a crop of black bear cubs as this year," he said.

Jim glanced up at the hanging carcass. "So I notice."

A plane landed on the lake and taxied to the float. A lean, hawk-faced man got out, dragging forth another small black bear, and sliding him toward the meat pole. Jim checked him out, too, as the first man looked on. "Damn," he grunted, "wish I'd been with you." I noticed the blood on his pants and even flecks of it on his black woolen underwear top.

"These old-timers resent a newcomer," the first man said. "I been here four years now. They ain't really accepted me yet. I tell them old dryballs they better get used to me, because I'm here to stay as long as I can plant potatoes and outrun meat."

We stopped in to visit an old artist with arthritic hands. Sam Pratt's past was in his paintings that crowded the walls of his little studio. There was a scene of wolves howling around a trapper's cache with draperies of northern lights in the background, an Arctic owl about to sink its talons into a galloping hare, a gold prospector being surprised by a bear.

"The country's changing," he said.

Then later on in a restaurant I noticed a sallow, square-faced character with high cheekbones. He stared at us with pale eyes. When we got up to leave, he said, "If you find any moose cows with machine-gun bullets in 'em, look me up, pal, will ya?"

"Old man Pratt is right," Jim said as we got into the car.

FOR SEVERAL DAYS A VISITOR FROM Sweden had been strolling the headquarters area with head down and hands behind his back. His nose was turned upward, and that physical characteristic symbolized his aloofness. I spoke to him several times, but he never acknowledged me with an answer and seemed totally involved in a haughty preoccupation. I was determined that any future conversation would be initiated by him. I guess Jim and Dave Spencer, the Game Manager of the Kenai Moose Range and a pilot of the department's amphibious plane, a Widgeon, had had a bellyful of him. Out of desperation, I suppose, Jim assigned me to take the gentleman on a patrol of Skilak Lake for a few days.

We hit some very rough water as we went. He sat regally in the bow and stayed that way even when the motor quit on me about two hundred yards out from the beach. I couldn't get the motor started. Finally I grabbed the oars and got us in. I was to learn later that the oil mixed with the gas was too heavy, but at the time I was certain that my poor rapport with all engines was still haunting me.

I tried my best not to endanger America's relations with

Sweden. My guest's constant expressions of "Pardon?" and "I must say" rivaled the Chinese water torture. He must have had a lot of servants in his native land.

At our beach camp, he sprawled luxuriously on the moss and meditated while I pulled and cursed at the outboard. When I finally struggled forward with it, he chose that precise moment to show me the jawbone of a moose he had found, and seemed immensely irritated that I wanted to set the motor down before listening to his dissertation.

While I cut spruce boughs for the bunks inside the tent I had pitched single-handedly, he sat head back against a tree trunk, his mouth open and his round belly rising and falling. After I got supper ready, he awakened just long enough to eat, and promptly went back to his snoring while I did all the chores.

Throughout the long night he complained vocally about my bough bed contributing to his rheumatism, and subconsciously with unintelligible mutterings and snorts.

The next morning I gave up on him ever greeting the day.

Finally I decided to fry my eggs anyway, for he gave no indication of coming out of his coma. Just as I picked up the salt shaker, an eye ogled at me and a voice said simply, "No salt."

He made not the slightest attempt to help break camp at all, nor even push the boat out after I had bracketed on the motor. He was afraid to get his feet wet, and instead of moving back toward the stern to make it easier for me to work the bow free, he stayed in the bow like an anchor and added to my swollen-faced struggles. I had given up trying to communicate.

One thing he did do was to identify crowberry and cloudberry for me as we prowled over "the Burn of 1947." He was lost in his scientific world of Latin family names, genera, and species. The crown prince waved his arm over the lupine, fireweed, aspens, and seedlings of spruce.

"We shall get a black bear and a brown bear," he decreed. "I shall collect them for the Swedish Museum. You shall get me a moose as well."

"Uh-uh," I grunted, patting the slung .348. "I shoot nothing unless you get some authorization."

He was very put out with my attitude, and he trailed behind me, sputtering in Swedish.

I checked several hunters, and much to my relief, my companion only spoke with his eyes and his bored gestures.

I was relieved to get back to Kenai.

"Jim," I said, "after this, I'd rather go it alone. My own nose is enough to wipe."

September 5, 1955

Dear Dad, Molly, & Mrs. Millet:

> *I just don't have the time to write these days. I just came in from a 12-day trip all by my lonesome. I took a boat and outboard up the swift, flowing Kasilof River that comes out of the 32-mile-long Tustumena Lake. I had my share of thrills. Especially coming down, when I hit a rock in the river. I thought I was going to lose everything. I grabbed an oar and paddled and crouched and came down through the boils of white water. Somehow I made the shore. I leaped out with the bow line and as the current caught the boat my arms felt as though they would come out of their sockets. I snubbed the line around an alder. I shouted above the noise of the river, "There, you ugly sonofabitch, I beat you."*

> *I was out checking moose kills.*

> *We are going out again any minute. This is certainly not the letter I would like it to be. Please excuse this brief letter and also the lapse in my communication with you. I just never know where I'm going to be. You can't mail letters when you're miles back in the brush.*

> *I should finish up here about Sept. 23rd. I should be home around the first of October or shortly before.*

> *Love to all,*

> *Sam*

THE GRAY, GREEN KASILOF, DISCOLORED BY the glacial silt of Tustumena, swept past, gnashing and heaving over the great boulders of its bed. It churned away in its wild hurry into Cook Inlet, leaving a harsh hissing that enveloped me like the warning of a giant snake. I didn't like its sound nor its color. I didn't like the idea of going up it at all. I would have felt more confident going down it with no motor to worry me. It was the motor that made me afraid.

But my instructions were to go upriver and check on any moose kills I found.

I let the 25 horse Johnson idle for a few moments in its veil of thin blue smoke. Then I eased her into gear and nosed the Wizard River Skiff into the vicious grab of the current. I was swept sideways. Quickly I poured on the power, recovered direction, and cleaved into the onrush. I waved to Jim, then turned to the serious business at hand. The Wizard parted the flow, snaking between white, bulging humps that warned of sunken boulders, and hugging the river turns. My outfit beneath a green tarp was bulked in the bow. My fingers were curled tightly around the throttle grip. I poised in a crouch, searching the humped water ahead of me. I was too damn tense.

Below Moose Rapids, I struck something—a rock or a "sleeper." Whatever it was, the opaque water kept its secret. The motor raced as the current hurled me backwards. I grabbed an oar, dug deep with the blade in an effort to skirt a seething boil that came at me like something thrown. I strained with loud grunts, but I couldn't turn the stern away. Dropping to my knees, I gripped the gunwales. The Wizard rocked and slapped through it, spinning in circles. When the bank loomed within reach, I grabbed at an alder branch. It ripped through my hands. I grabbed another. The bow rammed the bank.

I leaped over the canvas, snatched up the coiled painter, and vaulted to the edge just as the bow worked loose. My arms jerked out straight. I held on to the bucking line, digging in with my heels. Swiftly I took a turn around an alder butt. The skiff made a slow, stubborn swing into the current, then came in alongside like a tired fish to the net.

After I caught my breath, I replaced the sheared pin, and I started up the stretch of water just lost. Up I roared into the rapids, breasting the leaping, sharp ridges, ridges that rushed at me close together and staggered past on either side. I had the throttle wide open. The bow slammed. Icy spray shot over it and stung my face. My whole world tossed and fumed about me. I glanced back for an instant at the sunken bowls, the gnashing undulations, and then I was through the angry place.

I saw the knobby end of a snag rearing and disappearing before me like the head and neck of an aquatic dinosaur. "You're a 'preacher'," I said to it as I passed.

At intervals the motor bucked and lunged. The intervals came closer and closer together until I thought the stern would tear away. The entire boat shuddered. I hoped I could make the slack water.

I didn't.

The motor raced, then abruptly died. Off I went on another dash downstream, the trees on the banks streaking past. I almost pulled my arms out of their shoulder sockets, but I held on to handfuls of branches and managed to gain the land again.

It wasn't a pin this time. I pulled at the motor until I was exhausted. Damn the motor. I'd had enough of it for one day. I'd make camp. There were two choices. I could ride the river back down to the landing, or I could wait for Grant or someone else to come along and give me a tow up to slack water. Word could be sent back that I needed a mechanic or another motor.

The latter choice won out. I wasn't going back to Fish and Wildlife like a whipped puppy.

I pitched the mountain tent on a mossy knoll, drove in four green alder stakes until the tops were even enough to support a frying pan, and built my campfire in the enclosure with birch bark and the dry, bearded twigs of spruce.

Rain played on the tent canvas with a sound like static on a radio. Now a flurry of big drops blown from the spruce thumped the sides. I lay warm in my sleeping bag, listening to the maddened rush of the Kasilof.

I was one hell of a riverman.

JUST AS MY COFFEE WAS BOILING over in the little pail, an engine whined above the river's thunder. Around the bend came Grant, standing in the stern, a party of hunters crouched low and hanging on to the gunwales. I hailed to him, waving my hat, and he swung in close, throttling down just enough to hold his position. I told him my problem.

"I'll be coming back down in the morning," he shouted. "Give you a tow then. Too much of a load this trip. Don't try going downstream with a haywire motor. You'll end up crosswise on a rock."

His motors roared, and the boat leaped strongly against the flow.

He used two motors. They were Martins with throw-out clutches. If he hit something, he didn't shear a pin and lose his power. If one motor conked out, he still had the other one. That made more sense than the outfit I had.

A BOAT WAS COMING DOWNRIVER. IT wasn't Grant.

A fellow wearing a camouflaged duck hunter's hat was standing in the stern. He had two motors, too. A thin, tight-faced youth with a bone-handled revolver strapped on his hips sat in the bow. The gun looked too big for him. The boat went past my position, then swung wide, and approached me into the current. The helmsman ran the bow up hard so it climbed the banking before he shut the motors off.

"Grant couldn't make it," he said. "Too rough on the lake. He told me to drop down to help you out if he didn't show up across by eight. We'll tow you up to slack water."

"I appreciate it," I grinned. I'd been stranded for more than a day now. I was anxious to get going again. Patience had been the order of the day. A man couldn't rush help out here. He was just thankful to get it.

The tow began. The Wizard fishtailed violently. The towline

knocked one of the motors out of gear. Then the line was shortened. I stood in the stern, using an oar like a sculling blade, and the operation smoothed. Through the watery humps we labored until the current lost its bulges, and slid past in dimples. It was like coming out of a storm when we beached at camp.

All the way up I had been thinking what I could offer my rescuers. I had plenty of gas. I could top off their tanks. Of course, there was always money. I reached for my wallet.

I had a twenty, a five, and two singles in it. I decided the fiver and the gas should be enough. Since Grant had smilingly spurned a money offer the day previous, I figured my benefactor wouldn't be mercenary either.

"What do I owe you?" I asked.

"You paying for this . . . or Fish and Wildlife?"

I shrugged.

"Well . . . I don't want to soak you if it's coming out of your pocket, but it's worth twenty bucks to me."

I picked out my last twenty and gave it to him. Where could I spend it out here? I didn't even ask for a receipt. It just didn't seem like the Alaskan way at all.

I didn't offer any gas either.

―

I WORKED MY HANDS BLACK AND sore on the motor. The only response I could get was a feeble stutter. I felt the frustration one must feel who looks at symbols on a printed page and can't form them into words.

Along came Phil Ames of Fish and Wildlife, like a genie rising out of the mist on the river. He was immediately helpful. I had every confidence that he would fix the motor, because he attacked it in a manner that indicated he knew what he was doing. He discovered the high speed jet was closed, but that wasn't the true problem. Even though he got the engine started, it still rattled and bucked when he slipped it into gear. Then he found that the cam on the gear shaft was gone. He just shook his head.

"I'm headed downriver anyway," he said. "I'll get word to Jim.

You can stay here at my camp."

In the late afternoon, Rex Williams and Bob Bryson came upriver. Rex fixed the lower unit in the motor so that I had a forward gear but no reverse.

"Best I can do," he said. "I didn't have another motor to bring you. You know how it is. Any cuts made in the Department of Interior funds, you can bet it's Fish and Wildlife gets the axe. No extras in this outfit except haywire."

I asked them to stay for supper, but they had to get back to Kenai. As I waved to them, I wished I had Rex's savvy about motors.

Frost sparkled on the tent. There was ice in the water bucket. I huddled over the crackling of my fire and spread my hands over the flames that climbed toward them. After washing down bacon and eggs with several cups of strong coffee, I tidied up camp and left it ready for the next guest.

The motor started on the fourth pull. It looked as though I would make Bear Creek at last.

Mist steamed off the river. Wind rippled the slack water into a chop. As I entered the thirty-two-mile-long Tustumena Lake, the big swells rolled in to meet me. "When she's rough at the entrance," Phil had said, "stay off her. That means she's bumpy as a cob and mean as sin."

The waves came at me, sharp-crested and close together. They came on crazily, and I couldn't keep the bow quartered into them. I had already wasted so much time. I felt guilty that I wasn't doing my job. Stubbornly I kept on going. Spray splashed my face and chest. My hand felt numb and clubby around the throttle handle. The canvas had puddles atop it, and water sloshed around my moccasins. I was shipping too much of it. To hell with this foolishness. I'd never make it across. I'd have to hole up again. Better a live me than a drowned one.

I pointed the bow at a gravel beach. Wisps of cloud, like the swipes of a paintbrush, hurried past the spruce spires. The Wizard grated, pitching violently in the swells that smashed in and made the gravel rattle.

I secured the skiff, hauled out my packboard, and walked over the piles of moose droppings to a comfortable-looking spruce trunk. I propped the packboard against it, leaned back, and went to sleep.

~

WHEN TUSTUMENA GOT OVER ITS FIT, I made the run to Bear Creek Lodge in about an hour, and came riding in on the swells. A figure with long black hair, a plaid shirt, and khaki pants hitched up high on the hips with a wide belt waited on the beach. She looked like a Native Alaskan.

"You must be Amy," I said, smiling.

"That's right," she said. "Who are you?"

I introduced myself. She insisted I use the lodge bunkhouse instead of pitching the mountain tent nearby. She had no guests. She was here all alone with her little daughter, Saywood. Her husband worked in Anchorage and came in most weekends with a small plane. He landed on the glacier strip at the head of the lake, then made the ten-mile trip in a tiny skiff with a 3.6-horsepower motor to the lodge. They were acting as caretakers and were thinking of buying the old place. Amy served meals to hunters coming down the trail from the far camps.

She made no bones about it. I would have my meals with her. If it made me feel better, I could cut some wood and do some odd jobs that needed attention to pay for my keep. I had to admit that moose steaks were better than the grub I had packed along.

~

I SET OUT TO GO CHECK on local hunting camps. It was raining hard, but I took a chance that it would let up, and packed in over the trail that wound behind the lodge. That's what I had come to do. There had been too many stops along the way.

Alders twisted out of the shadows. Their branches dripped drops that thumped on the skunk cabbage leaves. I climbed steeply until I topped the ridge to where the trail forked into willows, scattered islands of spruce, and blueberries hugging

Far Camp in the Caribou Hills. Bruce Willard is at far right.

against crimson leaves. Here and there were groves of aspens, too, yellowed leaves shivering amongst the green ones.

Grazing horses were the first sign of the camp. They stood like white and chestnut statues in the grassy bowl. Their ears were stiffened, and they peered blankly at me as I came on. One dropped his head to graze. A bell tinkled faintly. And then they were all pulling at the grass again, lazily swinging their wispy tails.

I saw a white flag atop a spruce, then the smoke settled in the boughs like a patch of fog. I saw the rain-stained white canvas, and I heard the mutter of voices and the cackle of sudden laughter. *You better not sneak in as though it's a surprise raid*, I thought. A camp is a home in the wilderness, and a man should knock when he comes to call.

"Hello, the camp," I whooped. I could see men sitting around a fire in the fine rain. Some were standing beneath a canvas canopy. I raised my arm in greeting and strolled in. "I'm from Fish and Wildlife," I said. "Just dropping in to check your licenses and your kills."

I met Doc Pollard, a fine old gentleman guide, and his son

George. They made me feel at ease with their party of hunters from California. Doc wore a floppy red hat. He sat cross-legged and peered up at me from beneath the brim. It was with pride that he showed me the meat hanging in a canvas shed. The quarters were all cheese-clothed. To one side were the big racks sheathed in velvet. I liked the way Doc nuzzled and embraced one of the horses we passed. After checking all the licenses, I sat around the fire.

George was fleshing a black bear hide. An upright crotched pole stood on either side of the fire, and a peeled green spruce sapling was laid across them like a goalpost, high enough above the blaze so that the woolen socks that hung from them were in no danger of being scorched. Black skillets and pots dangled from nails. A mulligan pot simmered over the coals, a drift of steam escaping from beneath its cover. Sticks were jabbed in a semicircle around the fire, slanting away from it. Boots and moccasins were stuck on them. A man with a white apron was whittling out a soup ladle. From the corner of his mouth jutted a stubby pipe. Shavings clung to his pants, and others like unwound springs curled on his slippers. I'd seen him someplace before.

He looked at the brightness toward the south. "Looks like He's turning off the faucets," he said. Then he glanced at the mulligan pot and peered at me. "Have a bowl?"

"Sure."

The hunters watched me as if I were a bomb about to explode. "Now tell the truth," one said. "Isn't that awful?"

It was, but I couldn't say so. It tasted as though hide and hooves were in it instead of meat. "Good," I lied, struggling to swallow another spoonful. "You fellows just aren't hungry enough to appreciate it." The cook looked at the others as if he had proven a point.

"I'm still not convinced," the hunter said, grinning at the cook. "I still think you used some stock from a garbage scow bilge."

I thanked the group for its hospitality and moved off down the trail. Halfway to the lodge I suddenly remembered where I had seen the cook before. He was one of the men who dropped in on us at Nonvianuk on the Peninsula and represented the

Consolidated Airlines "Hotel" there. As big as Alaska was, it was still quite small at that.

—

WHILE I DROPPED SOME SPRUCE SNAGS and bucked them into stove-length pieces with a Swede saw, I checked out guides and hunters moving down the trail and coming in from the lake.

Grant and Ness dropped by on horseback. They looked just as much at home in the saddle as they did in the riverboat. Grant had a .450 Alaskan hanging on its sling from the pommel. Ness had a bone-handled knife sticking out of a squirrel skin sheath.

"Sorry about the rooking you took," Grant said. "I got shorebound that morning. I didn't figure he still had it in for Fish and Wildlife. Guess he figured he was getting back at them through you. They suspended his license once."

I watched them head up the trail. They made me think of a couple of likeable outlaws.

At ten minutes after seven in the evening Hank, Amy's husband, flew over the lodge. She was very excited. She filled some lamps and wondered if they'd be beacon enough to guide him into the beach, for it would be dark before he arrived from the glacier. I offered to go down and pick him up, but Amy would have none of that. Hank had to make the trip himself in his little boat. That was his way.

After what seemed an eternity we heard the faint whine of a motor coming out of the darkness. Amy got up on her tiptoes in an attempt to hold the kerosene lantern higher.

"Let me hold it," I said. "Your arm must be tired."

"I'll hold it up all night for him," she said proudly.

I reached up with the axe and sliced off a spruce limb. "Here, let me hang it on the stub." It swung higher, but Amy worried that he couldn't see it. She asked me to build a fire on the beach. Even that leaping blaze seemed inadequate to her for the homecoming.

Finally Hank arrived in his bathtub skiff. He had a neatly trimmed beard. His pale eyes seemed far away from the rest of him as he spoke.

"Great Scott!" he exclaimed. "I thought I was coming into Broadway."

Amy got her feet wet in her hurry to embrace him. I went to bed wondering if Hank realized how lucky he was.

I HAD PLANNED TO VISIT JESS and Bruce Willard at Far Camp in the Caribou Hills on the other shore of Tustamena, but the arrival of the Fish and Wildlife Widgeon in the late afternoon changed my plans for the morning. I was to meet Jim down at the Kasilof landing around noon. I had visited enough camps and checked enough hunters to keep the "Bush telegraph" lines busy for a spell.

As I pulled away from the beach, Amy and Saywood waved. Amy had a lot of courage, and I truly admired her. I was glad to be leaving because I was beginning to enjoy my stay too much.

The trip across to Caribou Island in Nikolai Bay was uneventful except for the way the motor acted. It didn't have a smooth song at all. I expected the worst. The river was very much on my mind.

As I moved into the suck of the current, I felt I was trespassing on private property, and the owner was waiting to leap out at me from ambush. When I throttled the motor down, it went into its river-shy act. It bucked and jumped out of gear several times until I kept a steady pressure on the lever. Was my old nemesis coming back to haunt me? *If it quits on me this time*, I thought, *I'll just stand up with an oar and ride to the landing like a riverman on a log.*

I was pushed by a great force that swept me along down a chute between fast sliding-away spruces. Several times I slewed sideways and shipped water over the gunwales, but on I shot, caught up like a bug spewed from a water faucet and swirling toward the drain. It was a thrilling descent. I was both scared to death and feeling the exhilaration of a ballcarrier shaking off tacklers and sprinting for the end zone. My old camp loomed for an instant and then it was behind me. I kept wondering about the rapids, yet it was all rapids and white water that hurled me along.

I throttled down some more because I was moving too fast.

The stern swept sideways.

CRUNCH.

I drove against something that killed the motor. For a moment I just hung on it. I expected to see the river coming up through the bottom or pouring in on me over the gunwales. Then I was catapulted, nearly losing my balance as the current heaved us free. I didn't even attempt to start the motor. I stood up, legs wide apart. I dug with the oar, dodging the ugly white boils coming at me, exerting myself with loud explosive grunts as I sped like a runaway vehicle downhill.

I rounded the bend. There was the landing coming up fast. I aimed right for it. With the painter coiled in my hand I leaped over the bow just before it hit the banking, scrambled ashore, and snubbed the line. Caught up in the current once again, the Wizard stopped as if it had slammed into a wall. My chest was heaving.

"You didn't get me, you son of a bitch," I shouted at the river gnashing past. "I beat you . . . I beat you!"

"YOU MEAN YOU PACK BACK INTO them camps alone?" the barber asked. He had the stub of a toothpick in the corner of his mouth. His eyes inspected me like an inquisitive bird. "That's sticking your neck out, ain't it?"

"I'm still here. Fools walk in where. . . ."

"You caught them with a cow or a calf and you could end up under a pile of brush. The way the grass grows in this country, you'd be covered up and nobody'd ever know where you were. I don't want your job. No sirreeee. Not in this country. You're doggone right. How'd you get into Tustamena?"

"Up the Kasilof."

He whistled. "Worst son of a bitch in the country. You got to know what you're doing on that one. You're doggone right."

I almost shrunk down under the apron. He didn't know what a greenhorn he had in the chair.

When I left smelling of Bay Rum, he grinned at me. "So long," he said, "and stay out of the brush."

⌐

I WENT ON A FEW AIR patrols in the Widgeon with Dave and Jim. I was a big-eyed kid on Christmas morning sneaking a peek through the balusters of the stairs at the presents I couldn't reach. We flew over glaciers that appeared as great puddles of plaster poured into weird-shaped molds within the peaks. I looked down on mountain slopes turning giddily as we banked. White blotches turned into Dall sheep and goats safe among their crags.

Jim got busier and busier with his paperwork and court appearances. I was assigned the car to patrol temporarily the ninety-mile Homer Road.

I didn't enjoy the roadblocks. Standing there for several hours waving a flashlight at approaching cars until they slowed and stopped: "Good evening. Have you been hunting or fishing today?" If they had, then the inevitable question: "May I check your licenses please?" The initialing and the probing of the beam in the car's interior. "Open your trunk please." I kept hoping I would always find things in order, and luckily I did. I would never make a good law-enforcement officer. I guess I wanted to help people and not have to punish them. The authority of the job never went to my head.

One day I stopped at the Ninilchik Inn. As I entered, the smell of freshly baked apple pie drifted to me. That was my introduction to Dave and Katherine Boyer. Dave had taught school up in the village of Koyukuk on the Yukon River for a year. Now he had a homestead here, a two-story house and the inn started. While we talked, he honed a big double-bitted axe he was planning to wield in the wood-chopping contest at the Ninilchik Fair. A volume of Robert Service's poetry exposed another bond between us.

But it was really Katherine who won me over with her wholesomeness. I couldn't take my eyes off her. Her fingers twined in the hair of her little girl who stared at me with her father's eyes.

I kept thinking of a line in one of Service's poems: "Hunger, not of the belly kind that's banished with bacon and beans. . . . "

Long after I left the inn, I kept seeing the radiance in Katherine's face as she looked at Dave when he spoke, and I wondered if ever a woman would look that same way at me.

September 5, 1955

Jim was quiet for a long time. I guess he just sat there, figuring what would be the best way to break the news to me the most tactful way.

"Sam, would it be disrupting your plans any if I laid you off ten days earlier? As slow as the hunting's been, it's rather pointless to keep the temporaries. Hard to find enough to keep them busy."

~

September 6, 1955
Dear Dad, Molly, & Mrs. Millet:

Well, it looks like I should be home sooner than I thought. My job here ends September 9. The moose season has been very slow. Fish and Wildlife, always on the lookout for cutting expenditures, seem to feel that the skeleton force of permanent employees can handle the job alone.

I should be staggering in anytime after the 12th of September.

Love to all,

Sam

My short-term employment had come to a close. I sent home what I thought I wouldn't need for the Alcan trip and took a flight to Kodiak.

I sat near two old-timers. One had a shock of gray hair that was discolored in places as if it had been singed over a campfire. He wore a ragged suit coat and boots. His partner sported a red, untrimmed beard and had big blue eyes that ogled you from over a nose like a lobster claw. They entertained me the whole trip as I eavesdropped. Several times I almost invaded their privacy when they mentioned places I had been.

"That sow on the Nonvianuk came foggin' up over the bank . . . poppin' her teeth and just a-slaverin' all over the place. I flew up and lit in an alder and there she was standin' with her paws up like she was waitin' to catch a fly ball. That alder kept hitchin' down. I hated to . . . but I had to shoot her."

"Four of them fellers working all day couldn't do enough work to flag a handcar. . . ." And on they chatted.

Before I realized it, the plane was slanting in for Kodiak.

CHAPTER 14

Driving Out

"Sam, you know right well you don't want to leave this country," said Dick. "Don't give up on it. Me and you got to figure something out."

We were watching Big John's jeep lurching skyward, then swinging on the boom to the deck of the *Expansion* out of Juneau. Some fishermen were mending seine to one side of us; others under a canopy of excited gulls were unloading a crab boat, tossing the grotesque shapes out of a hold and sliding them along down a trough. Each crab was picked up and dropped on its shell. A quiver of life and it kept on going; no movement after a second drop and it was flung over the side.

I had made up my mind. This big land had its hold on me, but the magnet of the blood was drawing me back to where home used to be. Dad was very close to retirement. Perhaps we could make that writer-artist team a reality after all. I was anxious to see Anna and the kids. Would the dog still know me? Or would he raise his back fur and rumble deep in his chest as I approached him?

"I've got to give it a try, Dick. If things don't pan out, I'll be back. You'll still be in the country . . . somewhere."

"Alaska's my home," Dick said, "but I ain't sure just what part yet. It's a great, big strawberry shortcake, and I only had a piece of it." He was watching the gulls plummeting. "Well, anyway, you two have a good trip down the road. John, I hope that filly on the other end is all you think she is. And, Sam, come ridin' up this way soon on a southeast wind."

"So long, Dick," I said, gripping his hand hard. "Keep out of the hot sun."

The last I saw of him as we drove away was the red bandanna he waved to us beneath a sky of gulls.

Ahead lay the first leg of our 2,700-mile journey down adventure road—the passage by boat from Kodiak to Seward, then a drive through Alaska and Canada on the "Soldier's Road," the highway that had been built in just eight months' time during World War II. After the war, they'd opened it up to civilians, and finally a traveler could drive between the South 48 and Alaska.

The *Expansion* ploughed through the turbulent Gulf of Alaska. The ocean fell steeply away beneath her bow and rose again in a froth that resembled lace changing patterns on a rich blue velvet. Doubled over the railing, a dough-faced mess boy retched.

"Hey," shouted the cook, "quit stickin' your finger down your throat. Stop showin' off and come in and wash the dishes."

We docked at Seward. I watched the crewman fastening the bridle slings to the jeep. Its headlights stared at me with the same spoiled-brat expression. It looked tiny beneath the green tarp folded across and lashed to its hood.

Resurrection Bay was full of jellyfish, delicate parachutes of protoplasm that shrunk and swelled as they drifted.

"Could I interest you in buying five acres of 'em," grinned one of the crew, noticing my curiosity. He signaled and the jeep lifted.

Big John had his large tool kit, complete with extra engine parts. Two spare tires and two gasoline cans added to my assurance, but in spite of Big John's vast mechanical know-how and his foresight, I felt the apprehension of driving down a lonesome stretch of road with the fuel gauge needle dipping past the empty mark.

Big John's 1942 jeep rests on the shoulder of the Alaska Highway.

I was the banker. We contributed fifty dollars each to the extra "kitty" wallet I had brought along. When that was used up, we would each make another deposit.

The paved road out of Seward to Anchorage opened up panoramas of mountains and golden displays of cottonwood leaves along dark-banked streams.

At Mile 67 we made camp for the night. We threw the tarp over a framework of spruce poles and tucked the excess under as a ground sheet for our sleeping bags. I cooked supper over a campfire while Big John tinkered with the transportation. When I saw him draining the radiator, I became uneasy.

"How come?" I asked.

"Leaks," he said. "Not too bad though. I didn't have time to fix it. I can't see losing antifreeze, so I'll drain it every night and fill it from a creek every morning. We'll have to stop and fill her now and then when she heats it up."

I didn't think we were going to make it.

The next day we passed between the Talkeetnas and the Chugach Range. Some of the mountains resembled great lumps of chunk chocolate, but the big boys had new snow all over their shoulders. Rabbits flashed before us, looking white-stockinged and dark-backed. They were changing into their winter robes. Everything crushed in the road made me swivel my neck for identification. Big John wasn't interested in roadside autopsies. He was busy monitoring the patient's heartbeat.

At Sheep Mountain, I talked Big John into stopping. He had a lot of patience with my inquisitiveness. I saw some Dall sheep, and having movie film to run off, I decided they would provide interesting footage. Big John did not share my enthusiasm. Lots of things had lost their old appeal to him lately. I remembered seeing the same symptoms in some of my boyhood pals just before they settled down.

I climbed up to find a deep canyon separating me from the browsing band of sheep. It would take too long to get any closer. I took some telephoto shots at several hundred yards. Not what I wanted, but I didn't want to keep Big John waiting too long. He had more serious thoughts on his mind than I did and more compelling reasons to get underway.

At one point, a hunter flagged us down. He held up a rabbit and something else that hung too long to be a rabbit. It was a young lynx. He pointed at a swale.

"The mother and another one's in there," he said excitedly. "Could you fellers flush 'em out for me?"

Big John and I took a wide circle and walked toward the hunter through a slender growth of aspens. We were about sixty yards apart. A gray apparition the color of dark smoke materialized and padded toward me. Lemon eyes glared at me from beneath tufted ears. The lynx crouched. *Damn it*, I thought, *no camera. . . .*

"Just stay put, old girl," I whispered, as I skirted her position. I didn't see the youngster at all.

The hunter was frustrated. He was careless the way he swung the shotgun's snout across our middles as he talked. "I can't understand it," he moaned. "Where'd they go?"

As we drove off, I told Big John what I had seen.

He smiled. "I saw the kitten," he said. "I figured it needed more help than that joker did."

At Chistochina, we splurged on a meal and joined some Indian

Sam poses for a photo at the start of the Canadian segment of the highway.

youths in their admiration of the pretty waitress.

THAT WAS THE COLDEST NIGHT YET. Ice floated down the river. The brush sparkled with a heavy sheathing of frost.

In the morning, a flat tire greeted us. Big John put on a spare while I broke camp. We decided to drive on and have breakfast in the lodge at Tok Junction sixty-five miles away. We were getting soft. So was the jeep. It groaned agonizingly before it started.

At the Canadian border, the Customs officer acted as though he had the same regard for the jeep as I did. He just shook his head sadly. We had to purchase a bond for it because it was considered a risk. Too many vehicles were breaking down on the gravel roads, and too many occupants were being stranded with too little funds. At least the bond would provide a form of insurance to curb government expense.

The tires drummed a different tune on the gravel and spewed a wake of dust that streamed out behind us and rose into the trees. The Yukon Territory mountains were different, too. They looked more severe, as if molded from steel instead of rock. Gleaming above the narrow spruce and the penciled saplings of willow, birch, and aspen, even the snow that powdered them glinted with austerity.

I was amazed at the number of porcupine casualties along the way. A strutting ruffed grouse was like seeing an old friend and made me think of Dad and all the times we had hunted that fine game bird together. I'd see him soon.

We passed through a land heavily forested and full of lakes, but there were no big trees at all.

At some point, Big John dropped behind a car that pulled a trailer. The dust was choking us and cutting down our visibility. Then we rounded a bend, and there was the trailer overturned in the road. The car was backing up toward the fugitive.

Big John and I stopped and supplied the beef to muscle the trailer upright. Then Big John and the magic of his tool kit made the hitch more secure, and once more the outfit was ready to travel.

"Thanks, boys," the driver said. "Now you go on ahead of me, and I'll swallow your dust for a spell."

I drooled over the beautiful lakes and streams we passed, but it was too damn cold to fish.

⌒

WHAT A MISERABLE NIGHT. I SHOULD have cut some boughs to pile on top of the ground sheet. We had traveled too long and darkness had descended upon us before we stopped. We had thrown up a hurried camp. The frost from the ground seeped into my bones. Several times I started to get up to cut some boughs, but Big John's soft snoring held me back.

"Never had any trouble sleeping," he once said. "I could sleep in a wheelbarrow."

Through the lean-to flaps, I could see the chilly points of stars glinting in the sky. Moonlight made long shadows of the stark trees. The flame of our campfire flickered feebly at a big chunk of cottonwood. I kept drawing my legs up in an effort to contract into a tight ball. I almost wished I was back at Nonvianuk, fighting the insect pests. At least it was warm then. The heap looked luminous, like a frosty ghost. Daylight took forever to break.

The morning proved no easier than the night before. Preparing breakfast, I knocked an egg against the frying pan edge. Nothing happened. The egg was frozen solid. So we settled for boiled eggs with our bacon. Big John broke the ice in the stream to perform his ritual of filling the jeep's radiator.

The jeep wouldn't start. Big John carried some coals in a shovel from the campfire and built a small blaze beneath the crankcase and the intake manifold. The welcome snort of the jeep a while later chased away my fears. Big John didn't act surprised at all, and after returning the area to nature once again, we were on our way.

We stopped at Burwash Landing on Kluane Lake. An Indian woman with black knee-length stockings beneath her skirt sold me a lynx skin for nine dollars while her children stared up at me and licked their fingers. That pelt would add a northern flavor to Dad's studio.

A few miles later, we came upon a vehicle down in a ditch. It had blown a front tire. The driver walked around puffing a cigarette into clouds. His wife held a baby close to her, trying to quiet the screaming. Luckily no one was hurt.

Big John hauled out the tow chain and tractored the car back up on to the road. Then we changed the tire for him. The man reached for his wallet. Big John held up his hand and shook his head. "Maybe you can help somebody down the road," he said. The look on the woman's face expressed more thanks than the words of both of them.

We began to understand why we'd paid for that bond at the border. Tires and parts of tires were strewn along the road as we drove. Some were even hung in trees. Every now and then a grim sign said, "Two killed here in 1951" or "Four killed here in 1949."

And on we went, bannering a dust trail between the trees.

THAT NIGHT I COULD SEE MY breath, but I slept warm. The lesson of the night before was not forgotten. A mattress of spruce boughs protected me from the frost.

Once again the jeep was reluctant to arouse in the morning. Once again, Big John gave it his special fire treatment to warm its innards and get it into a traveling mood.

About every hundred miles we spelled each other on the driving. With Big John beside me, even though he often dozed, I felt the jeep would behave. It just wouldn't dare to show how miserable it could be in the master's presence.

Before we arrived at Whitehorse, capital of Yukon Territory, we had two flat tires. We pulled into a garage back from the river. Big John had the spares repaired, and while he supervised the jeep's grease job and oil change, I strolled past the old riverboats and captured their names. *Klondike. Keno. Yukoner.* I examined a White Pass mail sled and dallied at the small cabin where Robert Service was said to have once lived. My imagination whirled with the pictures and sounds of what must have happened here fifty years ago.

Big John and I often kidded each other about failing to become sourdoughs. To reach that noble status, it was said you had to shoot a bear, take a leak in the Yukon, and sleep with a ... well, never mind. When I got back to the garage, I heard the toilet flush in the restroom. Seconds later Big John came out. He glanced meaningfully toward the river and grinned. "That takes care of one of them," he said. "Two more to go and I'll be a sourdough."

As I noticed the first lodgepole pines about twenty miles out of Whitehorse, the jeep became sluggish. Big John checked the points to find them burned. He fiddled for a time beneath the engine hood with his feeler gauge, mumbled some soothing words, and once more the jeep throbbed with power as if he had administered a syringe of adrenalin.

"Should have checked the points and plugs back at the garage," he said simply.

⌐

SWIFT RIVER WAS RUNNING ICE.

When we entered British Columbia at Mile 620, Big John's firearms were sealed. Border officials would recheck the tags when we entered the U.S. to ensure they had not been fired. I had sent mine home earlier. Rather than have my fly rod sealed, I bought a fishing license. I might fish farther on down, but I didn't think so. Big John was not a fisherman, and the lure of Kamloops rainbows were nothing compared to what beckoned him to the south.

"You'll catch an odd few," said the agent as he scrawled out my license.

A densely timbered land welcomed us. Tamaracks glowed like orange yellow torches out of the green of the lodgepoles and the spruce. The mountains beyond were huge, upended slabs of rock that gleamed white, silver, and gold in the sun.

At a gas station we met a young fellow who had totaled his father's car on the road more than a year ago. No insurance. He was staying on in the place of his misfortune, doing odd jobs until he had enough money saved to buy his dad a new car. Perhaps he was an example of how some of the country got settled along the highway.

At a Liard River rooming house we showered, shaved off the stubble, ate supper, and slept between sheets for a change.

⌐

BIG JOHN POURED SOME OF CRYSTAL clear Muncho Lake into the radiator. I was tempted to fish, but what I dreamed of catching was probably more than I would have caught. I was feeling the strong homeward pull, too. No more could I blame the hurry on Big John. The farther south we moved, the more momentum we gathered.

Outside of Port Nelson the stands of aspen, red pine, and spruce were as thick as hair. More and more often we had to stop to replenish the radiator's water supply. Big John made adjustments at intervals when the jeep didn't respond as he expected it to, or didn't hum the right tune to his practiced ear. The engine was his patient on the operating table, and he wasn't going to let it die.

We came upon a stranded family. A connecting rod had come through the car engine's block. Big John had the answer.

"We'll push you to Dawson Creek," he said, and that's what he did for 171 miles, the jeep powering the car up the steep grades, then holding back while it coasted down the other side. He would move up behind it again when it slowed, ready to boost it up the next hill.

The Dailey family couldn't thank us enough. They had been stranded for hours. Most of the traffic had been in the wrong direction. The little jeep had taken on the stature and the aura of a messiah. Big John would accept no money. When I suggested to him in private that we shouldn't make them feel totally obligated, he agreed to Mr. Dailey's offer of a meal in a restaurant with all the trimmings.

The fifteen-year-old daughter had stars in her eyes. They brimmed with tears. "As long as I live," she breathed with all the feeling of a Katharine Hepburn performance, "I'll never forget that little jeep and two wonderful Alaskans."

I guess the "Alaskan" part got to me and made me puff up like a turkey gobbler. For a moment I almost forgot that compliments were to be sniffed and not engulfed. Besides, Big John had done it all anyway.

⁓

WE WENT THROUGH PRINCE GEORGE AND then Quesnel and along the Fraser River in a region of Canada that had experienced its own gold rush. I loved every mile of glorious British Columbia. On the jeep lurched, lurched over the rough roadbed, but now more than ever I began to fear for its life.

Going into Williams Lake the patient suffered a serious setback. The rear end gave out. The gas line to the fuel pump had ruptured. Vital signs were fast draining away. Big John stood

Inspection and time for a drink.

back with his huge hands on his hips and made a decision. An operation was required. First, stop the bleeding. He bound up the gash in the gas line with tape. I donated my talents and some fly line to wrap over it as though I were winding a line guide onto a fishing rod. Then Big John performed major surgery, and disconnected the four-wheel drive, while I assisted with a generous intravenous feeding through the radiator.

We drove on, but now the jeep felt jointed in the middle. The front part of it threatened to run away from the rest of it. We limped into Williams Lake and kept on going.

The Fraser Valley was vivid with the reds and yellows of autumn. Along the Thompson River into Lytton, I was as tensed as a crewman on a flak-shattered bomber, hand on the ripcord, and ready to bail out at any moment. Big John had entrusted me with the wheel. I clenched it in a grip of rigor mortis. I could imagine the outside wheels turning and balancing on the lip of a precipice. When a bus suddenly came around a turn from the opposite direction, I was certain we were going to be forced over the edge. Big John gazed placidly into the abyss and made no comment at all.

We made the run to Hope, a little town in southern B.C., in the rain. With each drop in latitude, it had been getting warmer and warmer.

When we stopped at the U.S. border, the jeep wouldn't start again. The two of us pushed it across the line and into the South Forty-Eight. Back on American soil! Miraculously Big John was able to revive the jeep with some kind of a transplant or an engine massage.

When at last we pulled into Big John's yard at Renton, Washington, I expected the jeep to heave a death rattle, slant its wheels, and settle down tiredly on top of them. My travel, however, wasn't over yet.

The next day, the Seattle-Tacoma Airport was beckoning me for the flight east. Before locking up my gear, I decided to make one last check of the jeep's interior. Just when I was feeling sincere admiration for the old veteran, actually relating in a very positive way, I jammed my finger beneath its seat, drawing blood. "Well," I muttered, "if that's the way you want it. . . ." Snapping the pain from my finger, I walked toward the house. Stress noises from the sagging metal trailed me. I swear it sounded like laughter.

It had been immediately apparent to me on our arrival that Big John's girl thought more of herself than she did of him. He understood the ways of a four-wheel-drive jeep, but like me, he didn't understand women at all. Had he really made all this effort for her?

If the breakup that followed bothered him, he didn't show it. As I prepared to go, his great hand swallowed mine.

"You son of a gun," I said. "Your heart's bigger than you are, and some gal's going to discover it someday, even though you're not a sourdough."

We parted ways. It had been a hell of a ride.

⌇

FROM SEATTLE, I TOOK A FLIGHT to Boston rather than travel by bus again. I didn't want to prolong the trip across the land this time. After almost thirty-nine months, the cycle was completing itself. I kept thinking about the poem Dad had mentioned about the golden windows in his own cabin. There was a lot of truth in it, but when I thought about the big country I had left behind, I realized I had been right up to them, stared into them, and the gold was still there on the panes.

A Nest of My Own

I almost made it back to Alaska on the "southeast wind" Dick talked about. Things just didn't pan out. My stories didn't sell.

Then Dad, with all his plans to concentrate on what he loved to do at last, passed away just a few months after his retirement. It seemed like such a dirty trick. Death was his final rejection slip. Our dream of the writer-artist team vanished like the morning mist, but I didn't fall into the trap of feeling sorry for myself. That wasn't the Alaskan way at all. My savings almost gone, I had to adjust to the reality of employment. I wasn't going down without a fight for what I wanted, instead of what I had to accept. The writing, though, would have to wait. I had to strike out in another direction.

In the spring of 1957, a Marine buddy of mine, George Carchia, suggested I work for his uncle's landscaping outfit until I figured out what to do next. A carpenter by trade, George was as gifted with a fishing hook as he was with a hammer

Marine buddies Sam Keith and George Carchia during World War II.

and became my local fishing partner and lifelong friend. He lived in Scituate, Massachusetts, with his good wife, Betty, and offered me a room at his parents' house so I could live close by. On a frosty evening in January 1958, George invited the neighbors over to watch my Alaskan home movies. It was he who introduced me to Jane Marie Saltamacchia, a broad-smiling brunette who radiated warmth and instant interest in me and my adventures.

At last, the right woman, one worth waiting for. Jane was the force that lured me away from the North, the catalyst that brought the pieces all together. We were married on May 11, 1958, with George as our best man.

Fleming Clemson, the stream guard I'd met years ago, had first suggested that I go into teaching. Now Jane picked up the campaign. She made me feel bigger than I was. She was more interested in me than I was in myself. I had done things in Alaska I never thought I could do. Now I had to prove to her that I could do it again, this time back home.

I became a teacher.

I brought qualities beyond competence in a subject to the

Sam's wedding day, May 11, 1958. From left to right, sister, Anna Keith Anderson;
stepmother Molly Keith; bride Jane Keith; Sam and father Merle Keith.

profession. My experience was more than academic. I understood motivation, because I had felt it in the Alaskan rivers that raced toward their salt-water goal. I had sensed it in the salmon that overcame obstacles to get a job done. I knew something about patience and tolerance. They were in the mountains that withstood the winds that blasted them, the snows that covered them, the plants that clung to them, and the animals that grazed over them. I understood humility, for I had been awed in a land that loomed with giants of rock and ice. I had been dwarfed and frightened beside rivers that hissed like serpents. I had passed the stage of being too impressed with my own importance. And at last I had experienced love . . . the prime mover of them all.

Dad's boy had grown up.

One day I had a letter from Big John, and I smiled as I read it. He had never written me such a long letter before. He, too, had found a partner, Dottie, and now he was whole.

As I write these words, it is 1974, and my old friend Dick is still toting his own pack in far-away Alaska. All these years he's been the other me up there. He built that dream of his on the edge of the Alaska Range. His letters never fail to bring on a wistful stare. I envy what he does and where he is, but surely he must envy me as well, for I have Jane, who looks at me the way Amy looked when she held the lantern high at Tustumena to light the way home for Hank, or the way Katherine Boyer of Ninilchik looked when her husband spoke. And I have a daughter who looks up at me the way I once did at the mountains.

I guess a man can't ask for more than that.

On His Shoulders

BY LAUREL KEITH LIES

I learned about nature while riding on my father's shoulders. Our backyard woods were his other classroom. He taught me how to find buried treasure, like spotted salamanders hiding under logs, and to savor the heady aroma of wild grapes in fall. Whether cultivating the rich earth of his vegetable garden or casting a new fly into some remote, bubbling stream, Dad was always happiest outdoors. He spoke about his time in Alaska with a humble reverence that most folks reserve for church. It was something special to him, like his fifty-year friendship with Dick Proenneke.

Growing up, I always knew when Dad had received a letter from Dick. He'd almost dance back from the mailbox before announcing that he had something special to share at supper. Dick's spidery penmanship on the red and blue Air Mail envelope was unmistakable. My mother and I loved to listen to each letter and watch Dad's face glow as he read "the latest news from Twin Lakes."

In 1970, Dad did finally ride that southeast wind he wrote about back to Alaska, to visit Dick at his cabin. I was eight, and

Sam, Jane, and daughter Laurel in the summer of 1969.

can still remember the hot July night when we drove him to Logan Airport in Boston to begin his journey. Dad was suited up in his Red Devil long johns, a plaid L.L. Bean woolen shirt, jeans, and suspenders—sweating, but grinning from ear to ear.

It was during that visit that Dad suggested creating a book about Dick's experiences building his cabin and living the life he'd chosen, miles from civilization in a place accessible only by floatplane. Dick was the Alaskan adventurer, a one-of-a-kind outdoorsman who had documented his day-to-day life in photos, film, and journals. Dad was the gifted storyteller who wove Dick's raw materials into an Alaskan classic.

After the book's publication, some friction arose between the two old friends. Dick wrote in his letters about how pleased he was with the book and with the attention he received from people who had read it, including visits from Alaska Gov. Jay Hammond and singer/songwriter John Denver. Yet at the same time, he didn't care for the spotlight it shone on his private corner of the world, or for the number of people who arrived to see it for themselves.

Sam and Laurel, 1989.

Dad was disappointed in Dick's apparent change of heart about the book, a project of which he was very proud. Nevertheless, both men placed such value on the relationship that they buried their differences and continued to write each other, a correspondence and friendship forged in unforgettable experiences, which continued to the end of their lives. It's remarkable to think that between 1955 and 2003, Dad and Dick generated more than five hundred letters to each other. They were more than best friends; they were brothers bonded by a love for Mother Alaska.

My father passed away on March 28, 2003, at the age of eighty-two. Dick passed away just weeks later, on April 20, at age eighty-six. They had just given permission to filmmaker Bob Swerer to use text from *One Man's Wilderness* and Dick's films for a new PBS documentary, *Alone in the Wilderness*. The film would go on to become one of the network's top fund-raising programs of all time, but ironically, neither man would ever know how many new readers and viewers the documentary would generate.

I like to think that Dad and Dick are snowshoeing together somewhere in the mountains, proud to have introduced Alaska to a new generation of adventurers.

As for me, I am very grateful to my husband, Brian, for discovering Dad's forty-year-old manuscript, to our editors, Tricia Brown and Kathy Howard, and to Doug Pfeiffer at Graphic Arts for publishing it. I believe it proves that Sam Keith truly was the writer he always wanted to be, with a voice and story all his own.

I guess a daughter can't ask for more than that.

Keep reading for the first chapter of the book
One Man's Wilderness: An Alaskan Odyssey
By Sam Keith
from the journals and photographs of Dick Proenneke

ONE MAN'S
AN ALASKAN ODYSSEY
50TH ANNIVERSARY EDITION
WILDERNESS

BY **SAM KEITH**
from the journals & photographs of
DICK PROENNEKE
Foreword by NICK OFFERMAN

AN EXCERPT FROM

One Man's Wilderness

CHAPTER ONE

Going In

I recognized the scrawl. I eased the point of a knife blade into the flap and slit open the envelope. It was the letter at last from Babe Alsworth, the bush pilot. "Come anytime. If we can't land on the ice with wheels, we can find some open water for floats." Typical Babe. Not a man to waste his words.

This meant the end of my stay with Spike and Hope Carrithers at Sawmill Lake on Kodiak. I had driven my camper north and was doing odd jobs for them while waiting to hear from Babe. Their cabin in the Twin Lakes region had fired me up for the wilderness adventure I was about to go on. They seemed to sense my excitement and restlessness. I could use their cabin until I built one of my own. I could use their tools and was taking in more of my own. I also had the use of their Grumman canoe to travel up and down twelve miles of water as clear as a dewdrop.

I left my camper in their care. I waved to them as I heard the engines begin to roar, and then the land moved faster and faster as I hurtled down the Kodiak strip on the flight to Anchorage. Babe would meet me there.

May 17, 1968. At Merrill Field, while waiting for Babe to drop out of the sky in his 180 Cessna, I squinted at the Chugach Range, white and glistening in the sun, and I thought about the trip back north in the camper. It was always a good feeling to be heading north. In a Nebraska town I had bought a felt-tipped marker and on the back of my camper I printed in big letters, DESTINATION—BACK AND BEYOND. It was really surprising how many cars pulled up behind and stayed close for a minute or two even though the way was clear for passing. Then as they passed, a smile, a wave, or a wistful look that said more than words could. Westward to the Oregon ranch country and those high green places where I had worked in the 1940s. On to Seattle where a modern freeway led me through the city without a stop, and I thought of the grizzled old lumberjack who bragged that he had cut timber on First and Pike. Hard to imagine those tall virgin stands of Douglas fir and cedar and hemlock in place of cement, steel, and asphalt. Then the Cariboo Highway and beautiful British Columbia. Smack into a blizzard as I crossed Pine Pass on the John Hart Highway to Dawson Creek. And all those other places with their wonderful names: Muncho Lake and Teslin and Whitehorse, Kluane and Tok Junction, Matanuska and the Kenai. The ferry ride across the wild Gulf of Alaska and a red sun sinking into the rich blue of it. Sawmill Lake, and now Anchorage.

The weather stayed clear, and Babe was on time. Same old Babe. Short in body and tall on experience. Wiry as a weasel. Sharp featured. Blue eyes that glinted from beneath eyebrows that tufted like feathers. A gray stubble of a moustache. That stocking cap perched atop his head. A real veteran of the bush. "Watches the weather," his son-in-law once told me. "He knows the signs. If they're not to his liking he'll just sit by the fire and wait on better ones. That's why he's been around so long."

"Smooth through the pass," Babe said. "A few things to pick up in town and we're on our way."

We did the errands and returned to load our cargo aboard the 180. Babe got his clearance and off we went, Babe seeming to look over a hood that was too high for him. A banking turn over the outskirts of Anchorage, then we were droning over the mud flats of Cook Inlet on the 170 air-mile trip to Port Alsworth on Lake Clark. I looked down on the muskeg meadows pockmarked with puddles and invaded by stringy ranks of spruce. Now and then I glanced at Babe, whose eyes seemed transfixed on the entrance to Lake Clark Pass, his chin resting in one cupped hand. Meditating as usual. I searched the ground below for a moose, but we were too high to see enough detail.

Suddenly the mountains hemmed us in on either side—steep wooded shoulders and ribs of rock falling away to the river that flowed to the south below, here and there a thin waterfall that appeared and disappeared in streamers of mist. We tossed in the air currents. Then we were above the big glacier, dirty with earth and boulders yet glinting blue from its shadowed crevices. It looked as though we were passing over the blades of huge, upturned axes, and then the land began to drop dizzily away beneath us and we were over the summit. The glacial river below was now flowing in a northerly direction through a dense forest of spruce, dividing now and then past slender islands of silt, and merging again in its rush to Lake Clark.

There it was, a great silvery area in the darkness of the spruce— Lake Clark. We came in low over the water, heading for Tanalian Point and Babe's place at Port Alsworth. Years ago he had decided to settle here because it was a natural layover for bush pilots flying from Kachemak Bay and Cook Inlet through Lake Clark Pass to Bristol Bay. It had been a good move and a good living.

I spotted the wind sock on the mast above the greenhouse and glanced at my watch. The trip had taken an hour and a half. Down we slanted to touch down on the stony strip. On the taxi in we hit a soft place, and we wound up hauling our cargo of baby chicks, groceries, and gear in a wheelbarrow over the mud to the big house.

I helped Babe the next few days. We patched the roof of his house. We put a new nose cowl on the Taylorcraft, attached the floats, and there she was, all poised to take me over the mountains on a thirty-minute flight to journey's end.

May 21st. Mares' tails in the sky. A chance of a change in the fine weather and probably wind that could hold me at Port Alsworth until the storm passed over. I had been delayed long enough. Even Mary Alsworth's cooking could hold me no longer. Babe sensed my itchiness. He squinted at the mountains and gave his silent approval.

We loaded my gear into the T-craft. Not too many groceries this trip; Babe would come again soon. Seemed like a heavy load to me, and jammed in as we were, I found myself wondering whether the old bird could get off the water. We taxied out, rippling the reflections of the sky and the mountains. The motor shuddered and roared, and I watched the spray plume away from the floats. We lifted easily toward the peaks and home.

Below us a wild land heaved with mountains and was gashed deep with valleys. I could see game trails in the snow. Most of the high lakes were frozen over. I was counting on open water where the upper lake dumped into the lower, but the Twins were 2,200 feet higher above sea level than Lake Clark and could still be sealed up tight.

We broke out over the lower lake to find most of it white with ice. There was open water where the connecting stream spilled in, enough to land in. The upper lake had a greenish cast but only traces of open water along the edges. We circled Spike's cabin. Everything looked to be in good shape, so we returned to the open spot of water on the lower lake. I would have to pack my gear the three and a half miles along the shore to the cabin. As we sloped in for a landing, a dozen or more diving ducks flurried trails over the water and labored their plump bodies into the air.

After unloading, Babe and I sat on the beach.

"This is truly God's country," I said, my eyes roving above the spruce tips to the high peaks.

Babe said nothing for a few minutes. He was lost in thought. "Compared to heaven," he said finally, "this is a dung hill." He rubbed a forefinger against the stubble of his moustache and pushed the watch cap farther back on his head. "Nothing but a dung hill."

I looked at the water, at the stones on the bottom as sharply etched as if seen through a fine camera lens. "This is as close as I hope to get to heaven," I said. "This is here and now. Something I'm sure of. How can heaven be any better than this?"

Babe's eyebrows seemed to lift like crests. "Man!" he spluttered. "Man, you don't know what you're talking about! Your philosophy worries me. Why, it says plain in the Bible. . . ."

I knew he would get me around to his favorite subject sooner or later. "One life at a time," I said. "If there's another one—well, that's a bonus. And I'm not so sure of that next one."

Babe shook his head sorrowfully. "You better think on it," he muttered, rising to his feet. "You'll have a lot of time to do just that." He waded out, stepped up on a float, and squinted at me over his shoulder. "Man, your philosophy. . . ."

I pushed the plane toward deeper water. The T-craft coughed and stuttered into a smooth idling. Babe craned out the side hatch. He wondered, would the lake be open in a week? Ten days? He would be back inside of two weeks.

I watched him take off like a giant loon. He was really banking a lot on heaven. He said he was ready for the Lord to take him anytime. He was even looking forward to it. I just hoped that when the time came he wouldn't be disappointed. I watched him until the speck went out of sight over the volcanic mountains.

It was good to be back in the wilderness again where everything seems at peace. I was alone. It was a great feeling—a stirring feeling. Free once more to plan and do as I pleased. Beyond was all around me. The dream was a dream no longer.

I suppose I was here because this was something I had to do. Not just dream about it but do it. I suppose, too, I was here to test myself, not that I had never done it before, but this time it was to be a more thorough and lasting examination.

What was I capable of that I didn't know yet? What about my limits? Could I truly enjoy my own company for an entire year? Was I equal to everything this wild land could throw at me? I had seen its moods in late spring, summer, and early fall, but what about winter? Would I love the isolation then, with its bone-stabbing cold, its brooding ghostly silence, its forced confinement? At age fifty-one I intended to find out.

My mind was swarming with the how and when of projects.

Could I really build the cabin with just hand tools to the standards I had set in my mind? The furniture, the doors, the windows— what was the best way to produce the needed boards? Would the tin gas cans serve as I hoped they would? Was the fireplace too ambitious a project? The cabin had to be ready before summer's end, but the cache up on its poles? Surely that must wait until next spring. There were priorities to establish and deadlines to meet. I would need the extra daylight the summer would bring.

The most exciting part of the whole adventure was putting self-reliance on trial. I did not intend to break any laws. No meat would be harvested until hunting season. Until then fish would be a mainstay of my diet, along with berries and wild greens. I would plant a small garden more out of curiosity than actual need. Babe would supply those extras that provide a little luxury to daily fare. He would be my one contact with that other world beyond the range.

I looked around at the wind-blasted peaks and the swirls of mist moving past them. It was hard to take my eyes away. I had been up on some of them, and I would be up there again. There was something different to see each time, and something different from each one. All those streamlets to explore and all those tracks to follow through the glare of the high basins and over the saddles. Where did they lead? What was beyond? What stories were written in the snow?

I watched an eagle turn slowly and fall away, quick-sliding across the dark stands of spruce that marched in uneven ranks up the slopes. His piercing cry came back on the wind. I thought of the man at his desk staring down from a city window at the ant colony streets below, the man toiling beside the thudding and rumbling of machinery, the man commuting to his job the same way at the same time each morning, staring at but not seeing the poles and the wires and the dirty buildings flashing past. Perhaps each man had his moment during the day when his vision came, a vision not unlike the one before me.

A strange possessiveness seemed to surge through me. I had no right to call this big country mine, yet I felt it was.

I examined my heap of gear on the gravel. There were 150

pounds to be backpacked along the connecting stream and the upper shoreline to Spike's cabin. Many times I had gone over in my mind what to take. I knew what was available in the cabin but didn't want to use any more of Spike's gear or supplies than I had to. Things were valuable out here and hard to replace. Spread before me were the essentials. I organized the array into three loads.

I was sure I could pack two loads today, but just in case it was only one, I included in the first trip a .30-06 converted Army Springfield, a box of cartridges, a .357 magnum pistol with cartridge belt and holster, the packboard, the camera gear (8mm movie and 35mm reflex), cartons of film, the foodstuffs (oatmeal, powdered milk, flour, salt, pepper, sugar, honey, rice, onions, baking soda, dehydrated potatoes, dried fruit, a few tins of butter, half a slab of bacon), and a jar of Mary Alsworth's ageless sourdough starter.

The second pile consisted of binoculars, spotting scope, tripod, a double-bitted axe, fishing gear, a sleeping bag, packages of seeds, *A Field Guide to Western Birds*, my ten-inch pack, and the clothing. More bulk than weight.

The third pile held the hand tools such as wood augers, files, chisels, drawknife, saws, saw set, honing stone, vise grips, screwdrivers, adze, plumb bob and line, string level, square, chalk, chalk line, and carpenter pencils; a galvanized pail containing such things as masking tape, nails, sheet metal screws, haywire, clothesline, needles and thread, wooden matches, a magnifying glass, and various repair items; a bag of plaster of Paris; and some oakum.

Over the last two piles I spread the tarp and weighted its edges with boulders. Then I shouldered the first load, buckled on the .357, slung up the rifle and went off, swishing through the buckbrush with the enthusiasm of a Boy Scout setting out on his first hike.

The stream tinkled as it moved past its ice chimes. I saw an arctic tern dipping its way along the open place where the stream poured from beneath the ice. A wren-type bird kept flushing and flitting daintily ahead of me. His tiny body had a yellowish green cast to it, but he wouldn't sit still long enough for me to catch a good field mark.

A thin film of ice covered yesterday's open water between the edge of the lake ice and the shore. There had been a dip in the temperature last night. It was tricky going as I picked my way with quick steps over the patches of snow and ice and through stretches of great boulders and loose gravel. The pull of the packboard straps felt comfortable against my woolen shirt, and I could feel the warmth of the spring sun on my face. I wondered if at that moment there was anyone in the world as free and happy.

I crossed the single-log bridge over Hope Creek. Another hundred yards and I broke out of the brush to my pile of cabin logs. At first glance, disappointment. They seemed badly checked, but they were going to have to do. I leaned against them, resting the packboard, and took a little parcel wrapped in wax paper from a pocket. It was a piece of smoked sockeye salmon, a sample from some Babe had in the T-craft. Squaw candy, the Natives called it. I bit off a chunk. It was rich with flavor, and while I chewed, my eyes wandered over the peeled logs.

That had been a big job last July, hard work but I enjoyed it. It was cool in the timber, and there were mornings I could see my breath. I had harvested the logs from a stand of spruce less than 300 yards from where they were now piled. The trees could have been dropped with a saw but I chose to use a double-bitted axe. Pulling a canoe paddle through miles of lakes had put me in shape for the work.

Learn to use an axe and respect it and you can't help but love it. Abuse one and it will wear your hands raw and open your foot like an overcooked sausage. Each blade was nursed to a perfect edge, and the keenness of its bright arc made my strokes more accurate and more deliberate. No sloppy moves with that deadly beauty! Before I started on a tree I carefully cleared obstructions that might tangle in the backswing. It was fun planning where each should fall, and notching it for direction. Snuck! Snuck! The ax made a solid sound as it bit deeply into the white wood.

There is a pride in blending each stroke into the slash. A deft twist now and then to pop a heavy piece from the cut. Downward swipes followed by one from a flatter angle, the white gash

Dick at Spike's cabin, with its weather-grayed antlers.

growing larger as chips leap out and fall on the moss of the forest floor. Then the attack on the other side, the tree tipping slowly toward the aisle selected, gaining momentum, hitting with a crash. Moving along its fallen length, slicing off the limbs close to the trunk.

Then the peeling. Easier than expected. A spruce pole tapered into a wedge-like blade was worked under the bark until the layer gave way to expose the wet naked wood. Then the hauling. Green, peeled trunks, some of them twenty-footers, had to be moved to the site. I fashioned a log dragger. It was nothing more than a pole like a wagon tongue, a gas-can tin shoe on the end fastened to the log butt with a spike, a crossbar on the other. Back up to the rig like a horse, grab the crossbar in both fists, and take off with legs driving. The log, all slippery with sap, skidded over the moss, and with bent back I kept it going until I reached the piling place.

The sharp smell of spruce in the air, the rushing, powerful noises of the creek, the fit feeling of blood surging through the muscles. That was the way it was with all fifty of them. About a week's work—real bull work but I never felt any better. Folks say that axemanship is a lost art, but I like to think I found it again in those cool spruce woods.

The logs were a great deal lighter now than they were then and could be handled easily enough. I wrapped the smoked salmon in the wax paper and put it back in a pocket. It was time to be moving on. I was anxious to get to Spike's cabin to see if it was the way I had left it last September. About 500 yards more through the spruce and the willow brush and there it was, its weather-grayed moose antlers spreading just below the peak of the roof, a tin can cover on its stovepipe, and its windows boarded up. It had a lonesome, forlorn look. It needed someone to live in it.

I lifted the bar of the cabin door and pushed inside. Close quarters with the canoe in there. Spike's note was still a prominent part of the entrance. It read, "Use things as you need them. Leave things as you found them." From the looks of the place no one had been inside. If anyone had, he had been very neat about it.

The cabin had everything needed to set up housekeeping until my own place was completed. A good stove, two bunks, a roof that didn't leak, a table, and a small supply of cooking staples and the necessary tools to go with them. A small stack of dry wood inside, in addition to the supply outside that I had cut last fall. When my cabin was ready and moving day was at hand, I would leave behind a little more than I had found.

Including the brief stop at the log pile, the trip had taken an hour and three quarters. Not bad time with a load. I unslung the ought-six and set down the packboard. My shoulders felt as though they wanted to float to the rafters.

First thing was to move the Grumman canoe outside and make some room. Next I uncovered the windows to get rid of the gloom and climbed a ladder to take the tin can off the top of the stovepipe. When I got back with the second load, I would make a fire.

If I could travel the lake ice, I would use the canoe like a sled. I shoved the canoe onto the ice and found it was too rotten and thin. A strong wind would break it up. It was back along the beach the way I had come.

My second load was about sixty pounds. I huddled together what was left and spread the tarp over it, again weighting the edges with boulders. If the weather changed, the gear would be well protected. This time with the binoculars along, I would have an excuse to stop now and then and glass the slopes for game. With the naked eye you don't often see the big animals unless they are fairly close, and might think there are none in the country. Through the lenses, with the high slopes drawn into sharp definition, you can spot movement or something that changes shade.

On Black Mountain I saw six Dall sheep. Farther on against the skyline of Falls Mountain, there was a big band with lambs among them. Just before crossing the log bridge on Hope Creek I spotted a lone caribou feeding along the Cowgill Benches. I could make out the stubs of new antlers. As I plodded along I knew many eyes were watching me. Was the word being passed that I was back?

At the cabin, once more unloaded, I opened a jar of blueberries I had picked and put up in September. The winter had been hard on them. Juice was two-thirds the way up the jar with the shriveled berries on top. They had a strong aroma and a sharp taste.

I decided to save the last load for morning. I distributed what I had brought so far into readily available places. I placed the ought-six on wall pegs. I didn't figure on getting the barrel dirty for a long time.

With the fire going, the cabin took on a cheery atmosphere. A few fat flies awakened and buzzed about sluggishly. When I went outside to get an armload of wood, I stopped to look at the thin blue smoke pluming against the green darkness of the spruce. It began to look and feel like home.

Supper was caribou sandwiches Mary Alsworth had packed, washed down with a cup of hot beef bouillon. Then I got ready for morning. I uncovered the jar of sourdough starter, dumped two-thirds of it into a bowl, put three heaping teaspoons of flour back into the starter jar, added some lukewarm water, stirred and capped it. If I did this every time, the starter would go on forever.

To the starter in the bowl I added five tablespoons of flour, three tablespoons of sugar, and a half cup of dry milk, mixing it all together with a wooden spoon. I dribbled in lukewarm water until the batter was thin. Then I covered the bowl with a pan. The mixture would work itself into a hotcake batter by morning.

Babe did me a real favor flying me in today. I hope he's a better businessman with others. He's never yet charged me the going rate of $30 for his mail and grocery runs from Port Alsworth to Twin Lakes. He makes me feel like it would be an insult to question him about the price. "We are not piling up treasures on this earth," he says. I hope I can make up the difference in other ways.

My first evening was clear and calm. I wish some of those folks who passed me in my camper and waved could see this place. Mosquitoes are out and working on the sunburn I acquired while packing this afternoon. Listen to them singing a tune. Brings to mind a comment Babe made one time. "Can't be very good country," he said, "when even a mosquito wouldn't live there." By the sound I allow this is prime country. I wonder if there are any mosquitoes in heaven.